Prophetic Inspiration After the Prophets: Maimonides and Other Medieval Authorities

Prophetic Inspiration After the Prophets: Maimonides and Other Medieval Authorities

by

Abraham J. Heschel

edited by Morris M. Faierstein
Preface by Moshe Idel

Ktav Publishing House, Inc.
Hoboken, NJ

Library of Congress Cataloging-in-Publication Data

Heschel, Abraham Joshua, 1907–1972.
Prophetic inspiration after the prophets : Maimonides and other medieval authorities / by Abraham J. Heschel : edited by Morris M. Faierstein ; preface by Moshe Idel.
p. cm.
Includes bibliographical references and index.
ISBN 0–88125–346–4
1. Prophecy—Judaism—History of doctrines. 2. Mysticism—Judaism. 3. Spiritual life—Judaism. 4. Maimonides, Moses, 1135–1204—Contributions in understanding of prophecy.
I. Faierstein, Morris M. II. Title.
BM645.P67H47 1994
296.3'11—dc20 94–13623
CIP

Manufactured in the United States of America

Contents

Preface by Moshe Idel vii
Acknowledgments by Sylvia Heschel xiii
Abbreviations xv
Prophetic Inspiration in the Middle Ages 1
Did Maimonides Believe that He Had Attained the Rank of Prophet? 69
Index 127

Preface

Most of Prof. Abraham Joshua Heschel's thought and writings were devoted to ancient Judaism, biblical and rabbinic, on the one hand, and to the last important phase of Jewish mysticism, Hasidism, on the other. The medieval period is relatively less represented in his studies; his analyses of Solomon ibn Gabirol[1] and Maimonides, as well as a small study on a neglected Kabbalistic commentary on prayer[2] do not supply the unified survey that characterizes his book on the *Prophets,* his *Torah min ha-Shammayim,* or his monograph on Kotzk. They are, however, sufficient to enable us to conceive his vision of what he considered a desideratum for a more comprehensive picture of Judaism. The present essays of this volume constitute, together with the above-mentioned articles, part of Heschel's effort to present his view of the continuum of Jewish religious consciousness, starting from the Bible and ending in the modern period. Consequently, Heschel is to be considered as one of the very few thinkers of our times who endeavored to offer a comprehensive picture for the whole realm of Jewish religious phenomena, while simultaneously structuring a philosophy of religion of his own.

---

1. See "Das Begriff des Seins in der Philosophie Gabirols," *Festschrift Jakob Freimann,* Berlin, 1937, pp. 68–77; "Der Begriff der Einheit in der Philosophie Gabirols," *Monatschrift für Geschichte und Wissenschaft des Judentums,* vol. LXXXII (1938), 89–111; "Das Wesen der Dinge nach der Lehre Gabirols," *Hebrew Union College Annual,* vol. XIV (1939), 359–383.

2. See "Peirush 'al Tefilot," *Kovez Mada'i Likhvod Moshe Shor* (New York, 1945), 113–126 [Hebrew]. For more on this neglected commentary see Moshe Idel, "Ramon Lull and Ecstatic Kabbalah, A Preliminary Observation," *Journal of the Warburg and Courtauld Institutes,* vol. 51 (1988), 170–174.

In one of the following studies he complains that "there is no proper evaluation of the place of mystical experience in the life of Israel." Despite the formal assumption of the Sages that prophecy ceased, Heschel affirms that at least "the thirst for prophetic inspiration, the yearning for the sublime experiences of the supernatural has never died among us." This statement would indicate that he assumed that the search for a mystical experience is to be seen as a constant of Jewish life, just as Heschel assumed that God's search for human beings is such a constant. The essays translated below are detailed attempts to collect and analyze the evidence for the ongoing awareness of the prophetic experiences among medieval Jews up to the thirteenth century, namely, in the period that mediates between the main areas of his studies.

The two studies presented in this volume demonstrate convincingly that despite the halakhic formulation concerning the cessation of prophecy, many important medieval figures were described as prophets, even before or without any relation to the emergence of classical Kabbalah. This observation seems to me of paramount importance because it helps us portray the continuation of a variety of mystical practices and experiences which were not always related to the more crystallized schools of Jewish mysticism, Hasidei Ashkenaz and Kabbalah.[3]

The disparate nature of the evidence collected in the first essay may demonstrate that even outside the known mystical groups, Jewish masters were looking for, or at least respected, forms of mystical experience. In addition, the period covered in most of the material of this essay is important because the eleventh and early twelfth centuries have escaped systematic evaluation in modern scholarship, which has focused either on the evidence of previous

3. On mystical experiences in the period of the emergence of the Kabbalah see Gershom Scholem, *Origins of the Kabbalah,* trans. A. Arkush, ed. R.J. Zwi Werblowsky (Princeton University Press, Jewish Publication Society, 1987), 238–243.

centuries or on mystical phenomena described by later authors. This gap is filled by Heschel's essay, thereby allowing the emergence of a less rigid picture of the history of Jewish mysticism. In lieu of the assumption that the Gaonic period was devoid of a concern with mysticism, it is possible to argue that despite the absence of an organized group which focused on a mystical way of life, individuals were nevertheless attracted to mystical phenomena.

A crucial question which haunts many of the interpretations of phrases such as *ruaḥ ha-qodesh, horunu min ha-Shammayim,* or *bat qol,* is the status of these expressions: are they metaphors whose single role is to enhance the authority of a certain type of teaching,[4] or do they point to a feeling of revelation from above in the proper sense of the word. It is very difficult to generalize about the appropriate meaning of the evidence adduced by Heschel. Whatever the case, it is significant that metaphors of revelation serve as vehicles for establishing authority, even in instances when the authors might not have been practicing mystics.

Interestingly enough, for Heschel evidence of the existence of certain experiences is much more important than its conceptual contents. Thus, he follows the medieval understanding of the Hebrew noun *nevu'ah*; if in biblical Hebrew it stands for a very particular and structured experience, which is characterized by the moral and historical contents transmitted by the prophet from God to the people of Israel, in medieval Hebrew the term stands more often for a mystical experience even when the revelation of a special content is not involved in such an experience.[5]

If preoccupation with the metaphysical and historical content of Jewish mysticial writings is characteristic of Gershom Scholem's school, whether in the case of Kabbalah or that of eighteenth century

---

4. See Isadore Twersky, *Rabad of Posquières: A Twelfth-Century Talmudist* (Harvard University Press, 1962), 291–297; Scholem, ibid., 206–7.

5. See my *The Mystical Experience in Abraham Abulafia* (New York, Albany, 1988).

Hasidism, Heschel prefers to illumine the evidence concerning a sense of contact between human and divine. These emphases and sentivities can be properly described as the result of the different backgrounds that were formative in the spiritual physiognomy of the two thinkers: idealistic philosophy in the case of Scholem versus existential philosophy in the case of Heschel. Likewise, the historical, or what has been aptly designated as the "dramatical"[6] understanding of mysticism in Scholem's work differs from the conceptual approach of Heschel, who emphasized the additional importance of the emotional and contemplative elements. Heschel preferred to fathom the "consciousness of the pious man" in order to be able to "conceive the reality behind it."[7]

Heschel's second essay, dealing with the question of Maimonides' self-perception as a prophet, also stands apart from the main lines of modern understanding of this figure. Commonly portrayed as a sober philosopher, Maimonides was only very rarely conceived as someone who strove for a more mystical experience despite his lengthly elaborations on the nature of biblical prophecy; it is from the recent studies of David Blumenthal that a more spiritual picture of Maimonides is emerging.[8] The question of the nature of the relation between Maimonides' view of prophecy and that of Abraham Abulafia, which ends this essay, illustrates Heschel's effort to detect an organic link between what are, *prima facie,* distinct spiritual phenomena: Jewish philosophy and Kabbalah.[9]

---

6. David R. Blumenthal, "Maimonides: Prayer, Worship, and Mysticism," in D.R. Blumenthal, *Approaches to Judaism in Medieval Times,* vol. III (1988), pp. 12–13, note 1.

7. Cf. his *God In Search of Man: A Philosophy of Judaism* (New York, 1955), p. 8,

8. See his "Maimonides' Intellectualistic Mysticism and the Superiority of the Prophecy of Moses," *Studies in Medieval Culture,* vol. 10 (1982), pp. 51–68 and his study cited above.

9. On this issue see Moshe Idel, *Maimonide et la mystique juive,* (Paris: Le Cerf, 1991).

In the above studies, as in many of his other writings, Heschel was preoccupied with those parts of Jewish tradition that reflect a sense of the ineffable, without reducing Jewish spirituality to only a few of its manifestations.[10]

10. His *Torah min ha-Shammayim* is an interesting example of building a theological structure of ancient Judaism without ignoring the relevant material stemming from all the layers of Jewish religious literature. To a great extent, the medieval Jewish material adduced in the discussions in this volume is necessary for any analysis of Heschel's more comprehensive view of Judaism as a whole.

Acknowledgments

It is gratifying to me that after so many years these two essays written in Hebrew will now be available in English.

"Did Maimonides Strive for Inspiration?" was published in the *Louis Ginzberg Jubilee Volume* in 1945 by the American Academy for Social Research. "Inspiration in the Middle Ages," in the *Alexander Marx Jubilee Volume,* 1950, was published by the Jewish Theological Seminary.

Translation is an art that presupposes not only a high degree of accomplishment in the pertinent language but also a depth of understanding of the author's intent. My husband, just before he died, chose Rabbi David Wolf Silverman for the task of translating five of his essays, these two from Hebrew, and another three from German. I am appreciative of the time and energy Rabbi Silverman gave this project and the excellence of the translations.

I asked Rabbi David Shapiro, whom my husband held in high esteem, to review the translations. He translated all the Latin quotations of one of the essays, and added a number of insights. Alas, he suffered a stroke and was unable to complete the work he had begun. His death, a few years later, was a great loss to all who knew him.

Very valuable was the keen interest and advice of Prof. Avi Ravitzky of the Hebrew University. He read all five essays.

I would also like to thank Professor Fritz Rothschild and Rabbi Samuel Dresner for their advice and friendship.

Finally, under the aegis of KTAV, Dr. Morris Faierstein edited the essays, giving unstintingly of his time. I extend my appreciation to him and to all who have helped in various ways through these many years.

Mrs. Abraham Joshua Heschel

Abbreviations

B.—Babylonian Talmud.

EI—Encyclopaedia of Islam (Leiden, 1913–36).

EJ—Encyclopaedia Judaica (Berlin, 1928–34).

Guide—Guide of the Perplexed. trans. S. Pines (Chicago, 1963), page numbers refer to this edition. Page numbers in the original Hebrew version of these essays refer to the Vilna 1904 edition.

HB—Hebräische Bibliographie.

HUCA—Hebrew Union College Annual.

J.—Jerusalem Talmud.

J.E.—*Jewish Encylopedia*

JJGL—Jahrbücher für Jüdische Geschichte und Literatur.

JQR—Jewish Quarterly Review.

Kovez—Kovez Teshuvot ha-Rambam ve-Igrotav, ed. A. Lichtenberg (Leipzig, 1859).

MGWJ—Monatschrift für Geschichte und Wissenschaft des Judentums.

MJC—Medieval Jewish Chronicles, ed. A. Neubauer (vol. 1, Oxford, 1887; vol. 2, Oxford, 1895).

M.T.—Mishneh Torah.

MWJ—Magazin für die Wissenschaft des Judentums.

N.S.—New Series.

Orient. Lit.—*Orient literatur*

O.S.—Old Series.

PAAJR—Procedings of the American Academy for Jewish Research.

REJ—Revue des Etudes Juives

S.L.—Prof. Saul Lieberman.

t.—*Tosefta* (Vienna and Berlin, 1877–80), ed. M. S. Zuckermandel.

ZDMG—Zeitschrift der Deutschen Morgenländischen Geselchaft.

ZfHB—Zeitschrift für Hebräische Bibliographie.

Prophetic Inspiration in the Middle Ages (Until the Time of Maimonides)

I

It was the unanimous belief of the sages of the Talmudic era (may their memory be for a blessing) and also in the Middle Ages,[1] that with the death of Haggai, Zechariah and Malachi, prophetic

1. R. Saadia Gaon, *Sefer ha-Galui* I; *Kuzari* I:87, III:39; *Shirat Yisrael* (Leipzig, 1924), ed. B. Z. Halper, p. 52; *Megillat ha-Megalleh* (Berlin, 1924), ed. S. Poznanski, p. 44; *Ḥovot ha-Levavot,* translator's introduction; *Sefer ha-Kabbalah,* in *MJC,* vol. 1, pp. 50–51; *Kiẓẓur Zekher Ẓaddiq,* ibid., p. 88; *Seder Olam Katan* (Breslau, 1903), ed. S. H. Horowitz, p. 21; *Sefer Mitzvot Gadol,* introduction; *Sefer Yuḥasin* (London, 1857), ed. Z. Filipowski, p. 12; *Sefer Ikkarim* (Philadelphia, 1929), ed. I. Husik, III:11; *Commentary of Abrabanel* on *Guide of the Perplexed* II:32. Compare the words of the Karaite, Suleiman ben Yeruḥam, *Milḥamot ha-Shem* (New York, 1934), ed. I. Davidson, p. 43: "the Holy Spirit is not among us." On the reasons for the departure of prophecy, see the other essay in this book, n. 94. In addition to what is cited there, and in agreement with the dictum of the sages, "If Israel had not sinned, they would only have received the Pentateuch and the Book of Joshua" (B. Nedarim 22b), there were those who maintained that prophecy ceased in Israel, not because previous generations were unworthy of it, but on the contrary, they were righteous and the chastisements of the prophets were superfluous in their age. Cf. *Sefer Ḥasidim* (Frankfurt am Main, 1924), ed. J. Wistinetski, par. 544: "The Holy Spirit which inspired the prophets was absent during the period of the Second Temple, because idolatry had already been stamped out. In those days the evil impulse toward idolatry was slain. If not for the prophets of God, when the prophets of Baal [produced] wonders, [Israel] would have been completely converted to idolatry. Therefore, they were no longer in need of prophets. Moreover, the full measure of the Holy Spirit that had been destined to descend was already included in the pages of the twenty-four books [TaNaKH] and the Torah, as it is written, 'It is no longer in heaven' (Deut. 30:12)." The opinion of R. Joseph Shelomo Delmegido of Candia, *Meẓaref le-Ḥokhmah* (Basel, 1629), p. 15b, is typical: "By

inspiration ceased from Israel.[2] This perception, however, did not completely stand in the way of those individuals who yearned for prophetic inspiration to descend on them.[3] The sages did not decree: Keep away from prophecy. Those who declared that prophecy had come to an end would not deny that prophetic vision had not ceased. "Although prophecy ceased, communication continued through a *bat kol* [heavenly echo]." Indeed, the *bat kol* was "a kind of prophecy."[4]

---

my life, this is the reason for the absence of prophets . . ., viz., that because of our many sins, in every place that the people of God sojourn they reside in unclean alleys. Thus, the gentiles call the section of Hamburg where the Jews live and where I teach, 'Excrement Avenue' [*dreck allee*]. Thus, in most places you will find slaughterhouses adjoining synagogues. If it is forbidden to speak words of Torah in such stinking surroundings, how could the Holy Spirit rest upon us there? Even the apartments in the houses are filled with refuse, and when these are combined with the stains of the soul, how could the Shekhinah dwell together with them in the midst of their impurities?"

2. T. Sotah 13:2, J. Sotah 24b, B. Sanhedrin 11a, Shir ha-Shirim Rabbah 8.11.

3. I have written a separate essay on the yearning for prophecy in the days of the Tannaim and Amoraim. [This essay was never published—Ed.]

4. B. M. Lewin, *Oẓar ha-Ge'onim* (Haifa and Jerusalem, 1928–42), *Yoma* 9b; ibid., Sotah, p. 247; Ḥagigah, sec. 70. Cf. Rashi on Job 4:16, who explains *bat kol* as meaning "the sound heard at a distance when a man hits a hard surface with a hammer." This is what is meant by a *bat kol* issuing forth from heaven. [Cf. the margin of Yerushalmi, MS Leiden and MS Rome, end of Sotah, and also what is stated in the introduction to S. Lieberman, *Yerushalmi Kifshuto* (Jerusalem, 1935), p. 28.] The expression *bat kol shammayim* also occurs: "There is a difference between revelation to the prophets and revelation to the sages. The revelation to the sages was via a *bat kol* and to the prophets via a *kol* (voice). What is a *bat kol*? It is like someone who hears something from among the mountains, and the back of the mountains reflects the sound [an echo]. This is a *bat kol* from heaven, where God informs the sages concerning anything that is doubtful to them." Rashi's comment on B. Sotah 33a, "The Attribute which is appointed for this task knows the seventy languages, because it is prepared to transmit its message in whatever language is appropriate." In the Amoraic period, the term *bat kol* was used to indicate communication from heaven in a natural manner. Cf. B. Megillah 32a, "R. Johanan said: How do we know that use of a *bat kol* is permitted? Because it is

Another heavenly source from which later generations were to draw supernal knowledge was the dream. From the scriptural verse, "And I shall surely conceal My face on that day" (Deut. 31:18), which hinted at the departure of prophecy from Israel, Rava (or Rabbah) inferred that "the Holy One, blessed be He, said: Even though I do not communicate with them any more [in the clear light of day], I shall continue to speak to them in dreams."[5]

There were times when the sages, faced with a perplexing problem to which they could find no solution, resorted to dreams, through various means of inquiry and explication. They believed

---

written, 'Your ears shall hear that which sounds behind you' [Isa. 30:21]." Rashi comments: "If he had the intention to begin something, and he hears a voice saying either yes or no, he should follow it, and there is no suspicion [of necromancy]." J. Shabbat 6:3 tells of a similar *bat kol:* "R. Jonah and R. Jose went to visit R. Aha, who was sick. They said: 'Let us follow the message of the *bat kol.*' They heard the voice of woman telling her friend: 'Snuff out the candle.' They said to her: 'The candles of Israel are never snuffed out or extinguished.'" In Mishnah Yevamot 16:6, "They may allow a woman to marry based on a *bat kol* [that her previous husband is dead]," the dictum refers, apparently, to a "rumor," e.g., some sort of pronouncement or voice (cf. B. Gittin 89a). Cf. E. E. Urbach, "Halakhah u-Nevuah," *Tarbiẓ* 18 (1946), pp. 23 f. According to Nahmanides' commentary to Exodus 28:30, there are four levels of prophecy, and this is their order of rank: the Holy Spirit, prophecy, *Urim ve-Tumim,* and *bat kol;* cf. commentary of R. Bahya ben Asher to Deut. 33:8; *Shoshan Sodot,* p. 51b; *Tikkunei Zohar* 19; *Responsa of R. Isaac Alfasi,* resp. 1; *Megillat Ta'anit* (Lwów, 1906), ed. M. Grossberg, p. 60 n. 9. R. Eleazar Rokeach, *Sodei Razayya* (Bilgoraj, 1936), ed. Y. Kamelhar, p. 44, explains *bat kol* "because a 'daughter' represents the receptive principle," hence "the *bat kol* is audible only to the prophet and not to anyone in his vicinity." Cf. also R. Menahem Recanati, *Peirush al ha-Torah, Parshat Vayera.*

5. B. Ḥagigah 5b. According to the commentary of the Maharsha (R. Samuel Edels), the intent of this verse is to exclude the occurence of prophecy of the level of Moses, "which was face to face, however the prophecy which was communicated to the other prophets through a dream, was not closed off by reason of the hiding of God's face." According to this interpretation, Rava related this verse to the era of the prophets.

that the solution transmitted by the dream came from heaven. This activity was termed *she'ilat ḥalom* (asking questions via a dream)—a term known from the geonic period.[6] The process of *she'ilat ḥalom* was not at all comparable to other supernormal phenomena. It was achieved through the initiative of an individual who knew how to arouse the supernal powers, viz., the *ba'al ḥalom* (the dream master or dream-adept)[7] who then reveals that which is hidden.

6. *Shitah Mekubbeẓet,* Baba Meẓia 107b: "Rav traveled to a cemetery and performed a certain act; Rabbenu Hananel interpreted the act as referring to dream inquiry." Cf. *Arukh,* Avad 2 [cf. R. Judah Bargeloni, *Peirush le-Sefer Yeẓirah* (Berlin, 1885), ed. S. Z. Halberstam, pp. 41 f.; cf. J. Reifman, "He'arot al Sefer: Ḥukei ha-Torah," *Bet Talmud* 1 (1881), p. 249. S.L.] Rashi explained this passage: "He knew the art of necromancy and understood how each of the corpses buried there had died, viz., whether the death was in accordance with the allotted time span or whether it was through the power of the evil eye." The origin of the expression appears to be derived from I Samuel 28:6, "and Saul inquired of the Lord, but the Lord did not answer him, either by dreams or by Urim or by prophets"; cf. R. David Kimhi's commentary on the verse cited. Cf. *Midrash Eleh Ezkerah,* in *Bet ha-Midrash* (Jerusalem, 1938), ed. A. Jellinek, vol. 2, p. 64, concerning Rabbi Ishmael the High Priest, who ascended to heaven to inquire about the decree against the ten martyrs (*asarah harugei malkhut*) [the matter we are dealing with is the kind of dream that responds to a question, called αἰτητικοί, in contrast to φεόπεμπτοι, which come incidentally and are sent by God (see what Artemidorus wrote in his *Onirocriticon,* bk. 1, chap. 6, and bk. 4, chap. 2, and the beginning of chap. 3. Gentiles received the answers to dream questions through *incubatio.* Concerning questions relating to religious matters, see Yohanan (Hans) Lewy, *Annales du Service des Antiquites de l'Egypte* 44 (1946), p. 230. Strabo (*Geography* 12.35) relates that dream adepts—εὐόνειροι—customarily slept in the Temple in Jerusalem in order that their dreams would be successful. [T. Shabbat 6:7: "Change your garment, so that your dreams will be good ones" (according to the printed editions). Gentiles customarily slept on the hides of sacrifices in order for their dreams to succeed. Cf. what J. G. Fraser wrote in his commentary on *Pausanias,* vol. 2, p. 476, S.L.]

7. This expression is found in B. Sanhedrin 30a; *Avot de Rabbi Nathan* (Vienna, 1887), ed. S. Schechter, Version A, chap. 17, p. 66 (*Midrash Tanna'im* [Berlin, 1908–9], ed. D. Hoffman, p. 199). In t. Ma'aser Sheni 5:9, ed. M. Zuckermandel, the reading is "the man of dreams," and in J. Ma'aser Sheni 55b, it says "it came

The facets of the prophetic inspiration are many. Concerning the greatest of the prophets (i.e., Moses) it is written, "mouth to mouth I speak with him" (Num 12:8), while later prophets such as Zechariah and Daniel heard messages delivered through the mediation of an angel. The closure of prophecy was accompanied by the termination of the indwelling spirit; in its place there came an anonymous disclosure, e.g. the revelation of Enoch or the message mediated by Elijah. In the period under consideration, it was the appearance of Elijah which was the usual visual form. Whether awake or in a dream, it was Elijah, as the messenger specially appointed to supervise the covenant in the flesh performed on the eighth day of

---

to him in a dream." Mention is made of a "dream-adept" in B. Berakhot 10b. According to Rashi, ad loc., this locution refers to "the angel who sends dreams in the night." B. Sanhedrin 30a; cf. B. Berakhot 25b: In one case the agent is an angel, in the other it is a demon. In *Zohar* I:149b we read the following: "The dream was sent by means of Gabriel." Cf. also *Zohar* I:183a. According to B. Sotah 33a, Gabriel taught Joseph the seventy languages of mankind. Cf. *Sefer Ḥasidim,* ed. Wistinetski, par. 389. I have also discovered that "dream adept" is a title of Elijah. "Mordecai learned all that happened" (Esther 4:1). How was it made known to him? According to Esther R. 7.18: "From the mouth of Elijah," and similarly in the Targum: "Through Elijah the High Priest" (in *Targum Sheni:* "He saw it with the Holy Spirit"). And Rashi: "The dream-master told him that heaven agreed with him." It is worth noting the comments of R. Joseph Nachmias, in his commentary: "Mordecai learned all that had happened—from the people of the city, because it was public knowledge and not secret, the decree had already been issued in Shushan. In the midrash: In a dream, because they bowed down to an idol in the days of Nebuchadnezzar." Indeed, Rashi, with his usual lucidity, emphasizes that he learned from the master of dreams that the decree had also been sealed in heaven. Cf. *Manot ha-Levi* (Lemberg, 1911), p. 128a. It is interesting that in the language of Scripture, Genesis 37:19, "master of dreams" (*ba'al ha-ḥalomot*) means one who is accustomed to dream dreams or the interpreter of dreams (*Targum Onkelos:* "master of dreams." This Aramaic term in the second meaning is in MS Targum to Job 6:6, cf. J. Levy, *Chaldäisches Wörterbuch* [Leipzig, 1867–68], p. 261). Cf. A. Kristianpoler, *Traum und Traumdeutung* (Vienna, 1923) (*Monumenta Talmudica,* IV, 2, 1), p. 2.

the child's life,[8] who appeared to exceptional individuals, answering their questions, solving their uncertainties and granting them esoteric knowledge as well as precognition of future events. This visionary perception, which is well known to us from the period of the Tannaim and Amoraim, was taken to be a species of prophecy.[9]

In many generations there were people who claimed to be or of whom it was said that they were recipients of the Spirit. These exalted ones strove to enter the *Pardes* (lit. "orchard," synonymous with the heaven of the mystical esoterics) and to merit the infusion of supernal knowledge. Indeed, they believed that they had attained their goal. This achievement, although limited in terms of its impact upon the life of the masses, was of great importance in the spiritual

---

8. "For this reason the sages ordained that a place of honor is set for the angel of the covenant," *Pirke de Rabbi Eliezer,* end of chap. 29. Cf. the commentary of RaDaL (R. David Luria); cf. *Zohar* I:93a. The mohel customarily says: "This is the chair of Elijah, who is remembered for good." Cf. *Sefer Ḥasidim,* ed. Wistinetski, par. 585. And in *Sodei Razayya* of R. Eleazar Rokeach, p. 5: "He has many messengers; since there are circumcisions on the Sabbath in many places, how can he be here and there if the Sabbath boundaries exist higher than ten handbreadths?" Cf. B. Erubin 43a–b.

9. Cf. R. Judah Loewe of Prague (Maharal), *Neẓaḥ Yisrael,* chap. 28; and the statement of R. Abraham ibn Ezra at the end of Malakhi: "There is no doubt that he was seen in the days of our holy sages." Compare the song for the conclusion of the Sabbath, "Happy is he who has seen his face in a dream." Despite this R. Shem Tov ibn Shaprut explained, *Pardes Rimmonim* (Zhitomir, 1866), ed. E. Z. Zweifel, Baba Meẓia, chap. 4, the statement of R. Eliezer, "It will be proved from heaven. . . . they will send written queries to the leading rabbis and the heads of the academies in all the lands, and all of them responded that the halakhah is in accord with Rabbi Eliezer, and this was called a *bat kol.*" In chap. 7: Elijah was the name given to any one of their contemporaries who was imbued with the Holy Spirit. He was then deemed a holy man and given the name Elijah." Cf. *Seder Eliyahu Rabah* (Vienna, 1901), ed. M. Ish Shalom, introduction, p. 61. *Pardes Rimmonim,* ed. E. Z. Zweifel, notes. We also find an angel who explained a halakhah concerning *ẓiẓit* ("An angel appeared to R. Katina, etc. B. Menaḥot 41a), and it is interesting that Rabah bar Rav Huna, "the angel's disputant," disagreed with the angel's decision.

odyssey of the elect. The supremacy of natural reason could not slake desire. Many of the sages remained dissatisfied with the knowledge attainable by rational means. Their souls longed for the hidden wisdom conferred upon man by divine grace.

Only a shred of the wisdom of the earlier rabbis, i.e., the Talmudic masters, has come down to us. And it appears mainly in the Halakhah. The testimonies concerning the inner life of the sages are few. Isolated individual occurrences, whose worth was momentary and whose content made no difference in the conduct of religious law, were deemed unworthy of being written down.[10] Moreover, matters involving prophetic inspiration were matters about which one remained close-mouthed. He who had achieved this spiritual rung would seal his lips, bridle his tongue, and conceal it under a canopy of secrecy. Nevertheless, whoever seeks diligently will find sufficient material with regard to the attainment of this level of spirituality. This material includes the following:

a. Reports concerning those who merited the experience of prophetic inspiration.
b. Testimonies of individuals who were so infused.
c. Opinions of medieval sages as to whether prophetic inspiration could be attained by their contemporaries or by future generations.
d. A definite statement as to the desirability and feasibility of this pursuit.

The usual stance taken with regard to stories about prophetic inspiration and manifestation of Elijah does not generally regard

10. "There is no city in the land of Israel which did not contain prophets [and why were their prophecies not publicized?]; however, every prophecy which was for future generations was written down, those for a particular time were not written down." *Seder Olam* (Vilna, 1894–97), ed. B. Ratner, chap. 21, p. 46a. Cf. B. Megillah 14a.

these as actual events, but takes them as the product of popular imagination—and no more. Many of the spiritual giants of Jewry acknowledged that they had attained peaks of intellectual wisdom by dint of prophetic inspiration or through the agency of dream-inquiry. The common people, as was to be expected, would then weave an imaginative multicolored tapestry from the skeins thus provided by the elite. Despite these colorful accretions one cannot deny that the appearance of Elijah and similar phenomena were attestations to an experience, a spiritual fact of the soul, a witness to the spriritual level which the chosen few believed that they had reached.

This matter should not be taken lightly. Revelation is an indispensable groundwork for religion. He who denies apodictically and *a priori* the possibility of divine communication and sees, as it were, trickery will ultimately conclude that religion originates as illusion. We can neither prove nor disprove these experiences. Nevertheless, to understand the true spirit of Israel it is important to remember that in the heart of the faithful of Israel there is a firm belief that exceptional individuals are singled out for investiture with the divine presence which grants supernal communication, the gift of heavenly thought. From time to time sages have informed us that they have been infused with insights into the mysteries of the Torah by divine grace and that it was not by the power of their own intelligence that they achieved specific insights. The number known to us is very small and without doubt the number of those hidden and forgotten surpasses the number of those recorded and known.

Rav Hai Gaon writes: "Among the earlier sages, it was assumed that the Holy One, blessed be He, could work wonders through the saints, as He had through the prophets; He granted them awesome visions just as He had granted visions to the prophets."[11] Many of the great medieval sages believed in the descent of prophetic inspiration upon the saintly. "At first, God revealed His secret to the prophets

---

11. *Oẓar ha-Ge'onim,* Hagigah, p. 15; cf. pp. 18, 20.

. . . then to the righteous . . . and finally to the God-fearing, as it is written: 'The secret of the Lord [is transmitted to] those who fear Him.' "[12]

The words of Rav Avdimi of Haifa, viz., "From the day that the Temple was destroyed, the power of prophecy was taken from the prophets and given to the sages," were explained by Nahmanides in the following manner: "Despite the fact that prophecy occurring through apparitions and visions was removed from the prophets, the prophecy of the sages, which derives from discursive reasoning, was not removed. The sages knew the truth via the prophetic inspiration within them."[13] According to the Ritva (R. Yom Tov ben Abraham), the wise "attain through their intellect to a cognition of many matters which are beyond the reach of the unaided natural intellect."[14] The Almighty reveals to them "the true secret meaning of ambiguous matters."[15] Because of this, the Talmud will occasionally state with regard to the dicta of the sages: "These are naught but prophetic words,"[16] i.e., "there is no human discipline that enables one to make such fine distinctions; whoever made the statement

---

12. *Midrash ha-Gadol,* Genesis (Cambridge, 1902), ed. S. Schechter, pp. 754 f. Cf. Epstein, "Tereifot de-Ereẓ Yisrael" *Tarbiẓ* 2 (1931), p. 318: "The sages went to extraordinary lengths with regard to certain kinds of meat, so that Israel might be pure. Blessed be He Who revealed his secrets to them to fulfill what is written, 'The secret of the Lord is for those who fear Him' (Ps. 25:14)."

13. Commentary on B. Baba Batra 11a Cf. *Sefer Ḥasidim,* par. 1473: "There is a wisdom such that a person can see the meat and know whether the slaughterer had intercourse with his wife on the previous night."

14. *Ha-Kotev* on *Ein Yaakov,* B. Baba Batra 11a.

15. Rashi's comments on the words of R. Abiathar, a contemporary of R. Hisda: viz., "his teacher agreed with him." B. Gittin 7b. A different interpretation is offered by R. Joseph ibn Migash for the dictum "a sage is preferred over a prophet." I.e., a prophet is authorized to proclaim only that which is heard by him or whatever is put in his mouth; a rabbinic sage proclaims that which was transmitted orally to Moses at Sinai, even though he did not hear it." *Shittah Mekubbeẓet,* Baba Batra 12.

16. B. Erubin 60b, B. Baba Batra 12a, B. Bekhorot 45a.

was aided by the Holy Spirit [i.e., it is not rational and need not be accepted—trans.]."[17] Such opinions accord well with the words of R. Meir that "he who studies Torah for its own sake will receive the secrets of the Torah at the hands of heaven."[18]

However, not everyone thought that the prophecy of the sages was only an inner illumination, standing on the periphery of wisdom and a mere adjunct to rational inquiry. According to Rabbenu Nissim, "secrets concerning the world order that were hidden from the ministering angels" are made known to "whoever did not search out the future at the hands of diviners," but trusted the Holy One alone.[19] From another source we learn that in every generation there arise prophets in Israel who are masters of a unique kind of prophetic power. In the *Midrash ha-Gadol* we meet this astonishing midrashic statement, " 'The sceptre shall not pass from Judah' [Gen.

17. This is the explanation offered by the Tosafist R. Isaac the Elder, B. Erubin 60b, Tosafot s.v. *Ein.* According to other commentators, this statement was made in a disparaging manner: "This is comparable to one who prophesies in the name of God, and does not cite any reason for his statements." Cf. Rashi ad loc. R. Hananel's statement at that point is to the same effect. In addition we may cite the statements of R. Gershom, B. Bekhorot 45a and B. Baba Batra 12a: "These statements are, in principle, prophetic." The observations of R. Samson ben R. Abraham are also noteworthy, *Teshuvot Maimuniot,* relating to *Sefer Shofetim,* sec. 20: "It does not seem to be the case at all; a sage as authoritative as R. Hayyim, who, out of his vast erudition and acuity sought to permit that which had been prohibited by R. Joshua. For what he demonstrated was actually prophetic inspiration and the presence of the Holy Spirit, for we have found that the words of the Torah are poor in one place and rich in another." Nahmanides too writes in his *Ḥiddushim* on B. Shabbat 39b: "And in the Tosafot it is explained . . . these are words of prophecy."

18. Avot 6:1. This is the reading according to the *Maḥzor Vitry* (Berlin, 1889–97), p. 554. Cf. the explanation given there: "Secrets of the Torah, such as *Ma'aseh Bereshit, Ma'aseh Merkavah, Sefer Yeẓirah,* and a fortiori the remainder of the Torah." And in *Seder Eliyahu Zuta* (Vienna, 1904), ed. M. Ish Shalom, chap. 17: "And they reveal to him a secret from heaven and the mysteries of the Torah."

19. B. Nedarim 32a.

49:10]—this denotes sovereignty; 'nor the staff from his descendants'—this denotes prophet and scribe."[20] In the Syriac translation of the Torah which, through the Christian Church, preserved many rabbinic homilies, this was translated as follows: "The sceptre shall not pass from Judah nor the *dabkan* from his descendants."[21] What does the word *dabkana* mean? According to Ephraem the Syrian of Edessa (ca. 4th cent. C.E.)[22] and Bar Hebraeus (ca. 13th century C.E.)[23] the word means prophet. Who were the prophets of every generation? Did this refer to specific prophets? Were they the Merkabah mystics? The history of those generations has dropped into oblivion, and what we know about them is like a drop in the bucket. Perhaps in the earlier generations prophets flourished whose words and deeds have been forgotten. It is appropriate here to mention that in the *Zohar*, the disciples of R. Simeon bar Yohai are called "true prophets."[24]

---

20. Midrash Ha-Gadol Genesis, ed. S. Schechter, p. 737.

21. Ed. R. H. Heller, Genesis 49:10. R. Abraham ibn Ezra explains the words of the prophet Isaiah 59:21: "My spirit which is upon you, and the words which I have placed in your mouth, shall not be absent from your mouth, nor from the mouth of your children, nor from the mouth of your children's children—said the Lord—from now on, for all time," as a promise that "that the power of prophecy would never cease from their descendants," M. Friedlaender, ed., *Ibn Ezra's Commentary on Isaiah* (London, 1873–77), p. 104. Rashi sees here not a promise concerning prophecy but "that even in exile the Torah would not be forgotten by them." Cf. his commentary ad loc. See, however, the interpretation of R. Elijah Mizrahi on Deut. 18:19, "from the midst of your brethren, like me . . . to separate them from the magicians and the sorcerers . . . for you have no need for them, since you will always have prophets like me available to you. . . . they will take my place in every generation . . . and this is nothing more than a literal understanding of the text."

22. S. Poznanski, *Schiloh* (Leipzig 1904), Beilage 4; B. Zimmels, "Zur Geschichte der Exegese," *MWJ* 17 (1890), p. 153: Nor a judge who is a prophet in foretelling the future.

23. R. Schröter, "Bar-Hebraeus' Scholien," *ZDMG* 24 (1870), p. 498.

24. *Zohar* II:154a, "As for me, would that I be given an awakening of prophetic inspiration, to be among the disciples of the prophets, the true disciples of Rabbi Simeon bar Yoḥai, who make the upper and lower beings tremble, all the more so

We have reports from the eleventh and twelfth centuries of some extraordinary individuals who were called prophets.[25] Their visions, however, have not been transmitted to future generations. But the little that we do know concerning their life-style proves that this noble title was not conferred upon them for nothing. The title "prophet" was always held sacred in Israel and we may assume was never used lightly. "Empty words are not remembered." Even in

---

[that] I be among you. According to the Tosafists, Hillel had prophetic foreknowledge of the destruction of the Temple. Cf. B. Gittin 36b, s.v. *bi-zeman.* According to R. Baruch in the name of R. Hananel, "the incident concerning the oven of Achnai [B. Baba Meẓia 59b], where the walls of the Bet Midrash [were at first invoked] as proof [and then rejected], etc., and then rejected], etc., There was a student who fell asleep in the Bet Midrash and dreamed a prophetic dream." *Sefer Yuḥasin,* ed. Z. Filipowski, p. 33.

25. The name "prophet" (*navi*) attached to certain names: Benjamin Navi, author of the penitential hymn *Zekhor Berit Ezraḥi,* R. Judah ben Nathan Navi, Abraham the Physician Navi, *Manuscripti codices hebraici . . . J. B. de Rossi . . .* (Parma, 1803), p. 157, cod. 1371. According to Zunz (*Zur Geschichte und Literatur* [Berlin, 1845], n. 369; *Literaturgeschichte der synagogalen Poesie* [Berlin, 1865], p. 355, n. 2), Eliezer "Navi" is either an acronym for "his soul shall dwell in goodness and his seed shall inherit the land" (*Nafsho be-tuv talin vezar'o yirash ereẓ*) or a family surname. Cf. also M. Steinschneider, "Poeten und Polemiker in Nordspanien um 1400," *HB* 15 (1875), p. 55. Jacob Reifman follows the opinion of Zunz, cf. "Toldot Rabbenu Bahya," *Alumah* 1 (1936), p. 86, n. 53: "*Navi* was a name used by some of the Tosafists to denote the strict pietist who observed the laws of torts, the injunctions concerning blessings, and the admonitions of [the ethical laws] of Avot (cf. B. Baba Kamma 30a), because the acronym of *Navi* is Nezikin, Berakhot, and Avot." Both Zunz and Reifman used this method of acronymic allusion to suppress the "esoteric." This type of approach was also used by R. Nehemiah ben R. Abraham, author of *Divrei Navi* (Amsterdam, 1688). This problem was also treated by M.Z. Weiss, "Ha-Navi," *Ha-Ẓofeh,* 5 (1921), pp. 46–47; J. Müller, *Teshuvot Ḥakhmei Ẓarfat ve-Lotir* (Vienna, 1881), introduction; H. Gross, *Gallia Judaica* (Paris, 1897), p. 466. There is no doubt, with regard to the prophets whom I will mention later, that they were awarded this title because of their activity as prophets. Cf. G. Scholem, "Al Nevi'uto shel R. Ezra mi-Montcontour," *Tarbiẓ,* 2 (1931), p. 244.

Biblical days, there were prophets whose names alone are known to us, but whose words have not been transmitted to future generations. There is no doubt that the prophets who did arise in the Middle Ages were worthy of the name, but their deeds were forgotten in those mournful times of persecution.

II
Prophets

1. R. Samuel ben R. Kalynomos the Elder of Speyer (b. ca. 1084), the father of R. Judah the Pious and one of the great Kabbalists, is denominated in ancient sources by the title "the holy saint and prophet."[26] R. Samuel the Prophet excelled in learning and saintliness and wandered from place to place for seven or nine years in order to purify himself by living in "exile." He was among the first to make known the esoteric doctrine in Ashkenaz (Franco-German Jewry) as it had been taught him by his father. Of him it was said that he knew the secret names of God and that, upon one occasion, he "made mention of one of the names and the house of study thereupon became filled with light."[27] Of him it was told that he once "lifted his eyes heavenward and it seemed to him that he saw the heavens

---

26. *Darkei Teshuvah* of R. Eleazar Rokeach, the student and relative of R. Judah the Pious, at the end of *Teshuvot R. Meir ben R. Barukh* (Budapest, 1895), p. 160b; also *Teshuvot Maharshal*, sec. 29; *Meẓaref le-Kesef*, chap. 12; D. Kaufmann, "La Discussion sur le Phylactères,"*REJ* 5 (1882), p. 276; A. Epstein, "R. Shmuel ha-Ḥasid be-R. Kalonymous ha-Zaken,"*Ha-Goren* 4 (1903), p. 87; N. Brüll, "Beiträge zur Jüdischen Sagen und Sprachkunde im Mittelalter,"*JJGL* 9 (1889), p. 24. The author of the *Shalshelet ha-Kabbalah* (Amsterdam, 1697), p. 42a, saw "a small book which said at the beginning, 'This is the book of the pious ones founded by Rabbenu Samuel, the prophet, the father of R. Judah the pious.' "

27. Brüll, op. cit., p. 33. The author of this statement was perhaps a contemporary of R. Judah the Pious. Cf. Y. Kamelhar, *Ḥasidim ha-Rishonim* (Vác, 1917), p. 54.

open before him."[28] According to the legend, "he wanted to write down the year of the Millennium shortly before he died and he asked that a quill and ink be brought to him. Upon their being set before him, he died. After his demise he appeared to R. Judah the Pious in a dream and told him the date. The latter also tried to write down the date shortly before he died but the same fate befell him."[29] Perhaps it is he who is mentioned in the legend concerning "Samuel the true prophet," who delivered a homily on the Song of the Sea at a meeting of rabbis in the second-floor dwelling of R. Menahem Hordimsi; at the conclusion of his address [one of the listeners] raised a question about the tefillin knot. For its solution he called the angel Metatron before the company as well as Moses our teacher (may peace be upon him) and "even wanted to disturb the Shekhinah."[30] In *Pa'ane'aḥ Raza* mention is made of an anagogic commentary composed by R. Samuel the Prophet.[31]

28. Brüll, op. cit., p. 24.

29. A. Marx, "Ma'amar le-Shenat ha-Geulah,"*Ha-Ẓofeh* 5 (1921), p. 195.

30. *Shalshelet ha-Kabbalah,* p. 40. This story is republished by D. Kaufmann, "La Discussion sur le Phylactères," *REJ* 5 (1882), pp. 274–275. It is interesting that the *mitzvah* of *tefillin* occupies a special place in the visions of the sages, cf. below, nn. 44, 130, and *She'elot u-Teshuvot min ha-Shammayim,* secs. 2, 3, 26, 48, 49. Compare *Migdal Oz.* Hilkhot Tefillin 3:5: "Maimonides explains "in terms of what he received as a tradition from his teachers . . . yet Rabbenu Tam and many others maintained the view of R. Hai Gaon. Controversy raged over this issue until the Tosafists, our masters, decided to adopt the practice of both disputants. . . . Until we were informed by heaven that the controversy on earth is replicated above . . . and I am astonished that our eminent rabbi [R. Abraham ben David], who was an adept in Kabbalah, a recipient of the oral tradition, tried to decide this matter by dint of reasoned argument when it is one of the mysteries of the world."

31. "The commentary of R. Samuel Navi to *li-vehemah laḥmah,* which in gematria equals *ezba,* which represents the she-bear, devoid of nipples." D. S. Sassoon, *Ohel David. Catalogue of Hebrew and Samaritan Manuscripts in the Sassoon Collection* (London, 1932), no. 1103, in a MS dated 1356. [This would contradict the Radal's note in *Pirkei de R. Eliezer,* end of chap. 21 regarding the *Makhiri* on Psalm 147, p. 286. S. L.]

2. R. Jacob Tam (1090–1171), thought to be the greatest scholar, of his day, was known as "the great and holy Rabbi."[32] His disciple R. Hayyim ha-Kohen, one of the Tosafists, would say of him, "Had I been present when he died, I would have allowed myself to be defiled in his behalf."[33] R. Abraham ibn Ezra called him "the angel of God,"[34] and his pupil R. Eliezer ben R. Solomon called him "prophet."[35] According to the conventional view, Rabbenu Tam is not reckoned among those who gained knowledge of esoteric lore. Certain details about his life indicate that he was given to esoteric studies and that the title "prophet" was awarded him because of his supernal insights into that lore. R. Ephraim bar Samson, a thirteenth-century Biblical exegete, recounts that Rabbenu Tam engaged in "dream inquiries."[36] On the basis of another source, we learn that R. Tam asked numerous questions of heaven and received answers from there.[37] The forty-two-letter grammaton used by "the angels who

32. I. H. Weiss, "Iggeret Bikoret,"*Bet Talmud* 5 (1889), p. 257.

33. Tosafot, B. Ketubot 103b, s.v. *oto.*

34. *Kovez̤ Hokhmat ha-Ra'vah,* ed. D. Kahana, p. 80; *Omer ha-Shikkhah,* p. 127, 4; 28, 7. Ibn Ezra wrote Rabbenu Tam with humility: "I write to the greatest of the shepherds of God's people; may he deign to answer the lowliest member of that people." It is interesting that Rabbenu Tam writes of Rashi: "Far be it from us in any way to contest the opinion of the angel who has created us."*Sefer ha-Yashar* (Berlin, 1898), ed. S. Rosenthal, p. 11. Cf. V. Aptowitzer, *Mavo le-Sefer Ravyah* (Jerusalem, 1938), p. 97.

35. *Sefer ha-Yashar,* ed. Rosenthal, p. 132.; ed. Vienna, 1816, p. 78d: "And Eliezer entreated the prophet of Ramerupt, Rabbenu Jacob, the greatest of the shepherds."

36. H. Y. D. Azulai, *Shem ha-Gedolim, Ma'arekhet Gedolim,* Aleph, no. 230.

37. A. Neubauer, *Catalogue of Hebrew Manuscripts in the Bodleian Library* (Oxford, 1886), nos. 790, 2274. Rabbenu Tam's seeking an answer to a question through a dream is mentioned in the notes to R. Jonah Gerondi's *Sefer Issur ve-Heter he-Arokh,* chap. 20, *Din Kerumin.* Cf. M. Steinschneider, "Jakob aus Marvège, der Himmelscorrespondent," *HB* 14 (1874), p. 122, n. 1; ibid., p. 131, "I heard from Rabbenu Tam that he once asked a dream-master whether Jesus and Mary, his mother, were alluded to in the Hebrew Bible. The dream-master answered him: *elohei nekhar ha-arez̤* [Deut. 31:16] is equivalent to Jesus and Mary

were appointed to oversee increase of Torah learning,"[38] which was known in the circle of Hai Gaon,[39] and of which Rashi wrote, "it is not known to us,"[40] was known to R. Tam.[41] In an essay by R. Eliezer Trevish of Frankfurt (a famed Kabbalist whose archives contained many manuscripts) there is found a prayer of R. Tam, which begins, "I entreat you, Michael, Gabriel, and Raphael, that you stand in prayer before the King of Kings, the Holy One, blessed be He."[42]

---

in gematria." Steinschneider thinks that the reference here is to R. Jacob ha-Levi, but in the extant literature the latter is never addressed by the title "Rabbenu Tam." Moreover, dream inquiries were not the monopoly of R. Jacob ha-Levi; they were a widespread phenomenon in that period (see below on dream inquiries among the Ḥasidei Ashkenaz); there is no need to assume that in all those sources there is a confusion between the names of R. Jacob ha-Levi and Rabbenu Ya'akov Tam. Cf. also *Teshuvot ha-Radbaz,* sec. 340; H. Michael, *Or ha-Ḥayyim* (Frankfurt a.M., 1891), p. 251. Also noteworthy is the fact that in *Sefer ha-Yashar* (Vienna, 1816), 85b, Rabbenu Tam relates: "When the dream-master, six months after the death of the holy Rabbi Samson, queried him, it seemed as if he were still alive." According to V. Aptowitzer, *Mavo le-Sefer Ravyah,* p. 420, the person referred to here is R. Samson of Falaise, the grandfather of R. Samson of Sens, one of Rabbenu Tam's most eminent contemporaries.

38. *She'elot u-Teshuvot min ha-Shammayim* (Lwów, 1929), ed. R. Margulies, sec. 9.

39. See below, n. 168.

40. B. Kiddushin 71a. Cf. Rashi, B. Avodah Zarah 17b; B. Sanhedrin 101b; Rashi, in B. Sukkah 45a, explains the seventy-two-letter name of God by combining the verses *va-yisa, va-yavo va-yet* [Exod. 14:19–21]. According to R. Hai Gaon, "the letters [of this name of God] are not known."

41. B. Ḥagigah 11b, Tosafot, s.v. *ein doreshin:* "Rabbenu Tam explained *Ma'aseh Bereshit:* The forty-two-letter name of God which issues from the very first verse of Genesis and its immediately succeeding verse."

42. R. Yuspa Hahn, *Yosef Omeẓ* (Frankfurt a.M., 1928), par. 484. This prayer was brought to my attention by Prof. Louis Ginzberg. Rabbenu Tam deals with the concept of *Sar ha-Olam* in B. Yevamot 16b, Tosafot, s.v. *pasuk zeh.* According to Rashi, B. Sanhedrin 44b, it is permitted for a man to supplicate angels to aid him in his prayers.

An allusion to R. Tam's belief that the Holy Spirit invested him may be seen from his couplet: "And the teacher shall teach in the manner of a wayward rebellious son, but upon me there rests the spirit of the creator."[43] The author of the *Shalshelet ha-Kabbalah* relates:

> It was transmitted to me by many of the Sages of that generation, among them the disciples of the gaon R. Leon d'Moreal and also from three of the elders of the generation whom I consulted individually and they all said that they had received the tradition from their elders . . . that when R. Tam and R. Ephraim the Great son of Isaac Ratisbon [Ratisbon died in 1175/4935] were teaching together in the yeshiva in Regensburg, it so happened that one day they were involved in a complex discussion concerning the knot of the tefillin when R. Ephraim claimed that one ought to tie the knot daily, as it was written, "and you shall bind them for a sign upon your arm." R. Tam claimed that there is no obligation to do so daily. They argued pro and con until R. Tam became so angered that he stood upright and roared, "Moses our Teacher, descend." Three times he cried out in this manner until Moses appeared and R. Tam then said to him, "I claim that it is not obligatory to tie the knot of the tefillin daily—and that in the Torah you received from God you have not been enjoined so!" Moses agreed and then departed.[44]

---

43. Tosafot, B. Avodah Zarah 34a, s.v. *dorinah.* The statement refers to R. Ephraim of Regensburg. Cf. *Kol Bo,* sec. 96, and in *Sefer Amarkal* (in *Festschrift zum siebzigsten Geburstage David Hoffman's* [Berlin, 1914], p. 118), where we find a slightly different formulation. Cf. Aptowitzer, *Mavo,* p. 167, p. 321.

44. *Shalshelet ha-Kabbalah,* 40b. According to legend, Ibn Ezra created "a creature in the presence of Rabbenu Tam and he exclaimed: 'Behold what has been wrought by the holy letters!' Then he ordered it to turn around, and it returned to its previous state." Cf. *Commentary attributed to R. Saadiah Gaon to Sefer Yeẓirah* 2:5. "R. Tam relates: 'I have been told by my father, who heard it from his teachers, that when the liturgical poet R. Eleazar Kalir composed the hymn *Ve-Ḥayyot asher hena meruba'ot la-kise,* he was then in a forest and fire flashed about him. And the sages of Lorraine, who were his teachers, attested to this. And Simon ben R. Isaac the Great, who was well versed in miracles, gave similar testimony.'" *Shibbolei ha-Leket,* sec. 28; *Maḥzor Vitry,* sec. 325, p. 364. Concerning R. Simon

Another witness to R. Tam's involvement with asking questions of heaven is found in R. Mordechai Yaffa, the author of the *Levushim*, known for his caustic attacks against those who believed in dreams.[45] He states,

> I have found another reason proffered in the name of R. Tam, who was once asked, "Why is it that we recite the 145th Psalm aloud in the presence of the Torah scroll, while this is not done on weekdays?" A *bat kol* answered from heaven, "because of the acronym it contains." These are: [The first word, *AShReI*;] After he drinks [the Kiddush] [*YoSheVei*;] The Seventh day God chose, [*VeiTeKha*], Bless First Waters and Fill the Goblet with Wine, [*Od*]; Fowl and Meat and Fish [*YeHaLLeluKHa*;] Three Meals, Dress Whites and Change Your Cloth [*SeLaH*;] End, Make Havdalah. All this applies to the Sabbath, and so too to Festivals, which are also called Sabbaths. Thus far have I heard.[46]

---

ha-Gadol, cf. Y. Heilprin *Seder ha-Dorot* (Warsaw, 1882) 4, 856 (p. 196), "There is a tradition that R. Simon implored the Holy One, blessed be He, that he should not see the persecution, and he died three days prior to it." Rabbenu Tam explained the Talmudic statement that God never brings obstacles through the righteous "as referring to forbidden foods, because this is particularly offensive to the righteous." He believed that "it would be impossible for him not to be apprised of the forbidden nature of the food." *Sefer ha-Yashar* (Vienna, 1816), sec. 355. Cf. B. Shabbat 12b, Tosafot, s.v. Rabbi Nathan: "And thus R. Eleazar Kalir composed [a *Kedushah* where] the letters of the word 'Jacob' represent that portion of the *Kedushah* which begins 'and each of the angels cried one to another' to 'the throne of his heavenly glory' as an analogue of the divine chariot. And he placed the paper on which he had composed his holy *Kedushah* on the waters of the river, the paper did not move from its position, as if it could not move because of the glory of the throne."From *Sefer Gematriot*, in A. Freimann, introduction to *Sefer Ḥasidim* (Frankfurt a.M., 1924), p. 5.

45. *Levush ha-Orah, Vayeshev; Levush Ir-Shushan,* sec. 255, par. 9.

46. *Levush ha-Tekhelet* (Venice, 1620), sec. 286, par. 1.

In Rabbenu Tam's circle there were a few scholars who were themselves occupied with esoteric wisdom. His brother-in-law and disciple, "our Holy Teacher"[47] Rabbi Isaac ben R. Samuel of Dampierre, the famous Tosafist, known as the Elder Rabbi Isaac, was wont (according to legend) to ascend heavenwards at night, where messages would be given him by the ministering angels,[48] a spiritual level attributed to the Merkabah mystics.

3. R. Ezra the Tosafist (ca. beginning of 13th cent.) was called R. Ezra the Prophet[49] or the Prophet from Montcontour (Dep. Vienne, France), undoubtedly because he too delved into mysteries. According to the testimony of one who may have been his contemporary, R. Ezra ascended "to heaven and asked for the date of the Millennium." He addressed Haggai, Zechariah, and Malachi—each one in his own name wrote down three verses containing the name of God.[50] From other sources we learn "that the soul of the prophet of Montcontour ascended heavenwards and there heard the holy angels singing that particular poem before the Lord that entire phrase. When he awoke he was reminded of the phrase. He recounted the incident to his students and then wrote down the entire poem."[51] Once the prophet of Montcontour, the grandson of R. Abraham ibn Ezra, ascended to heaven and there espied a student, who, while other members of the heavenly academy stood up to praise the Lord, remained

47. *Ha-Terumah,* beginning of Hikhot Sheḥitah; I. H. Weiss, "Toldot Rabbenu Ya'akov Tam,"*Bet Talmud* 3 (1883), p. 225.

48. From a commentary on Avot MS, 1, cited by A. Marx, "Ma'amar al Shenat ha-Geulah" *Ha-Ẓofeh* 5 (1921), p. 195.

49. Tosafot, B. Gittin 88a, s.v. *ve-dilma;* B. Shevuot 25a, s.v. *ve-Rav; Mordecai,* end of Yevamot; *Tosafot Rabbenu Pereẓ* to B. Baba Kamma 23b; See Gross, *Gallia Judaica,* p. 337.

50. A. Marx, *Ha-Ẓofeh* 5 (1921), p. 197.

51. Cited in the MS of the book by R. Moses Botarel; cf. also G. Scholem, "Al 'Nevi'uto' shel R. Ezra mi-Montcontour,"*Tarbiẓ* 2 (1931), p. 244; idem, "Od al 'neviuto' shel R. Ezra mi-Montcontour," *Tarbiẓ* 2 (1931), p. 514.

seated. The prophet was astonished and asked him, "What is your great merit, that you are privileged to remain seated while all the others are standing?" He answered, "Because all my life upon the conclusion of my prayers I would recite the following with great intention and devoutness: 'Who can retell the mighty deeds of the Lord, whose glory is manifest in the heavens—whose divinity and loving-kindness and righteousness are manifest in the earthly regions. He is King. He is just—He speaks and He fulfills.' "[52]

4. R. Troestlin the Prophet, who, it appears, lived before the year 1235, wrote the following in his prophecy, "Alas, ye heavens, for Israel have not repented and are not putting their minds to repentance; many Messianic dates have passed because of the sins of Israel, especially many opportunities for redemption have been lost due to the magnitude of our sins."[53] One of his interpretations, on the verse "O God, may You be adored forever," is extant, as is a prayer to be recited before undertaking a journey which has the superscript, "Received from our master, our teacher, R. Troestlin the prophet of Erfurt."[54]

---

52. According to a Vatican MS; cf. N. Fried, "Od al 'Nevi'uto' shel R. Ezra mi-Montcontour," *Tarbiẓ* 2 (1931), p. 514; M. Steinschneider, "Miscellen,"*HB,* 9 (1869), p. 115; idem, "Zur Pseudepigr. Literatur,"*HB* 4 (1861), p. 23. According to the opinion of H. Gross, *Gallia Judaica,* p. 376, R. Ezra the Prophet is mentioned in *Minḥat Yehudah al ha-Torah* (cf. *Da'at Zekenim mi-Rabotenu Ba'alei ha-Tosafot* [Leghorn, 1783], p. 75b.). I have also found this in the *Likkutim* in the name of R. Joseph of Marseilles in the name of the *Navi,* but his name is not specified.

53. According to A. Marx, *Ha-Ẓofeh* 5 (1921), p. 198, the date of composition of this commentary would be sometime between 1220 and 1235.

54. JTS MS Adler 1161, pp. 27–28. In another form it is found in Bodleian MS 1816, fol. 102b, according to G. Scholem, *Major Trends in Jewish Mysticism* (Jerusalem, 1941), p. 370. On the basis of a somewhat gross anthropomorphism found there, the date of the author's life should be advanced to the eleventh century; "For God says, I sit astride the divine beasts, looking like a Jew, for the Holy One, blessed be He, is comparable to an old, bearded scholarly Jew." This mode of thought demonstrates that R. Troestlin the prophet was close to the esoteric savants

5. R. Abraham the Prophet, known to us from only one source which quotes his interpretation of the verse "and the ravens [*orevim*] brought him bread and meat" (I Kings 17:6). There are those who interpret this as alluding to merchants. R. Abraham the Prophet asked of Elijah, who responded, "*Orevim* is a scribal error; the *resh* precedes the *bet* instead of the reverse. Thus the word should denote passersby (*overim*)—namely that passersby brought him bread and meat."[55]

6. The first head of the Academy of Narbonne, "an ancient seat of Torah learning whence Torah went forth to all lands,"[56] and which was also a center for Kabbalistic speculation, is mentioned in the *Sefer ha-Kabbalah* of R. Abraham ben David as being R. Jacob the Prophet-Gaon, ben R. Moshe ben R. Abun.[57] Apparently, he lived about the middle of the eleventh century. Rabbenu Tam says of R. Joseph Tov-Elem (Bonfils), "all his days he served the wise in the

---

clustered around the *Shi'ur Qomah.* Cf. also A. Marx, *Ha-Ẓofeh* 5 (1921), p. 201, n. 49.

55. MS Sasson 349, *Ohel David,* p. 1102. Is this the R. Abraham ben R. Samuel the prophet (born ca. 1130; cf. V. Aptowitzer, *Mavo* p. 308) who was the head of the academy in Speyer? According to legend, this R. Abraham was not interested in esoteric lore (cf. Brüll, op. cit., p. 33). But in Bodleian MS 2644, A. Neubauer, *Catalogue of the Hebrew Manuscripts in the Bodleian Library* (Oxford, 1886–1906), vol. 2, p. 41, a reference is made to his being a Biblical exegete: "He commented on Lamentations according to the interpretation of R. Eliezer of Worms, who received it from his father, our teacher, R. Judah, who received it from R. Abraham, who in turn received it from R. Samuel the Pious."

56. *The Travels of R. Benjamin of Tudela.*

57. Neubauer, *MJC,* vol. 1, p. 83; cf. S. Poznanski, *Babylonische Geonim im nachgaonäischen Zeitalter* (Berlin, 1914), p. 107. A. Neubauer, "Documents Inédits," *REJ* 10 (1885), p. 104; H. Albeck ed., *Eshkol* (Jerusalem, 1935–38), introduction.

presence of (our Rabbi) the prophet,"[58] referring apparently to R. Jacob the Prophet.[59]

7. R. Elijah the Elder, the son of R. Menahem of Le Mans, the author of *azharot,* a disciple of Rabbenu Gershom the Light of the Exile, and the halakhic disputant of R. Joseph Tov-Elem (Bonfils),[60] is addressed in many manuscripts as Elijah the Prophet.[61] Even R. Moses Botarel called him "the great rabbi and kabbalist."[62]

8. R. Sheshet ben Benveniste, the prince of Barcelona (b. ca. 1110), who, in Al-Harizi's words, was the "pillar of the world and the foundation-stone of all pietists"[63] and in his day was known as the "elder-prophet," was a man "on whom the spirit of the Lord dwelt.'[64] This title was not a metaphorical hyperbole. R. Joseph ibn Zabara emphasized that his high achievement was the result of his simplicity, humility, probity, and piety—all those traits which R. Pinhas b. Yair had enumerated as prerequisites for the attainment of prophetic inspiration.[65] In his youth R. Sheshet had studied in Narbonne and perhaps was close to the circle of kabbalists in that city who, according to tradition, were themselves deemed worthy of the appearance of Elijah.[66] He apparently believed that the Holy

58. *Sefer ha-Yashar,* ed. Rosenthal, p. 89; cf. I. H. Weiss, "Toledot Rabbenu Ya'akov Tam," *Bet Talmud* 3 (1883), p. 260.

59. Cf. H. Albeck, *Eshkol,* introduction.

60. *She'elot u-Teshuvot Maharal,* sec. 29; *Shibbolei ha-Leket ha-Shalem* (Vilna, 1887), ed. S. Buber, no. 28.

61. Rosenberg, *Kovez̩ Ma'asei Yedei Geonim* (Berlin, 1856), p. 109.

62. *Peirush Sefer Yez̩irah* 5:1, 1:1; cf. A. Jellinek, "Die kabbalisten Familie . . ." *Der Orient, Literaturblatt* 12 (1851), p. 546.

63. *Taḥkemoni* (Warsaw, 1895–99), ed. A. Kaminka, gate 46, p. 350.

64. R. Joseph ibn Zabara, *Sefer Sha'ashuim* (New York, 1914), ed. I. Davidson, p. 145.

65. *Sefer Sha'ashuim,* pp. 146 ff.

66. Cf. below, pp. 32ff.

Spirit rested upon the sages of Narbonne.[67] In one of his poems he describes a vision that came to him in a dream: "I saw an angel standing before me; his spirit came to me and I began to prophesy: Oh, you who seek visions, listen to my words—the Lord, who has embittered my soul, is now good to me; He has said that He will answer me in my time of trouble."[68]

III
The Approximation of Prophecy

Rabbenu Kalonymos of Lucca ben R. Moshe ben R. Kalonymos, a contemporary of Rashi, was "a very great sage and composer of liturgical poems for all the festivals."[69] According to legend, he became acquainted with the future fate of his son through a dream.[70] Of him it was related in the Tosafot: "Three matters were made known to him as though via prophecy at the time of his death."[71]

---

67. "From the day that the Holy City was destroyed, the light of knowledge [*ner binah*], Narbonne was not extinguished, and the Holy Spirit rested upon me [returned?]"—a metaphorical depiction of R. Sheshet ibn Benveniste upon his becoming the chief rabbi of Narbonne. Cf. D. Kaufmann, "Lettres de Scheschet," *REJ* 39 (1899), p. 66.

68. Ibid., p. 223. R. Sheshet was an admirer of Maimonides; cf. Dr. Frankl, "Ein handschriftliches Schreiben des Scheschet über Maimuni's Wirksamheit,"*MGWJ* 25 (1876), p. 511.

69. *Shibbolei ha-Leket ha-Shalem,* no. 28.

70. Brüll, *JJGL* 9 (1889), pp. 36 ff.

71. End of B. Menaḥot. Compare L. Ginzberg, *Geonica* (New York, 1909), vol. 2, pp. 55, 57. Aptowitzer, *Mavo,* p. 393. The belief that the terminally ill could discern matters through the "eye of the soul" was widespread among the sages (cf. *Ẓiyyoni,* Vayera: "it is impossible to deny what experience has demonstrated"). Cf., e.g., Sifre, Behalotekha 103, Bamidbar Rabah 14.37; B. Berakhot 28b. "The Philosopher [=Aristotle] has written in his treatise on Sleeping and Waking that the terminally ill, whose sensory powers have declined, are able to peer into the future due to the strengthening of their imagination. The latter organ is no longer

As yet there is no proper evaluation of the place of mystical experience in the life of Israel. The thirst for prophetic inspiration, the yearning for sublime experiences of the supernatural has never died among us. Despite efforts to keep it hidden [out of modesty], it makes its appearance in investigations which apparently are only of halakhic import. The primary principle among these mystics is: it is not the theory but the practice which alone matters. Even among the circle of Hasidei Ashkenaz, who tended to keep at a distance from mystical experience, there was a belief that all of the "secret things" which were initiated above, i.e., in heaven, were reserved ultimately for those who were completely righteous. Nevertheless a flavor of those mysteries was made available to masters of esoteric lore.[72]

The phenomenon of mystics (esoterics) who were renowned as prophets apparently ceased after the twelfth century.[73] Later masters

---

distracted by the interference of the sensory powers. Much of this can also be found in the Talmud, viz., that statements made on the deathbed are given credence as if they were prophetic." R. Simon ben Zemach Duran, *Magen Avot* III:4, p. 72b.

72. *Sefer Ḥasidim,* ed. Wistinetski, par. 1056, p. 268. "The prayer Barukh She'amar was composed by the Men of the Great Assembly in accordance with a text that descended from heaven." Cited in the name of *Or Zaru'a, Turei Zahav,* on Oraḥ Ḥayyim 51:1.

73. In recent centuries we know of only one person who was given the title of prophet, viz. "the great and pious sage, our teacher, Zechariah Mendel, of blessed memory, who at the end of his days, became chief rabbi of the Holy Land and was buried there. I have heard it said that the sage Pinehas Hurwitz, the rabbi of Frankfurt am Main, in his lifetime was called by the name Zechariah the prophet." *Menorat Zechariah* (Frankfort am Oder, 1776), introduction. Cf. M. Zunz, *Ir ha-Ẓedek* (Lwów, 1874), p. 115, and the statements of H. N. Dembitzer, *Kelilat Yofi* (Cracow, 1888–93), vol. 1, pp. 78–80, who casts doubt on this tradition because "it is well known . . . that from the time that prophecy ceased in Israel . . . no man has ever been called prophet even by way of exaggeration."In A. Marcus, *Keset ha-Sofer* (Cracow, 1913), Bereshit, p. 15a, it is written: I have in hand an old Bible with a Yiddish translation printed in Wilhelmsdorff, 1623, [with a commentary] *Sod Mesharim* by R. Obadiah the Prophet, whose name is mentioned only in this book and not in any other . . . he seems to have been a contemporary of the

were never given this appellation.[74] The yearning to attain prophetic

---

disciples of R. Joseph Colon . . . this Bible bears the *haskamah* of the Maharsha [R. Samuel Edels] and all the great men of that generation." This book is not mentioned in A. Freimann's essay, "Annalen der Hebräischen Druckerei in Wilhelmsdorff," *Festschrift zum siebzigsten Geburtstage A. Berliner's* (Frankfurt a.M., 1903), pp. 100–115, and I have been unable to locate it in the library of the Jewish Theological Seminary of America. The name R. Ephraim the Prophet of Regensburg, which is mentioned in *Seder ha-Dorot,* Fourth Millenium, 930, according to the *She'elot u-Teshuvot Maharshal* as well as in I. H. Weiss, "Toledot Rabbenu Ya'akov Tam," *Bet Talmud,* 3 (1883), p. 258, without reference to the Maharshal's responsa, which were available to them, is a mistake arising from scribal error. In the first edition, *She'elot u-Teshuvot Maharshal* (Lublin, 1574), no. 29, there is a reference to R. Ephraim *ha-Gevir* from Regensburg, and the same name is found in the Fürth 1768 edition. Indeed, the Lublin 1599 edition reads: "R. Ephraim *ha-Gevi.*" Perhaps it should be read *ha-gibbor*—cf. B. Pesaḥim 36a, Tosafot, s.v. *ba-Makom:* "Rabbenu Ephraim bar Ephraim *ha-gibbor.*"

Addendum

My friend the librarian R. Hayyim Lieberman has called my attention to the following volume: *Sefer ha-Magid Nevi'im Rishonim im Peirush Rashi* and Yiddish translation *Agudat Shmuel,* named after R. Samuel, son of the great sage, rabbi, and pietist, R. Moses, of blessed memory, of Lugatch, which he had selected and edited from many old books, "including the notes of R. Obadiah the Prophet of Guratam," published in Amsterdam in 1699. [Cf. also H. Lieberman, "Al HaG"Ha De-R"W," *Ohel RH"L* (Brooklyn, 1980), vol. 1, pp. 310–329, ed.] In the introduction the author recounts his travels in "an Arab land." In one place he found "more than 80,000 heads of households . . . speaking Hebrew, just as we Ashkenazi Jews do; they told me that they were descendants of the tribe of Benjamin who had resided there from the time of the first exile . . . and they had a printing press which they brought from their land, when they were exiled(!)." Cf. M. Steinschneider, *Catalogus Librorum Hebraeorum in Bibliotheca Bodleiana* (Oxford, 1852–60), no. 2454.

74. E.g., "the prophet of Avila" (*Teshuvot ha-Rashba,* pt. 1, no. 548; cf. Brody, *EJ* 3:780–781); David Reubeni (cf. *MJC,* vol. 1, p. 146; Y. Baer, *Toledot ha-Yehudim be-Sefarad ha-Noẓrit* [Tel Aviv, 1945], pp. 184 ff.); the lad who prophesied in the time of Gersonides (*Milḥamot Adonai* II:7); Moses the prophet in the days of R. Hasdai Ibn Crescas (A. Jellinek, *Bet ha-Midrash,* vol. 6, p. 142, no. 13); H. Graetz, "Ein Pseudo-Messias im 14. Jahrhundert," *MGWJ* 28 [1879], p. 79). Cf.

rank was a matter for individuals, not for public disclosure.

On the other hand, there were those who felt quite strongly that there was no contemporary need for prophets.[75] In his caustic style, R. Moses Taku attacks "the retarded bumpkins, heretics (*minim*; is this a deliberate play on the Hebrew word for "believer," *ma'amin*?) seeking to become prophets and habituating themselves to the enunciation and continual repetition of holy names; at times, as they concentrate on the enunciations and become confused, their bodies collapse with weariness —the soul becomes dominant, and breaks through all barriers, achieving the capacity to envision far-off things. But after the passage of some time the power of the divine name that he enunciated departs from him and he once more returns to his former state of mental confusion."[76] These words leave the impression that the subject he is complaining of was a widespread phenomenon in his day. R. Jonah the Pious of Gerona, who lived in the thirteenth century, explains the Talmudic statement "he who prays must set his eyes downward and his heart upward" as meaning, "i.e., that he think of himself situated as in heaven—removing from himself all [thoughts or desires] of mundane pleasures or bodily enjoyment

---

F. Baer's article, "Eine jüdische Messiasprophetie auf das Jahr 1186 und der dritte Kreuzzung," *MGWJ* 70 (1926), pp. 113 ff.; idem, "Ha-Maẓav ha-Politi shel Yehudei Sefarad be-Doro shel R. Yehuda ha-Levi," *Ẓion* 1 (1935), p. 20. Cf. also *Me'ora'ot Ẓvi* (Warsaw, 1838), pp. 51b ff.

75. "Walk before Him wholeheartedly; look to Him alone and do not seek after future things." Rashi on Deut. 18:13. "Whoever engages in invoking angels . . . will come to a bad end. . . .therefore, let a man distance himself from doing these things and let him not inquire after dreams . . . there is no greater good for man than that he pray to God . . . even some prophets who were martyred did not invoke the Name; rather they prayed to Him, saying, If He does not hearken to our prayer, we are unworthy of being saved." *Sefer Ḥasidim,* ed. Wistinetski, par. 211; "If you see a man prophesying about the Messiah, know that he occupies himself 'with magical powers and demonic rites.'" Ibid., par. 212; cf. also, par. 1450—"and in this time when there are no prophets."

76. R. Kircheim, "Sefer Ketav Tamim," *Oẓar Neḥmad* 3 (1860), p. 84.

as the ancients have said, 'if you desire to have proper intention, divest your body from the soul.' "[77] A hint of this is to be found in the words of R. Jacob Baal ha-Turim, "This was the practice of the early pietists, viz., they would isolate themselves and concentrate upon their prayers,[78] so that ultimately they would divest themselves of their bodies;[79] their spiritual intellect would then dominate so

77. "According to my teacher and rabbi (may the Lord watch over and protect him)," *Talmidei Rabbenu Yona al Berakhot,* chap. 5.

78. "Our revered sages said: Why are Israel's prayers not answered? Because they do not invoke the Divine Name appropriate to that particular occasion, nor do they concentrate their minds upon the work of unification, and understand that this is a wondrous matter. It was in this way that the wise, holy, and pure sages would shoulder the yoke of the kingdom of heaven. And it was through prophetic inspiration that they could know, understand, and comprehend that which was ordained to be—whether for good or ill, or between one juridicial decision and another; and they would then hear a heavenly voice proclaim, 'Blessed be His glorious kingdom for ever and ever.' " A. J. Heschel, "Perush al ha-Tefillot," *Kovez̦ Mada'i le-Zekher Moshe Schorr* (New York, 1944), pp. 118 ff. [Cf. *Pirkei de Rabbi Eliezer,* chap. 8.]

79. The notion that the prophets of Israel had transcended their bodies and were in a state of ecstasy when they were infused with the Holy Spirit originated with Philo; cf. A. J. Heschel, *Die Prophetie* (Warsaw, 1936), pp. 15 ff. Philo employed this idea with regard to Moses. Cf. *Zohar* I: 171a: "Moses heard the voice and would stand on his feet fully erect and aware . . . the rest of the prophets would fall on their faces, their limbs would weaken and tremble and they could not understand the matter clearly." Cf. ibid. III: 268b. According to Maimonides, the prophets, "when they had the prophetic experience, their limbs trembled, their physical strength failed them, their thoughts became confused; and thus, their minds were left free to comprehend the vision they saw." They were "filled with fear and confusion and became physically weak." (*M.T.,* Hilkhot Yesodei ha-Torah 7:2, 7:6). "When the prophecy comes upon the prophet . . . his powers weaken and his body becomes useless, and he becomes so frightened that he almost expires." This is the level of the prophet who falls into a deep sleep, "when all his feelings became useless and his mind was empty, as in a dream." Cf. also, *Mose Maimuni's Einleitung zu Chelek im arabischen Urtext und in der hebräischen Uebersetzung* (Berlin, 1901), ed. J. Holzer, seventh principle. In *Sefer Ḥasidim ha-Yashan* [ed. R. Margulies], par. 773 we read: "When the souls of the prophets are bound up in love, their heart cleaves to

that they approached the rung of prophecy."[80] Messianic excitement was aroused many times not by prognosticators of the end-time, but by proclamations by harbingers of good tidings who appeared as prophets and announced the time of the Millennium of wonders. In the sixth century, close to the time of Muhammad, one of these living in Arabia, wrote, "Prophecy has come to me concerning the House of David—graciously bestowing serenity upon my soul."[81] The fact that the Jewish community was inclined to accept messages of this

---

God as if they are not in this world. Therefore it is written: 'What did that madman come to you for?'[II Kings 9:11]." On transcending the body as the condition for supernatural knowledge, cf. R. Moses Ibn Ezra: "We have found it written in the wisdom literature of antiquity, that whoever is capable of divesting himself of his body, his senses, and his emotions, and restrains himself from the pursuit of the mundane is thereby rendered capable of ascending to the higher sphere, where he will receive his just reward. . . . A master of epigrams has stated: 'Which of you is closest to God? He whose soul leaves this world, though he dwells within it.'" *Arugat ha-Bosem, Ẓion,* 2 (Frankfurt a.M., 1842), pp. 120 ff. Against this, R. Moses Taku writes: "This is said apparently of people who are not expert; but those who are practiced in this matter—no injury occurs to their bodies; they do not tremble and fall," R. Kircheim, "Sefer Ketav Tamim," *Oẓar Neḥmad* 3 (1860), p. 85. Cf. also Abraham Ibn Ezra, Commentary on Psalms 139:18: "The body rests and the soul cleaves to the supernal soul, then he will see marvelous sights . . . different from any other dreams." The expression *hitpashtut ha-gashmiut* (divestiture or transcendence of matter or of the body) first appears at a later period. For R. Judah Ibn Tibbon, the Hebrew term *hitpashtut* signifies extension in space. The whole section in *Sefer ha-Turim* is an admixture of the spirit of Ḥasidei Ashkenaz and the intellect of the Spanish savants. R. Moses Isserles, *Darkei Moshe,* sec. 91, maintains that the essence of prayer for Maimonides is transcendence of the body.

80. *Tur,* Oraḥ Ḥayyim, sec. 98.

81. H. Z. Hirschberg, "Ikvot ha-Mashiaḥ be-Ereẓ Arav be-Mei'ah ha-Ḥamishit veha-Shishit aḥar Ḥurban Bayit Sheni,"*Sefer Zikaron le-Vet ha-Midrash le-Rabbanim be-Vina* (Jerusalem, 1946), p. 115. According to S. D. Goitein, "Inyanim Yehudim be-Sefer Ansab El Ashraf El Bladri," *Ẓion* 1 (1935), p. 78, the Jews appeared to the Arabs as the bearers of supernatural knowledge.

kind testifies to the belief of the people that prophetic inspiration was within the range of possibility.

Maimonides recounts how R. Moses Al-Dar'i, who came to Andalusia in 1122, announced publicly that "the Messiah had appeared and that the Lord had revealed this to him in a dream. He did not, however, consider himself to be the Messiah. People flocked to him and believed his prophecies, and later he began to prophesy about matters which came true." In his performance of sign-events (miracles), he demonstrated to all that he was indubitably a prophet.[82]

Maimonides relates that during the days of the First Crusade, at the beginning of the twelfth century, there were "important men in Cordoba, the capital of Andalusia, who were devotees of astrology and agreed that the Messiah would appear that very year. Night after night they would make an invocation through a dream inquiry in order to know whether the Messiah would be a native Andalusian. They finally concluded that a certain man, Ibn Aryeh, esteemed a pietist, one of the teachers of the populace, [was to be the Messiah]. They performed miracles and predicted future events, just as Al-Dar'i had done, until they captured the hearts of the masses. But when this whole affair became known to the elders and sages of our community, they gathered in the synagogues and summoned Ibn Aryeh, gave him lashes and punishments and excommunicated him for remaining silent about this matter and allowing these people to employ his name without interference and not rebuking these

82. *Iggeret Teiman,* trans. Jacob Mann, "Tenu'ot Meshiḥiot . . ." *Ha-Tekufah* 24 (1928), pp. 355 f. Cf. the other essay in this volume, pp. 73ff. In a responsum to the scholars of Lunel concerning the Biblical portions encased in the tefillin. Maimonides writes (*Teshuvot ha-Rambam* [Jerusalem, 1934], ed. A. Freimann, p. 9): "And R. Moses Dar'i, who followed your practice in this matter, and when he emigrated from the west to the land of Israel, his tefillin were like yours, but when he was shown the words and arguments of the sages of old, he threw away his tefillin (and donned others) in accordance with the order that we have described." M. Steinschneider's opinion, as expressed in *Jewish Encyclopedia* (New York, 1904) 4:440, 5:70, is unwarranted.

people for a sin against our faith. They did likewise to all of his followers."[83]

From the text of a letter sent to the Jewish community of Alexandria we learn of a "prophet whose prophecy and piety cannot be doubted, since his predictions have come to pass . . . who performed signs and wonders . . ., who explained Talmudic difficulties which, until then, had been unresolved and revealed Biblical secrets as well." This prophet lived in France and prophesied that in 1226 "the ingathering of the exiles would begin and our master Elijah would appear . . . [and] in the year 1233 Messiah the son of David would appear . . . and the Kingdom would be restored to the daughter of Jerusalem."[84]

In Santurbo, close to the city of Catania in Sicily, there appeared in the twelfth (or the thirteenth) century, a woman who prophesied and claimed, "Thus I have been mandated by the mouth of the Holy One." The entire community, according to an eyewitness, saw her "fall upon her face, implore and cry . . . while saying. . . , 'Thus has the Holy One sworn to me in the presence of the angels and Moses our teacher—that the end-time is near.' "[85]

We have a book entitled *The Child's Prophecy* in which Nahman Katofa prophesied concerning the redemption and the changes which would befall the Jews and the nations in the end of days. The book contains five prophecies in Aramaic and is written in acronymous stanzas. The author and time of composition are unknown to us.

83. See Mann, ad loc. Concerning another kind of Messianic personality, cf. *Iggeret Teiman* (Vienna, 1874), ed. D. Holub, p. 50. Cf. also A. Marx, "The Correspondence Between the Rabbis of Southern France and Maimonides about Astrology," *HUCA* 3 (1926), pp. 349, 356 ff.

84. S. Assaf, "Te'udot Ḥadashot al Gerim ve-al Tenu'ot Meshiḥiyot," *Ẓion* 5 (1940), pp. 116, 124. He believes that this man is R. Ezra, the prophet of Montcontour.

85. J. Mann, "A Messianic Excitement in Sicily and Other Parts of Southern Europe," *Texts and Studies* (Cincinnati, 1931), vol. 1, pp. 39ff. Cf. A. Aeshcoli, "Al ha-Tenuah ha-Meshiḥit be-Sicilia," *Tarbiẓ* 11 (1940), pp. 207–219.

It has been estimated that the author lived at the beginning of the twelfth century.[86]

Claims to prophetic states are advanced also by the founders of sectarian movements. Abu Issa of Isfahan, who lived in the eighth century, and who was the founder of the Issa'ites, a sect which survived him for some two hundred years, "thought of himself as a prophet." He was an ordinary tailor, unable to read or write; nevertheless he produced, unaided, many books. Such an event (according to his followers) would have been impossible for a man not endowed with the prophetic spirit.[87] His disciple, Yudgan, and a follower of Yudgan's, Mushka, also looked upon themselves as prophets.[88]

---

86. H. Y. D. Azulai, *Shem ha-Gedolim, Ma'arekhet Sefarim,* s.v. *nevu'at ha-yeled; Shalshelet ha-Kabbalah* (Amsterdam, 1697), p. 35; cf. G. Scholem, "Ha-Mekubbal R. Abraham ben Eliezer ha-Levi," *Kiryat Sefer* 2 (1925), p. 117. A. Strauss, *Toledot ha-Yehudim be-Mizrayim ve-Suriya* (Jerusalem, 1944), p. 129.

87. A. Harkavy, "Le-Korot ha-Kitot be-Yisrael," in H. Graetz, *Divrei Yemei Yisrael* (Warsaw, 1893), trans. S. P. Rabinowitz, vol. 3, p. 501. S. Poznanski, "Meyassedei Kitot be-Yisrael bi-Tekufat ha-Geonim," *Reshumot* 1 (1920), pp. 209–213. *Abu-'l Fath' Muh'ammed asch-Schahrastani's Religonsparteien und Philosophenschulen* (Halle, 1850), ed. T. Harbrucker, prt. I, p. 255; Maimonides, *Iggeret Teiman.* He also said that the Talmudic sages have reached the level of the prophets; cf. B. Z. Dinur, *Yisrael ba-Golah* (Tel Aviv, 1926), vol. 1, pp. 161–164.

88. S. Poznanski, op. cit., p. 213; J. D. Eisenstein, *Ozar Yisrael* (New York, 1907–13), vol. 5, pp. 36–95; *EJ* 9:549. Among the Falashas there arise occasionally "prophets who wander about from city to city to speak in the name of God and to admonish their listeners that they should return to God, observe the commandments of His Torah; they also predict future events. The Falashas honor them and bring them gifts." A. Epstein, *Eldad ha-Dani* (Pressburg, 1891), p. 166.

IV
Attainment of Prophetic Inspiration and the Development of the Kabbalah

The attainment of the rung of the Holy Spirit and prophecy was the strongest wish of the great Kabbalists.[89] It was a traditional belief

89. "In this world, the sages, with the aid of the Holy Spirit, are able to grasp seven *sefirot.*" Nahmanides, *Sha'ar ha-Gemul* (Naples, 1490), p. 27b; *Migdal Oz, Hilkhot Teshuvah,* chap. 8, "I refer now to the tradition received from the mouths of the ancient scholars; we know for a truth that R. Sherira Gaon and R. Hai Gaon were adepts at this art of Kabbalah which they received as an oral tradition transmitted from one generation to the next, from one gaon to his successor; they all knew how to invoke and use the names of *Hekhalot Zuta* which enabled them to travel great distances with extreme rapidity and to mount the ladder of prophecy with all its attendant powers." *Sefer ha-Malbush,* in *Ohel David,* p. 445. Cf. M. Steinschneider, "Zur kabbalistischen Literatur: IV. Isak Kohen," *HB* 18 (1878), pp. 21 ff. G. Scholem, "Sidrei Shimusha Rabah," *Tarbiẓ* 16 (1945), pp. 197 ff. Naḥmanides, in his *Commentary to Job,* chap. 33, *Mikra'ot Gedolot* (Venice, 1517), writes: "Should you seek to understand the noble secret, then set your mind and your reins to learn [i.e., understand well what I am about to say] and repent your sins; so that the cloud may be lifted from your face and you will see the King and the Bride with your own eyes, and you will see the forthcoming redemption." And R. Isaac of Acre, *Me'irat Einayim, Ekev,* writes: "He who merits and attains the secret of cleaving [to God] will in turn attain the secret of equinamity. After that, the secret of contemplation. After this stage is reached, he will attain the rung of the Holy Spirit, and afterwards that of prophecy; he will prophesy and foretell future events." Apparently, Nahmanides saw prophecy as something which happens in every age: "In the souls of a few men there appears to be a prophetic capacity such that they are able to foresee future events. The man does not know from where this power comes, but if he isolates himself a spirit comes to him and says: Thus will be the future in a certain matter. The philosophers call this man a *kahin* ['prophet' in Arabic], and they do not know the cause of this phenomenon, but the matter has been confirmed by eye witnesses . . . and this man is deemed a prophet because he prophesied what came to pass."Cf. his commentary on Deut. 3:2. Cf. the commentary of R. Abraham ibn Ezra on Isaiah 44:25, "for some souls have this power of intense contemplation." Cf. his commentary on Exod. 3:9. Cf. also R. Judah al-Botini's *Sefer Sulam ha-Aliyah,* especially the chapter which deals

among these esoterics that the secrets were revealed to the Kabbalists by Elijah himself. This opinion, which contributed mightily to the diffusion of the Kabbalah, was already widely prevalent in Kabbalistic circles in the thirteenth century.[90] According to this

---

with the methods of contemplation and cleaving which result in the investiture by the Holy Spirit; cited by G. Scholem, *Kitvei Yad be-Kabbalah* (Jerusalem, 1930), p. 225.

90. Eight different views have been advanced regarding this matter.

(1) The best-known source is the statement of R. Menachem Recanati, *Perush al ha-Torah,* Naso. The first edition (Venice, 1523) was unknown to scholars, and their quotations from this work are invariably drawn from the second edition. the first edition says: "The pious R. Isaac, son of the master, who was third after Elijah." This is also found in the R. Shem Tov Gaon's *Keter Shem Tov,* printed in R. Judah Koreit's *Sefer Ma'or va-Shemesh* (Livorno, 1839), p. 35b: "I received this as an oral tradition stretching back to R. Isaac, son of the master, from my teacher, who said about him that he was the third successor of Elijah." The phrase "third after Elijah" can have two meanings: either that R. Isaac received the tradition from a student of Elijah's and Elijah is included in the line of those who are enumerated (this would be the explanation of the phrase as given via the stylistic rendition of the *Meirat Einai'im;* cf. below, the second source), or that he received it from a pupil twice removed from Elijah (the style of the fourth source). What is common to both is that R. Isaac was not himself deemed worthy of a visitation by Elijah. If the author believed that Elijah had appeared to R. Isaac, he would not have concealed this fact. According to this source, it is impossible to deduce with exactitude who it was that was the beneficiary of an appearance by Elijah.

(2) R. Isaac of Acre's *Me'irat Einayim,* Beshallaḥ, JTS MS 878, p. 26a; MS 877, p. 78b, cites the opinion of the *Keter Shem Tov* that R. Isaac the Blind was the third after Elijah, with the additional explanation: "His father, R. Abraham ben David (Rabad), was the second to Elijah, since he received it from Elijah."

(3) *Meirat Einayim,* loc. cit.: ויה"ב שנ"ד דער"ט thus in MS 878, and should be ?דעת"ו;, in MS 877 it is ויש"ד and its meaning is: "And I, Isaac the humble, the son of Samuel, watched over by God, from Acco, may it be rebuilt and firmly established" (cf. M. Halperin, *Notarikon* [Tel Aviv, 1930], p. 86, according to *Kerem Ḥemed* 9 [1856], p. 146), "I have it as a tradition that R. Jacob the Nazirite was the person who received it from Elijah and that R. Abraham ben David received it from Rabbi Jacob the Nazirite and that R. Isaac the Blind received it from his father, R.

Abraham ben David. If so, R. Isaac is the fourth to Elijah." According to R. Judah Hayyat's Commentary to the *Ma'arekhet ha-Elohut* (Mantua, 1555), chap. 14, R. Isaac was called "the fourth to Elijah."

(4) We find the following in Rabbi H. Y. D. Azulai' *Shem ha-Gedolim, Ma'arekhet Gedolim,* s.v. Rabad the second: "R. Isaac the Nazirite received it from Elijah the Prophet, and after him, R. Jacob the Nazirite, and from him it was received by the Rabad and his son R. Isaac the Blind, the fourth to Elijah." An analysis of the sources demonstrates that their common denominator is the tradition concerning R. Isaac the Blind and the source of his wisdom. Apparently, the oldest tradition lies in the statement that R. Isaac was the third or fourth to Elijah .The various attempts to clarify the evolution of the Kabbalistic reception from Elijah to R. Isaac resulted in different conclusions:

Me'irat Einayim	*Explanation #2—Ḥayyat*	*Keter Shem Tov—Recanati first ed.*
R. Isaac is fourth to Elijah		R. Isaac is third after Elijah
Azulai MS	*Me'irat Eynayim,* 2nd explanation	*Me'irat Eynayim,* 1st explanation
Elijah is revealed to R. Isaac the Nazirite.	Elijah is revealed to R. Jacob the Nazirite.	Elijah is revealed to R. Abraham ben David, author of the *Hasaggot*

(5) MS Halberstam, no. 388, p. 19b. Cf. S. Z. Halberstam, *Kehilat Shelomo* (Vienna, 1890), p. 109: "Elijah revealed himself to our teacher R. David, the Chief Judge (the father of Rabad, author of the *Hasaggot*), and opened before him the gate of prayer through the utilization of the Kabbalistic art; he in turn transmitted this knowledge to his son, who then conveyed it to his son, R. Isaac the Blind."

(6) R. Shem Tov, *Sefer ha-Emunot* (Ferrara, 1556), gate 4, chap. 10. The same formulation is also found in the JTS MS: "There is a tradition among some of the later authorities that Elijah revealed himself to the great teacher, R. Abraham the Pious (author of the *Eshkol*) . . . and his son-in-law, the Rabad received this from him."

(7) R. Joshua ibn Shueib. *Derashot* (Constantinople, 1523), *Pineḥas* (and in JTS MS 1340), "And in the time of Rabad, we have heard, Elijah was revealed to him." According to the author of *Sefer Yuḥasin* (ed. Filipowski), p. 220, the reference is to Rabad, the author of the *Hassagot.*

(8) In Recanati's *Peirush le-Torah* (Venice, 1545), Naso, p. 173d, and in the Lublin 1595 ed. (printed in R. Mordecai Jaffe's *Levush Or Yikrat*), p. 142b, the following was added to the first source: "He revealed himself to R. David the Chief Judge and taught him the art of Kabbalah; he transmitted this to his son the Rabad, to whom he appeared also; he in turn transmitted it to his son, R. Isaac the Blind . . . and Elijah appeared also to him. He transmitted

notion, Elijah had appeared to Kabbalistic masters living in Provence in the twelfth century and at the beginning of the thirteenth, namely, R. Abraham ben R. Isaac, the second Rabad, the author of the *Eshkol*, and the chief rabbi of Narbonne;[91] R. David; the son of R. David, Abraham of Posquières, the third Rabad, the author of the *Hassagot* on Maimonides and the son-in-law of the author of the *Eshkol*; R. Isaac the Nazirite; R. Jacob the Nazirite ben R. Saul of Lunel and the colleague of the author of the *Hassagot*; R. Isaac the Blind, the son of the author of the *Hassagot*.[92] According to another source, "There lived in Narbonne a wondrously wise and hidden master who had received wisdom from a sage and rabbi. Even his wise and holy teacher attested to the fact that Elijah the Prophet appeared to him from one Day of Atonement to the next."[93]

R. Abraham ben David, the author of *Hassagot*, "the greatest judge in the land" (Rabbenu Asher), "the greatest among the teachers" (R. Solomon ibn Adret), "the greatest among the generations"

---

it to two of his students, the first was R. Ezra who wrote a commentary on the Song of Songs and the other was R. Azriel, and after them this tradition was passed on to Naḥmanides." Clearly, this addendum, which contradicts the beginning of his work, was not written by R. Menachem Recanati. It is missing from the first printed edition and also from JTS, Adler MS, no. 2503. Indeed, on the title page of the venice 1545 edition we find: "printed . . . with an addendum of some dicta of the *Zohar* and other sections from various books." R. Meir ibn Gabbai, *Avodat ha-Kodesh* II:13, apparently quotes the statement of Recanati according to the Venice 1546 edition; similarly *Meẓaref le-Ḥokhmah* (Basel, 1629), p. 15a; cf. *Derekh Emunah* at the beginning of the book, Question 2. It is in this form that these statements are to be found in the books of later Kabbalists; cf. *Pardes Rimonim*, Sha'ar 3, chap. 3. *Eẓ Ḥayyim*, introduction.

91. It is appropriate here to emphasize the importance of the words of R. Sheshet ben Sheshet concerning Narbonne, which have never been noticed by scholars. Cf. above, n. 67.

92. On the place of these savants in the development of Kabbalah, compare G. Scholem, "Hatḥalat ha-Kabbalah," *Knesset* 10 (1947), pp. 179–228.

93. MS Sassoon, *Ohel David*, I, p. 444. Cf. G. Scholem, "Sidrei de-Shimusha Rabah," *Tarbiẓ* 16 (1945), p. 205.

(Meiri), "one of the greatest of the world's saints,"[94] who was deemed so holy that descendants of the priesthood [who are forbidden to come into contact with the dead—trans.] occupied themselves with his burial,[95] admitted that he had many times received insight into Talmudic matters via the Holy Spirit. In his *Mishneh Torah*, Maimonides had legislated that a myrtle whose top had been severed was ritually fit for use in observance of the mitzvah of the four species. R. Abraham ben David attacks this view and says: "Many times over the past years prophetic inspiration has appeared in our *bet-midrash,* and we concluded that such a myrtle is unfit."[96] At various points in his writing he states, "Make your ears into a funnel and hear the word of the Lord . . . blessed be God, who has revealed his secrets to those who revere Him."[97] "I wish to inform the reader of this book that whatever is written in these pages I received, not from a teacher or a rabbi, but only with the aid of God, who teaches man wisdom . . . the reader should know that what is found here is secret lore, as it is written, 'The secret of the Lord is made known to those who revere Him.' "[98] In the very same critical note where he says of Maimonides, "This is only his personal opinion, I do not know where he derived it," he maintains that "Ezra knew that the

94. *Oreḥot Ḥayyim* II, p. 102.

95. *Sefer Yuḥasin,* ed. Filipowski, p. 220.

96. *M.T.*, Hilkhot Lulav 8:5; cf. R. Menachem Meiri, *Magen Avot,* pp. 115–125.

97. *M.T.,* Hilkhot Mitamei Mishkav u-Moshav 7:7.

98. Introduction to his commentary on Eduyot. Cf. his commentary on Sifra, Aḥrei Mot 1:12: "Originally I thought otherwise, but I was then vouchsafed an explanation from heaven." As I. H. Weiss has noted, *Sifra* (Vienna, 1862), introduction, p. viii, it is impossible to take this statement as mere metaphor. In another place, Rabad concludes a responsum on civil law: "My brother, here is the answer to your question, as heaven has made it known to me," *Temim Dei'im,* sec. 50. This language is also found in *Shitah Mekubbeẓet,* Baba Meẓia, p. 102a: *Ba'alei ha-Nefesh* at the end of *Sha'ar ha-Shammayim.* Cf. *Temim Dei'im,* sec. 59; sec. 11: "Concerning your question, I am obliged to answer in terms of what has been conveyed to me by the Creator and not from my own wisdom, for I am unworthy." And in sec. 3: "As the Creator will convey to me the secret that has been revealed

sanctity of the Temple and Jerusalem would be renewed in the future to an eternal sanctity when God's Glory [is revealed] to the world. So it has been revealed to me as a secret which God makes known to those who fear Him."[99] It is not to be doubted that R. Abraham ben David never used such expressions casually[100] and that he was certain he had reached the level of prophetic inspiration.

It was also related in the Book of Ahimaaz concerning R. Shefatiah (ca. 9th cent.) that he had precognition of events through the agency of prophetic inspiration.[101]

V
Divine Illumination

In the eyes of many of the sages, the investiture of the Holy Spirit was not limited to knowledge of esoteric matters. R. Abraham ben David was not alone in maintaining that inquiry and discursive reasoning are not the only means of acquiring knowledge.[102] R. Isaac the Tosafist[103] said of R. Isaac Alfasi the halakhist, "A man

---

to us." Cf. sec. 227. Cf. the commentary of R. Yehonatan of Lunel on R. Isaac Alfasi, Ḥullin, chap. 4, p. 87.

99. R. Menachem Meiri, *Bet ha-Beḥirah,* chap. 6, halakhah 14. R. Moshe ibn Habib, *Shemot ba-Areẓ,* "Kappot Temarim," p. 12b (Sukkah 32b), says that the words of Rabad are hyperbolic. Cf. *Shem ha-Gedolim, Ma'arekhet Gedolim,* Aleph, no. 10.

100. Cf. *Sefer Yerei'im* Amud ha-Yirah 34: "Therefore, let a man beware of jesting and making merry by saying, 'Thus has the Lord said to me.' " Cf. *Hagahot Maimuniot,* Hilkhot Akum 5:8.

101. A. Neubauer, *MJC,* vol. 2, p. 124; cf. p. 119: "And behold, the angel of the Lord appeared to them in a vision"; cf. D. Kaufmann, "Die chronik des Achimaaz von Oria," *Gesammelte Schriften* (Frankfurt a.M., 1915), vol. 3, pp. 14–22.

102. Cf. above, p. 8ff.

103. This may be R. Isaac of Dampierre; cf. above, p. 19.

would weary himself to little or no avail in the writing of such a work without having the divine presence resting on him."[104]

The master-rabbi of all generations, R. Solomon Itzhaki (Rashi), "precise to a fault in the use of language, who could allude to novellae through the change of but a single letter in a word," and who fasted, according to legend, 613 times before writing one word of his commentary on the Torah,[105] hinted that he had been granted divine illumination. Since one must take great pains in interpreting every stroke of Rashi's pen, how much the more so is one forbidden to derogate in any way that which he says in his commentary on the Temple structure in Ezekiel, "And as for me, neither teacher nor helper aided me in explaining this entire matter. So it has been shown me from heaven."[106] Rashi, who composed most of his commentaries on the basis of previous authorities, occasionally writes, "I have never heard nor found the correct interpretation of this verse . . . but I say" or "my heart has told me."[107] We have insufficient evidence to decide whether the words of R. Menahem ben Zerah, the student of R. Judah, the son of Rabbenu Asher (d. 1374), are based on an ancient tradition, viz., "The Holy Spirit rested on Rashi and his mastery of the Talmud was so overwhelming, enabling him to write commentaries on the Babylonian Talmud."[108] A reference to the possibility of visions and dreams is also contained in *Sefer Ḥasidim,* viz., "If a man is so meritorious that heaven itself is opened

104. Cited by R. Menachem ben Zeraḥ, *Ẓedah la-Derekh,* introduction.

105. *Shem ha-Gedolim,* s.v. Rashi.

106. This may be found in his commentary on Ezekiel 42:3 in the first two editions, Venice 1523–28 and Venice 1568, and also in JTS MS 346, p. 6a, which was apparently written in twelfth-century France. Interestingly, in some nineteenth-century editions, the publishers found this section repugnant and eliminated it completely! A. J. Levy, *Rashi's Commentary on Ezekiel* (Philadelphia, 1931), pp. 40–48, also deleted this sentence. Cf. also Rabad's language, above, n. 98.

107. Ezek. 29:21, Exod. 28:4.

108. *Ẓedah la-Derekh,* introduction; cf. "Likkutim mi-Divrei Yosef Sambari," in Neubauer, *MJC,* vol. 1, p. 127.

up before him, he should thereupon ask the Holy One, blessed be He, that he grant serenity and satisfaction to all his creatures."[109] According to another source, it was Rashi's custom to make inquiries of Heaven.[110]

This yearning to achieve knowledge through divine illumination also occurred among medieval Jewish philosophers.[111] They believed "that the ancients knew many things through divine illumination";[112] that "it was possible that thought could attend to something that was non-conceptual and incomprehensible"[113] and that "the heart could visualize that which the eye could not see." There are times when a man grasps a proposition inwardly and does not know how this comes about, since he heard no voice speaking to him.[114]

The view that a poet writes with the aid of divine grace, i.e., of the muse appointed for poetry, also appeared in the Middle Ages. Despite the fact that this view is different from the concept of

---

109. *Sefer Ḥasidim,* ed. Wistinetski, par. 426; and in the Bologna ed. [R. Margulies, ed.], par. 1146: "And were it not for the fact that men speak of what they see, they would perceive many more things, as do the animals, who see and do not speak."

110. "We have been informed that in former times Rashi had reached this spiritual rung," MS *She'elot u-Teshuvot min ha-Shammayim,* mentioned below, n. 151. Rashi believed in the power of practical Kabbalah, cf. B. Sanhedrin 62b, "Rabah created a man by means of *Sefer Yeẓirah,* where he learned to combine the letters of the Divine Name." Cf. also ibid. 67b, R. Hanina and R. Oshaiah "combined the letters of the Divine Name with which the world was created." Cf. above, n. 40.

111. I have devoted another essay to this topic. Cf. [the other essay in this volume] and that of B. Z. Dinaburg, "Aliyato shel R. Judah Ha-Levi le-Ereẓ Yisrael," *Minḥah le-David: Le-Yovel ha-Shive'im shel R. David Yellin* (Jerusalem, 1935), pp. 157–182.

112. R. Abraham ben David, *Emunah Ramah,* II, 4a, p. 58.

113. *Musarei ha-Filosofim,* I, p. 17.

114. R. Abraham bar Ḥiyya, *Megillat ha-Megalleh,* p. 41; cf. the introduction by J. Guttmann, p. xviii, also idem, "Ueber Abraham bar Chijja's *Buch der Enthüllung,*" *MGWJ* 47 (1903), p. 467, n. 1.

Despite the fact that this view is different from the concept of prophetic inspiration, both as to its essence and its origins—Homer, Hesiod, Pindar, Virgil, Plato, and Cicero ranged on one side; the prophets and the Tannaim on the other—[philosophy] did not refrain from mixing them.

According to Saadia, a poet was also denoted a prophet in the Hebrew language. "The band of prophets mentioned in I Samuel 10:5 is, in reality, a chorus of poets. And the meaning of the words 'and you shall prophesy together with them' is 'you will poetize without prior thought.'"[115] There was one thinker who opposed those who pegged their free and easy use of the divine spirit to the authority of the "mighty oak"—Maimonides. "The empty claim of those vain men, viz., that when a man is inspired to write poetry, this is to be reckoned as an incursion of the Holy Spirit—-God forbid that this be taken as the opinion of Maimonides, the unrivaled one amongst the Geonim."[116]

Even the discoverers of truths in the realm of knowledge spoke of their discoveries as the consequence of heavenly inspiration.

---

115. *Commentary to Sefer Yeẓirah* (Paris, 1891), ed. M. Lambert, p. 17; R. Moses ibn Ezra, *Shirat Yisrael,* p. 45. R. Judah al-Ḥarizi speaks of the Spanish poets in terms normally reserved for prophets; compare *Taḥkemoni,* Gate 18, 1; 18, 4; 50. Concerning the poetry of R. Judah Halevi, he said: "It is as if it emanates from the starry heavens or from the Holy Spirit."Gate 3, 6.

116. Commentary to *Sefer Yeẓirah* attributed to Rabad, 1:10 (Mantua, 1562), p. 51a. R. Jacob says in the book of his father, R. Abraham Gavison, *Omer ha-Shikheḥah,* p. 125c, that "poetics is noble and sublime and is majestic and more powerful than all other arts. The masters of the arts and the disciplines have all agreed that whoever is an adept of this art is not devoid of visitations from heaven, and that the Holy Spirit leaps and sparkles among them."And in the name of R. Saadiah ibn Danan: "all the poets may be prophets." Cf. also his introduction. Cf. the statement of Rashba, "The books of the Greeks were composed by seers; their authors were called prophets and seers." *Minḥat Kena'ot* (Pressburg, 1838), p. 45; H. Gross, "Zur Geschichte der Juden in Arles," *MGWJ* 31 (1882), p. 513. Concerning the question of inspiration and its relation to prophecy, see my book *Die Prophetie,* pp. 40 ff.

"exalted savants,"[117] said of the founders of the discipline of Hebrew grammar, "God revealed to them the secrets of the Hebrew tongue and its grammar."[118] And R. Solomon Parhon writes of his teacher R. Judah Halevi "that the Creator revealed to him matters which had not been made know to R. Saadia, the chief among the philosophers."[119] R. Jonah Ibn Janah, the most eminent Hebrew grammarian, says more than once that his discoveries had been hidden from other scholars and "were not aroused within them";[120] they were transmited only to him via heaven, "and it was as if I prophesied about them in an actual prophetic state."[121]

117. *Shirat Yisrael,* p. 52.

118. Ibid., p. 63.

119. *Maḥberet ha-Arukh,* introduction, p. xxii. Cf. also S. Munck, *Notice sur Abou'l-Walid* . . . (Paris, 1851), pp. 65, 194.

120. "That which we have discovered concerning these marvelous things and the proper assumptions which have not been revealed except to us, nor did others feel it, was done by God's grace and goodness towards us." *Sefer ha-Shorashim* (Berlin, 1893–96), ed. W. Bacher, p. 64. "You have shown wondrous insight in interpretation, and nobody but us has realized this, but the Creator, may He be exalted, has extended us this understanding and prepared this knowledge for us, through God's goodness towards me." Ibid., p. 411. [ואסאל אללה אל האמי פי דלך] Abulwalid, *Takrîb wa-Tashîl, Opuscules et Traites* . . . (Paris, 1880), ed. H. Derenbourg, p. 269; cf. *Sefer ha-Rikmah* (Berlin, 1929), ed. M. Wilenski, 98, 20. W. Bacher, *Leben und Werke des Ibn Ganâh,* p. 14, n. 81 (מה ד״ץ אממה מנא); W. Bacher, *Die Bibelexegese Moses Maimunis* (Budapest, 1896), p. 100, n. 3.

121. Cf. *Sefer ha-Rikmah,* p. 24; "For I have not attained this art, except through diligent inquiry, investigation, and continuous exertion, day and night, coupled with a consuming desire, as if I were prophesying a prophecy."

VI
The Dream as a Transmitter of the Divine

This is not the place to describe the opinion of the ancients about dreams, about the realistic or fantastic elements in them. It is enough to refer to the words of R. Sabbatai Donolo in his commentary on *Sefer Yeẓirah*, Part I, "Just as the Creator knows future events, so too a man may, in a state of spiritual tranquility and bodily rest from labor of a mundane character, slumber and sleep, and the spirit of life will rest from its preoccupation with bodily needs. He will then see in his dreams future events, the spirits of the dead and places he has never seen or other great things of astonishing character." Indeed, a considerable number of the sages believed that many matters had been conveyed to them in a night-time vision.

R. Moses Ibn Ezra devotes an entire chapter of his *Shirat Yisrael* ("The Poetry of Israel") to answering the question "concerning the testimony of some individuals who claimed that they wrote poetry in their dreams" and concludes that "it is impossible to deny that some poems and essays are composed in dreams. We ourselves have heard of this from famous men among our own people, men of truth who would not lie and upon whose intellect and trustworthiness one can rely." R. Moses Ibn Ezra cites the dream of R. Hai and the verse which R. Samuel ha-Nagid saw in his dreams. R. Isaac ben Giyyat also relates how he was once occupied with the composition of a poem about the tribulations and persecutions that had befallen his native city of Lucena. In a dream he composed verses from which it became clear to him how he could fashion his poem. He cites the opinion of "one of the wise men among our people" that there are dreams which "are conveyed by means of a divine power which causes the soul to know matters about intelligibles." At times, "the

Creator will move the soul to arouse it and make it aware of that which will take place and befall it in the future."[122] R. Solomon Ibn Gabirol was directed in a dream to write a didactic poem, wherein he could describe the grammatical principles of the Holy Tongue.[123]

So strong was the belief of many of the sages, viz., that information could be conveyed to them from on high, that at times they relied upon their dreams for decisions in matters of Halakha.[124] R. Eliezer ben Nathan (a contemporary of Rabbenu Tam), according to legend a miracleworker and capable of traveling long distances in an instant,[125] relates in his book:

> In the year 1152 it so happened that my son-in-law Eliakim poured kosher wine from a jug into a chalice from which a non-Jew drank, which made the vessel unusable. He asked me whether the wine was still to be considered kosher. I asked him in return if the chalice was dry; he answered yes. I then declared the wine fit for use by Jews. One Sabbath afternoon after lunch as I lay sleeping I dreamed that my father-in-law, my teacher, appeared and read out loud the verse "they who drink wine from bowls and eat swine!" and I interpreted this in the dream that it was referring to the non-Jews who drank forbidden wine. Upon awakening, I knew that he had appeared so as to inform me that the wine was unfit, because the chalice had not really been dry. I thereupon took the chalice and tested it and let it stand for two days and one night. The chalice was still not dry. I knew then that my

---

122. *Shirat Yisrael,* pp. 103–105.

123. *Shir Anak,* in *Shirei Shelomo ibn Gabirol* (Berlin, 1924), ed. H. N. Bialik and Y. Ravnitzky, vol. 1, p. 109. J. Egers, "Shirei R. Shelomo ibn Gabirol,"*Jubelschrift zum neunzigsten Geburtstag des Dr. L. Zunz* (Berlin, 1884), pp. 18–23, 193.

124. On this problem, cf. E. E. Urbach, "Halakhah u-Nevuah," *Tarbiz* 18 (1946), pp. 6 ff.

125. Brüll, *JJGL* 9 (1889), pp. 23, 38.

authorization of the wine had been in error. I prohibited the wine in the cask and I and all who had drunk from it fasted for two days.[126]

Concerning R. Isaac the son of R. Moses of Vienna, the author of *Or Zaru'a*, it is related that he was hesitant as to the correct spelling of R. Akiva's name—whether it ended with an *aleph* (a) or a *heh* (h). He had a dream where he saw the verse "light is sown for the righteous and joy for the upright in heart" (Ps. 97:11). The last letter of the words of this verse make up the name R. Akiva ending with a *heh*. And that is the reason he entitled his book *Or Zaru'a* ("Light is Sown").[127] He himself writes about this matter: "And because of the great love with which the Lord had enlightened my eyes, I found his name written in this verse."[128] And R. Menahem ben R. Jacob of Worms (d. in 1203) relates that "a dream-master once told him why the blessing is formulated as "on the circumcision." The blessing *al ha-milah* corresponds to the ages of Sarah and Abraham when the commandment concerning circumcision was given to Abraham—the word *al*, "on" in Hebrew is numerically equivalent to 100 [Abraham's age at his circumcision]; the word *ha-milah* is equivalent to 90—an allusion to Sarah's age [at the birth of Isaac].[129] R. Moses of Coucy

---

126. *Even ha-Ezer* (Prague, 1610), sec. 26, p. 14b; and in the note, *Gilyon Mordechai,* Avoda Zarah, chap. 5, *remez* 858. His father-in-law was R. Eliakim ben R. Joseph of Mainz.

127. *Seder ha-Dorot,* Sixth Millenium, s.v. R. Yitzhak Or Zaru'a [= *Seder ha-Dorot ha-Shalem,* Jerusalem, 1985, p. 218a].

128. *Or Zaru'a,* Alfa Beta (Zhitomir, 1862).

129. *Zikhron Berit la-Rishonim,* "Kelalei ha-Milah le-R. Gershon ha-Gozer," p. 130. H. Gross, "Das Handschriftliche Werk Assufot,"*MWJ* 10 (1883), pp. 65, 80. [And in the Commentary to the Torah, MS Parma, according to S. Schechter, "Notes on a Hebrew Commentary to the Pentateuch in a Parma Manuscript," *Semitic Studies in Memory of Alexander Kohut* (Berlin, 1897), p. 489; "It once happened to a man who was a *sandek* at one circumcision and upon returning to play the same role at another ceremony was told by the dream-master not to participate,"etc. S.L.].

was motivated to write his *Sefer Mitzvot ha-Gadol* ("The Great Book of the Commandments")[130] because of a dream. R. Elijah of Londres [London] believed that he had dreamed a prophetic dream.[131] R.

---

130. "At the beginning of the sixth millennium (1220) I had a dream where I was told to write a Torah scroll in two parts. When I carefully contemplated the dream, I discovered that the two parts betokened a book of positive commandments and one of negative commandments. Therefore, I, Moses ben Jacob, have undertaken to write the two books. . . . with reference to prohibitions, too, I dreamed that the following was said to me: You have forgotten the essential element: 'Take care, lest you forget the Lord your God' [Deut. 8:11]. For I had not thought to include this command among the enumerated prohibitions; Maimonides too had not listed this one. When I considered this matter deeply in the morning, I saw that it was a fundamental principle in the worship of God. I listed it in its proper place, among the fundamental principles. God knows that in my opinion (!) I do not falsify when it comes to dreams." *Sefer Mitzvot Gadol,* introduction; prohibition no. 64. "In the year 4995 after the creation [1235 C.E.] there occurred a heavenly sign of chastisement. In the year 4996 [1236 C.E.] I was in Spain, rousing the people to repent, and the Lord strengthened my hands in the dreams of both Jews and Gentiles and in discerning the appearance of the stars (Explanation: he was unequaled as an interpreter of dreams, R. Solomon Luria, *Amudei Shelomo,* positive commandment no. 3.), and the Lord stretched forth His goodness over me and the earth trembled, and everything shook before the Lord. Many turned in repentance, and tens of thousands accepted the commandments of tefillin, mezuzah, and ẓiẓit. The same occurred in all the other lands where I traveled." Ibid. Cf. H. Malter, "Dreams as a Cause of Literary Composition," *Jewish Studies in Honor of Kaufmann Kohler* (Berlin, 1913), pp. 149–203; M. Schreiner, "Le Kitab al-Mouhâdara wa-l-Moudhâkara de Moïse b. Ezra et ses sources," *REJ* 22 (1891), p. 64; R. Margulies, *She'elot u-Teshuvot min ha-Shammayim,* with notes of *Or ha-Shammayim,* introduction, where he has collected a great deal of material on dreams and the Holy Spirit.

131. "And I was queried in my dreams as to why we recite this prayer on the Sabbath—'that there be no sorrow or trouble for us on the day of rest' and not 'that we be spared sorrow or trouble on the day of our rest,' viz., why do we not pray for our own good rather than for the good of the day? In my dreams I answered: Were the latter formulation to be adopted, it would imply that sorrow and trouble occur to us on the other six days . . . and I awakened from my sleep and realized it was a real prophetic dream and not just one which had the conventional one-sixtieth

Eliezer of Beaugency maintained that the exegesis of a difficult verse had been explained to him in a dream.[132]

It was a commonly held belief that many matters were conveyed to mankind by the spirits of the deceased who appeared to human beings in visions of the night. At the beginning of the twelfth century, three days after his demise, Rabbi Amnon, the author of the Unetaneh Tokef prayer, appeared to R. Kalonymos ben R. Meshullam (after his thumbs and big toes were cut off because he refused conversion to Christianity) and "taught him that liturgical poem . . . he also commanded him to send it to every part of the diaspora so that it might be his witness and monument. The gaon [R. Kalonymos] did his bidding."[133] R. Ḥayyim Vital relates that after his death Rashi appeared to his grandson, R. Samuel.[134]

---

measure of prophecy within it." Y. N. Epstein, "Perishat R. Eliyah mi-Londres," *Mada'ei ha-Yahadut* I (1926), p. 63.

132. "Now this explanation came to me in a dream; out of my great anguish to know the meaning of this verse I fell asleep over the book, and I then saw a man giving me a scroll to read, and at the head of the third column, it was written, *ha-atikim ha-atidim, ha-ẓiẓim, ha-zeitim,*" R. Eliezer of Beaugency, *Peirush al Yeḥezkel u-Trei Asar* (Warsaw, 1913), ed. S. Poznanski, p. 97. Cf. also *Sefer Sha'ashuim,* p. 8.

133. The author of the *Or Zaru'a,* end of *Hilkhot Rosh Hashanah,* sec. 276, found the story in a MS of R. Ephraim ben R. Jacob of Bonn; Cf. also *Hagahot Asheri,* Rosh Hashannah, chap. 1; *Shalshelet ha-Kabbalah* (Amsterdam, 1697), 47b. Cf. I. Davidson, *Oẓar ha-Shirah veha-Piyyut* (New York, 1929), vol. 2, pp. 199 ff. Even the prayer Vehu Raḥum was ordained, according to legend, as a memorial to the miraculous vision given in a dream to a sage "who feared sin but was not a great scholar." Cf. L. Zunz, *Literaturgeschichte der synagogalen Poesie* (Berlin, 1865), p. 16; I. Elbogen, *Der Jüdische Gottesdienst* (Frankfurt a.M., 1931), p. 524.

134. "And he was awakened. He said to him: 'Who are you?' The answer came: 'I am Solomon your grandfather; stand up, wash your hands in purity, and you will learn from me the pronuciation of the hidden Name, since I have taught you everything but this.' He followed the instructions, and he sat next to him, but

According to legend, on the very night that Maimonides completed his *Mishneh Torah*, Moses our Teacher appeared to him.[135] According to another legend, Maimonides, upon his demise, appeared in a dream to one of the Egyptian rabbinic authorities and informed him as to the matter of his burial.[136]

---

remained invisible while he taught him." H. Y. D. Azulai, *Shem ha-Gedolim*, s.v. Rashi.

135. *Seder ha-Dorot*, Fourth Millenium, no. 927 (p. 204).

136. Joseph Sambari, *Divrei Yosef* (Berlin, 1896), pp. 34–35. Adjacent to the city of Folush, one day's journey from Bagdad, R. Petaḥiah in the twelfth-century saw "a grave, and a fine building was built over it." "It was said of him that he came in a dream to a fine rich Jew and said: 'My name is Bruzak, and if you construct a fine building on my grave, you will have sons born to you.' He built the house and sons were born to him. They did a dream inquiry and asked who was buried there. The answer was: 'I am Bruzak and I have no other name.'" *Sibbuv R. Petaḥiah* (Jerusalem, 1905), ed. A. Greenhut, p. 12.

VII
The Appearance of Elijah and Dream Inquiries in Western Europe

During the time of the Crusades, it was widely believed "that Elijah appeared openly, and not in a dream, to men of select lineage."[137] Thus he had revealed himself to R. Eliezer, the son of R. Judah the son of R. Eliezer the Great. Those were days of desperate longing for the coming of the Messiah. Rabbi Tuviah, the author of the book *Lekaḥ Tov,* wrote in an epistle, "Signs and wonders have occurred in our land. Even Elijah the Prophet has appeared." In a city close to Constantinople, Jews who had seen Elijah banded together in fellowships. The Jewish community refused to believe them and they were excommunicated.[138]

Legend relates that R. Samuel the Prophet said to his son, R. Abraham, "My son, the time is ripe for your brother, Judah. Know that you will be head of the academy the rest of your days, but your brother Judah will know what is above and what is below; nothing will remain hidden from him and he shall be a Master of the Divine Name."[139] It was said of R. Judah the Pious that he had the power of precognition of future events.[140] An incident is told concerning R. Judah ben Schneur, the head official of Speyer, who "visited with him [R. Judah] on the eve of Passover; when they reached the hymn Ki Lo Na'eh, R. Judah the Pious became very happy. R. Judah danced and clapped his hands from excessive joy . . . and I heard that then R. Judah the Pious said to him that Elijah the Prophet, of blessed remembrance, was here with us! Then R. Judah said,

137. J. Mann, "Tenu'ot Meshiḥiot be-Yemei Masa'ei ha-Ẓelav ha-Rishonim,"*Ha-Tekufah* 23 (1925), p. 256.

138. Ibid. Cf. also F. Baer, "Eine jüdische Messiasprophetie auf das Jahr 1186, und der dritte Kreuzug,"*MGWJ* 70 (1926), pp. 113 ff.

139. N. Brüll, *JJGL* 9 (1889), p. 33.

140. Ibid., p. 28.

'Woe is me, for I was not worthy enough to be conscious of his presence.' R. Judah the Pious replied, 'Be happy, for the opposite is true—Elijah was closer to you than to me.'" However, R. Judah the Pious was not thought of as a prophet. The tradition is this: "If a pious man lived in the days of the prophets he is called a prophet; in the days of the Tannaim he would have been regarded as a Tanna and in the days of the Amoraim he would have been considered an Amora."[141] "When it came time for him to die, the leading men and students of the city visited him. He ordered that the house and the space before his bed be swept. He said to his visitors, 'Do you see anything?' They answered, 'We see nothing—except that in the dust before your bed there is written the word *ḥasid* [pious].' He thereupon said, 'Give me ink and quill, and I shall write down the date of the redemption and disclose it to you.' The moment the quill was placed in his hand, he died."[142]

It is also told of the grandson of R. Judah the Pious, R. Eleazar, that once, while he was blowing shofar on Rosh Hashanah in his study hall, his wife heard a man in the house of study laughing. She asked her husband, "Who can this be who makes merry while you blow the shofar?" She importuned her husband with this question until he answered, "It is Elijah the Prophet who entreats me to sound the shofar; I do it so ineptly that he laughs at me."[143]

R. Ephraim b. R. Isaac of Ratisbon (called R. Ephraim in the Tosafot and in the Codes [d. 1175]), and himself a Tosafist and praiseworthy liturgist, a student and disputant of Rabbenu Tam, relates that Elijah appeared to him. R. Ephraim opposed the

---

141. Ibid., pp. 22–23. Cf. Y. Kamelhar, *Ḥasidim ha-Rishonim,* p. 30.

142. N. Brüll, op. cit., p. 43. According to *Sibbuv R. Petaḥiah,* ed. A. Greenhut, p. 7, R. Judah ha-Hasid did not want to record the time of redemption. Cf. *Sefer Ḥasidim,* ed. Wistinetski, par. 212.

143. Brüll, op. cit., p. 22. According to legend, Elijah revealed himself to R. Isaac, the father of Rashi; Cf. L. Ginzberg, "Hagadot Ketuot," *Ha-Goren* 9 (1922), pp. 54 f.

observance and preservation of any custom that did not appear in the Talmud and he mocked those who claimed that "the custom of Israel constitutes Torah." "Not only did he seek to uproot ancient customs that were repugnant to him in his own town, but in every place that he visited, he would seek out customs that deserved to be uprooted and he wished to abolish them."[144] Because of this predilection, he stirred up controversy and quarrels with contemporary sages. But he was firm in his opinions and stormed at those who refused to listen to him. Once he had a meal of turbot. At night an old man with silver hair and a great long beard appeared to him. The old man was carrying a container filled with creeping things that were shouting at him, 'Come and eat.' He was revolted and stepped back saying, 'They are the creeping things of the sea!' The old man replied, 'They are just as permitted as the swarming creatures you ate today.' When he awoke he knew that Elijah had appeared to him. From that day forward he disallowed the eating of turbot."[145]

---

144. V. Aptowitzer, *Mavo le-Sefer Ra'avyah,* p. 322.

145. *Tashbaẓ Katan,* sec. 352; *Hagahot Asheri,* Avoda Zarah, chap. 2, sec. 41. The author of *Or Zaru'a,* Piskei Avoda Zarah, sec. 200, heard this "from the lips of the holy R. Judah *ha-Ḥasid* . . . whoever eats turbot will not be accounted worthy of eating Leviathan." Rabbenu Ephraim "permitted this fish, and on that same night he dreamed that he was brought a bowl of crawling things to eat, whereupon he grew angry at the server. The latter said: 'Why are you angered, did you not declare them permitted food?' Rabbenu Ephraim became angery at this and awoke. He then recalled his authorization of the turbot on that very day. He rose and broke all the pots and bowls from which he had eaten." R. Ephraim is mentioned in the story concerning the appearance of Moses, cf. above, p. 17. [The words of R. Isaiah the Elder of Trani in his responsa are interesting, MS Cambridge (according to S. Schechter "Notes on Hebrew Mss. in the University Library at Cambridge," *JQR,* O.S. 4 [1892], p. 98): "Despite the fact that dreams are not to be considered as warranted evidence either pro or con, and one should not rely on them, Elijah appeared to me in a dream and I asked him concerning the lung adhesions which many people consider permissible in a slaughtered animal. He answered that all adhesions which are in places where they do not naturally grow rendered the animal

Among the German pietists it was a widespread custom to seek out the correct interpretations of dreams via the invocation of angels. A pietist once inquired the meaning of a dream from his companion in the Garden of Eden (i.e., an angel).[146] The most eminent of the pietists saw here proper grounds for caution, and they warned, "Let a man distance himself from such doings, neither to inquire after the meaning of dreams himself nor invoke the aid of others in doing so . . . If a man think, 'It is better that I make a dream inquiry so that I might know which is the best wife for me to marry,' his enterprise will never succeed. Nothing is more proper for a man than to pray to the Holy One, blessed be He; and if one goes on a journey, let him not say, 'I shall invoke the angels to guard me on my way,' rather let him entreat the Lord to safeguard him."[147] And R. Isaac of Corbeille tells us that R. Judah the Pious would warn his disciples not to set out on their wedding journeys for fear of bandits. They disregarded his warning and journeyed safely back and forth, but only by dint of (continual) invocation of the divine name (as a protective talisman). Upon their return he said to them, "You have lost your portion in the world to come, unless you repeat your journey without invoking the divine name and thus expose yourselves to death." They went forth and were slain.[148]

One of the Tosafists, R. Jacob ha-Levi the Zaddik of Marvège, would, as a matter of course, ask guidance of heaven "on halakhic matters in areas of juristic doubt, and when it came to deciding issues

---

unfit. The difference between the Ḥasidei Ashkenaz and the Italian rationalists is only a matter of formulation S.L.].

146. *Sefer Ḥasidim,* ed. Wistinetski, par. 80; Rashba, *Minḥat Kenaot* (Pressburg, 1838), p. 29, relates "that he received clear and distinct information to the effect that the Ḥasidei Ashkenaz engaged in practices utilizing demons; they would bind the demons by oaths, use them as messengers, and utilize their services in many ways."

147. *Sefer Ḥasidim,* par. 211, cf. par. 379, p. 116.

148. *Amudei Golah* (Cracow, 1596), mitzvah 3.

between conflicting authorities. He would do this by isolating himself through prayer and pronouncement of the divine names. He would then receive answers to his questions." "Great and wonderful deeds and decisions were performed by him."[149] This was his normal procedure whenever there was doubt concerning a halakhah: He would command that the doors of the study hall be locked, then God would appear to him in a vision and resolve all the difficulties. Thus anyone seeking the solution to a problem would have it answered by God. And this was known to everyone, for he was in a trancelike state until some specific matter was brought to the entrance of his study and immediately he was awakened from his sleep.[150] His collection of responsa has come down to us with the title *Responsa from Heaven.*[151]

149. *Teshuvot Radbaz,* sec. 532. Cf. the introduction of R. Margulies, *She'elot u-Teshuvot min ha-Shammayim.* [In MS Parma, Commentary to the Torah, according to S. Schechter, "Notes on a Hebrew Manuscript to the Pentateuch in a Parma Manuscript," *Semitic Studies in Memory of Alexander Kohut* (Berlin, 1897), p. 488: R. Joseph ben R. Isaac asked R. Isaac of Rome about this verse in a dream, and he explained it, etc. S.L.]

150. JTS Enelow MS 682. Cf. A. Marx, "A New Collection of Manuscripts," *PAAJR* 4 (1933), p. 153.

151. Published together with the *Teshuvot ha-Radbaz,* vol. 5 (Livorno, 1818); *She'elot u-Teshuvot min ha-Shammayim* with the critical notes of *Keset ha-Sofer* (Cracow, 1895); with R. Margulies' critical notes, *Or la-Shammayim* (Lwów, 1929). Cf. M. Steinschneider, "Jacob aus Marvège der Himmelscorrespondent," *HB* 14, p. 122; H. Brody "Einzelschriften," *ZfHB* 1 (1896), p. 7; H. Gross, *Gallia Judaica,* pp. 364 f.; B. Cohen, *Kuntres ha-Teshuvot* (Budapest, 1930), no. 803; cf. *Shibbolei ha-Leket,* no. 157; "We do not require the dreams of R. Jacob of Marvège nor the solution he received through a dream query. . . . indeed, we do not pay attention to dreams since we have a rule that it [the Torah] is not in heaven"; cf. E. E. Urbach, "Halakhah u-Nevu'ah," *Tarbiẓ* 18 (1946), p. 22, n. 186. H. Y. D. Azulai, *Shem ha-Gedolim,* s.v. Jacob ha-Ḥasid; *Birkei Yosef,* Oraḥ Ḥayyim 604b. In JTS EMC MS 682; JNUL, MS 90, cf. I. Joel, *Reshimat Kitve Yad ha-Ivri'im* (Jerusalem, 1934), no. 220; *Kiryat Sefer* 2 (1925), p. 117; H. Rosenberg, "Ḥibburei Rav H. Y. D. Azulai . . . ," *Kiryat Sefer* 5 (1928), p. 159.

Apparently, R. Jacob did not employ divine names nor did he invoke angels,[152] but would pray and entreat the Lord that He "might charge the holy angels whose realm was dream-inquiries" to answer his queries.[153] From one intimation, we can infer that he would [awake from his trance] to find a written responsum before him.[154] When the answer appeared unclear, he would repeat the question as many as three times[155] on the same night(?)[156] or on the succeeding night; he would "seek to explain the answer to me or replace it with a more lucid one."[157] In one answer it was said, "We have made this known to you, O chosen man."[158] When he demanded to know whether the replies he had been receiving "had emanated . . . from the Holy Spirit . . . or whether they came from another spirit," the answer came, "In truth it is the word of the Lord."[159] Most of his questions concerned liturgical matters and forbidden foods. "He also asked the date of the future redemption, but he did not find the answer written down before him."[160]

We know the description of the condition of the questioner of dream inquiries from another era. It is related concerning R. Michael the Angel, "that he would devise inquiries; his soul would ascend to heaven to propound his questions. He would remain shut away

---

152. "Is it permitted to utilize the Holy Name of forty-two letters to invoke and bind the angels appointed over the Torah so that one might become expert in all he wishes to learn, or the angels in charge of riches or power so that one might find favor in the eyes of princes, or is it forbidden to utilize this? They answered: Holy, holy, holy is the Lord of Hosts. He alone will provide for you in all your ways." *She'elot u-Teshuvot min ha-Shammayim,* Margulies ed., sec. 9.

153. Secs. 3, 5.

154. Cf. below n. 160.

155. Secs. 5, 10, 16; 22.

156. Sec. 22.

157. Sec. 32.

158. Sec. 43.

159. Sec. 5.

160. Sec. 71.

in his room for three days and specifically ordered that it not be opened. People would peep through the lattice-work and see him prone upon the ground, motionless as a stone. Thus he would remain shut away for three days like a corpse upon its bier, neither stirring nor moving: after three days he would come to life and stand up; it is for this reason that he was called R. Michael the Angel.[161]

161. Cf. *Sefer ha-Kabbalah le-R. Abraham bar Shelomo, MJC,* I, p. 105. R. Simon ben Ẓemach Duran, *Magen Avot,* III, chap. 4, p. 72b, mentions "those who occupy themselves with dream queries while awake. Just as my father and teacher told me that his grandfather had asked and received true answers while in a waking state." So, too, R. Abraham Ibn Ezra writes in his Commentary on Exodus 14:19, "In *Sefer Raziel* [it is written], he who desires to make inquiry through dreams, let him read the following verse of seventy-two letters at the onset of night: 'In the thirtieth year' [Ezek. 1:1]." And in another place he writes: "A man mentions the holy names or the names of angels in order to know God's will or to make known that which is secret; then the Holy Spirit is revealed to him; his flesh, which is truly maggoty and wormy, like a garment [to the soul], shudders and trembles before the onrush of the Holy Spirit; he cannot suffer its force. He becomes like one who is about to fall in a dead faint; he does not know where he is, he does not perceive or know or feel anything through his body, but his soul sees and hears, that is called a seer and a visionary." Cited by R. Moses Taku, in R. Kircheim, *Sefer Ketav Tamim, Oẓar Neḥmad* 3 (1860), p. 85. Compare to Commentary of R. Abraham Ibn Ezra on Ps. 139:18, D. Rosin, "Die Religions philosophie Abraham Ibn Esra's," *MGWJ* 42 (1898), p. 205, according to MS Breslau. Cf. *Oẓar Neḥmad,* ibid., p. 97: "Ibn Ezra was involved with demons, who always accompanied him; he could discern supernal secrets from the entrails of a steer, secrets which even the angels were not privy to; nevertheless, the demons would give him access to them. I have heard it from Englishmen, among whom Ibn Ezra later died, that he was once riding in a forest and blundered into a pack of black dogs who surrounded him and stared at him; they were undoubtedly demons, for when he emerged from the forest he fell sick and died from that illness." And on p. 96: "Ibn Ezra wrote reasons that were mad . . . all of them were products of nightmares which appeared to him as if he were writing under the influence of the Holy Spirit." And in *Ma'amar Eẓ Ḥayyim* by R. Isaiah ben Joseph of Tabriz (cf. G. Scholem, *Kitvei Yad ba-Kabbalah* [Jerusalem, 1930], MS no. 15, p. 42), the author cites the following from Ibn Ezra's Commentary to the Torah: "Behold, the doors and gates of the [divine name] are locked; no man can tell me the secret things; and this yearning to know burns in

VIII
Elijah's Appearance and Dream Inquiries in Geonic Circles

Even among the geonim, the lords and masters of the Torah in Babylonia, there were those who yearned for visions similar to those conferred upon the prophets.[162] It was said that Elijah had manifested himself to some of the geonim.[163] R. Sherira Gaon said of R. Joseph

---

my heart and the glowing coal is not extinguished. There came a day and I was aglow with hope; I dreamed that I beheld a clear bright light . . . and it was the father of the wise and the chief of the prophets, my master, Moses, of blessed memory . . . and he said to me, 'I see that you long for the divine secrets and to know the meaning of the name of God. . . . now I shall hint as to its meaning, and if the Lord has granted you [an understanding heart], you will then know it.' This he did. I then awoke in great joy and wrote down what I had heard so that I might not forget it." According to Ibn Ezra's story, "an Arab king named al-Zafah . . . fasted for forty days, so that the master of dreams might permit him to translate the book [*Kalilah Wa'dinah* in Sanskrit] into Arabic"; cf. M. Steinschneider, "Zur Geschichte der Uebersetzungen aus dem Indischen ins Arabische,"*ZDMG* 24 (1870), p. 356. On the procedure of dream divination, cf. *Sefer Raziel* (Amsterdam, 1701), pp. 3a, 33b, 40a; Commentary of R. Moses Botarel on *Sefer Yeẓirah* 4:3. Cf. *Yefei Mar'eh, Ma'aser Sheini,* chap. 4: "Our eyes have witnessed how many of the learned have relied on the divinatory power of dreams through the aid of the art of Kabbalah to receive true and faithful answers."

162. Cf. B. M. Lewin, *Oẓar ha-Ge'onim,* Ḥagigah, p. 13.

163. According to the story in *Sefer Ḥasidim,* ed. Wistinetski, par. 630, p. 169, R. Hai Gaon traveled each year to Jerusalem from Babylonia, in order to circumambulate the Mount of Olives, during Sukkot. He laughed after the meal and said: "I purify myself on Hoshana Rabah and Elijah walks with me; that is why, when he talks with me, those behind and before me are kept at a distance. I once asked him: 'When will the Messiah come?' He answered: "When the Mount of Olives is ringed about by priests." I then took all the priests I could find, perhaps there were among them enough priests. Elijah then said to me: 'The priests that you see are all dressed in costly robes and tread the earth arrogantly; not one of them is a true descendant of Aaron, with the exception of one who stands in the rear, who is despised by his fellows and is clothed in rags. Indeed, he rejects honor and hides

bar R. Abba, the head of the Yeshiva of Pumbeditha (ca. 9th cent.), that one day in his old age, while immersed in thought, he said to the scholars, "Make room for the hoary-headed one who has appeared to me." The sages saw no one, but understood that he meant Elijah and they cleared a large space. What is customary today, viz., "that a space is cleared on the right of the master who sits at the head of the academy," derives from this incident. R. Sherira did not relate this as a folktale. His grandfather, R. Judah, was the scribe of R. Joseph "and was his aide in all matters pertaining to the academy during the latter's lifetime."[164] According to another tradition, R. Judah maintained that "Elijah the Prophet appeared in the academy of R. Joseph many times."[165]

During that era, there lived in Bagdad a certain R. Aaron the son of R. Samuel, known to R. Eleazer, the author of *Roke'aḥ*, as "the father of mysteries." Of him it was told that he performed miracles by invoking "holy names"[166] and was "able to restore wandering spirits of the dead to their resting places." He left Babylonia and journeyed to the city of Lucca, Italy, where he spread the knowledge

---

his identity; he limps on one leg and on his other side he lacks an eye. This is a true priest, a descendant of Aaron.'" R. Ḥai said: "By my life, I laughed that the only one among them who was truly a priest had bodily defects." Cf. V. Aptowitzer, *Meḥkarim be-Sifrut ha-Geonim* (Jerusalem, 1941), p. 25. "We have an oral tradition to the effect that Elijah manifested himself even in the days of the geonim. The reason he does not appear in our times is due to the failure of our generation and because of our sins; no man is worthy of his reappearance." R. Joshua ibn Shueib, *Derashot, Parshat Pineḥas.* Cf. *Shem ha-Gedolim,* s.v. geonim: "And I have seen in books and heard from the scribes that Elijah revealed himself to some of the *ge'onim.*"

164. B. M. Lewin, ed., *Iggeret Rav Sherira* (Haifa, 1921), pp. 109 f.

165. Rabad, *Sefer ha-Kabbalah, MJC,* vol. 1, p. 64; *Kiẓẓur Zekher Ẓaddiq,* ibid., p. 92. In these sources this gaon is named as R. Joseph bar Judah (!). It is claimed that "he was a great pietist and well versed in the miraculous," ibid., vol. 1, p. 64.

166. R. Moses Botarel, commentary to *Sefer Yeẓirah* 4:3.

of Torah and transmitted "mysteries" and especially the "mysteries of the authorized prayers" to R. Moshe ben Kalonymos.[167]

In the tenth century, Nisi Naharwani, the head of the Babylonian Academy (Kallah), a sightless man, but one of extraordinary spirit, was honored above all in his generation as a master of miracles and secrets. Close to the year 920, when David ben Zakkai was appointed exilarch, R. Kohen-Zedek, the head of the academy of Pumbeditha, opposed him and refused to accept his authority, despite the fact that the head of the Sura academy together with all of his faculty blessed ben Zakkai and accepted him as the exilarch. A three-year controversy then ensued between the two leaders of the age which was harmful to them and harmful to the nation and which was liable to bring confusion and dissension into the camp of Israel. It was then that Nisi intervened "in a peaceful manner hoping that he could establish his [ben Zakkai's] authority over the academy of Pumbeditha, and that Kohen-Zedek, the head of the academy, would accept him. One night Nisi unlocked all of the gates of Babylonia by pronouncing the divine name. Four (according to another version, fourteen) locked doors gave way before him until he reached the presence of Kohen-Zedek, who was studying in the middle of the night. When the latter espied him, he ran towards him and asked why he had come. Nisi replied, "By my life, I did not come into your room until I opened up four locks." Kohen-Zedek then asked, "What do you want of me now?" Nisi answered, "Do as I direct." Thus the gaon and the exilarch were reconciled.[168]

---

167. *Megillat Aḥima'aẓ MJC,* vol. 2, pp. 112 ff.; Cf. H. Gross, "Zwei kabbalistische Traditionsketten des R. Eleazar aus Worms,"*MGWJ* 49 (1905), p. 696; D. Kaufmann, *Gesammmelte Schriften,* III, pp. 5–11.

168. R. Nathan ha-Bavli, *MJC,* vol. 2, p. 79. The Arabic version was published by I. Friedlander, "The Arabic Original of the Report of R. Nathan Hababli,"*JQR,* O.S. 17 (1905), pp. 747 ff. His hypothesis on p. 760, n. 9, is far-fetched. Cf. also S. Poznanski, "Inyanim Shonim li-Tekufat ha-Geonim,"*Ha-Kedem* 2 (1908), p. 106, n. 6; L. Ginzberg, *Geonica* (New York, 1909), vol. 1, pp. 32 ff. Rav Nisi composed

Legend tells that some of the geonim were masters of dream inquiries. R. Saadia Gaon did not know how many letters there were in the Torah; he invoked an angel by pronouncing the divine name and was then supplied with the information.[169] R. Sherira sought to determine the arrival of the Messiah through dream inquiry;[170] and

---

a *vidui* and various liturgical poems; cf. I. Davidson, *Oẓar ha-Shirah veha-Piyyut,* vol. 4, p. 452; *Ha-Kedem,* ibid.

169. H. Y. D. Azulai, *Shem ha-Gedolim,* s.v. Saadia. Cf. "Otiyot le-Rabbenu Saadiah," at the end of *Likkutei ha-Shulḥan Arukh shel ha-Ari,* (n.p., 1783). According to R. Moses Botarel, *Peirush le-Sefer Yeẓirah* 4:3. Rav Saadia, Rav Hai Gaon, and Maimonides all indulged in divinatory dreams. Saadia tells us that "when the wicked saw that I had written . . . a book in Hebrew, divided into sentences, with all the necessary punctuation signs and diacritical marks, they began circulating slanderous gossip that my book was claiming prophetic status."*Sefer ha-Galui,* p. 3b. He was suspected "on the grounds of denying the cessation of prophecy." A. Harkavy, *Zikhron la-Rishonim* (Vilna, 1881), vol. 5, p. 160. Despite the fact that we are loath to lend ourselves to "slanderous gossip," the circulation of this suspicion throws light on the mentality of that epoch. When one seeks to spread a slanderous rumor about a person, he will choose only a believable tidbit, one to which the listener will give credence. But we have no proof that Saadia was in pursuit of the Holy Spirit. He repelled those who accepted a literal interpretation of his claim to being inspired from above (*hei'anoto mi-marom,* A. Harkavy, *Zikhron le-Rishonim,* vol. 5, p. 166, line 12). For all that, he prayed for the restoration of prophecy in the Shaḥarit service (cf. *Siddur Rav Saadia,* p., 80, "Send the Redeemer and let him redeem us and bring us happily to our land, with the light of your presence among us, and the vision of your prophets in our midst"). He believed that with the advent of the Redeemer, all the children of Israel would become prophets; "If an Israelite should travel in any land and say: 'I am an Israelite,' they will say to him, 'Tell us what will happen tomorrow or what happened yesterday,' which was a secret to them. And when he does tell them, it will become clear to them that he is indeed an Israelite." *Sefer Emunot ve-De'ot* (Leipzig, 1864), ed. D. Slutzki, p. 125. Cf. the other essay in this volume, n. 100. According to MS *Sefer ha-Ḥayyim,* R. Saadia knew "that on the basis of *Sefer Yeẓirah,* it was possible to fashion a golem." *Sefer Yeẓirah with the Commentary of Abu-Saḥal Dunash ben Tamim* (London, 1902), ed. M. Grossberg, p. 7, n. 1.

170. "Likkutim mi-Divrei R. Yosef Sambari," *MJC,* vol. 1, p. 117; R. Menasseh ben Israel, *Nishmat Ḥayyim,* treatise 3, chap. 6: "Rav Sherira Gaon once engaged

R. Hai imposed an oath on the angelic master of dreams and a hint concerning redemption was revealed to him.[171]

R. Hai Gaon testified that R. Abraham Gaon Kabassi could foresee the future through the movements of tree leaves on days when there was no wind. "He would wrap the tree in sheets. This is a glorious science. He would make known great wonders by means of which human beings would recognize the truth."[172]

---

in a dream-query, and they read before him a verse . . . this hinted at the answer to his question, but he did not understand. He renewed his question and then the matter was fully explained to him."

171. J. Kobak, "Likkutei Batar Likutei," *Ginzei Nistarot* 3 (1872), p. 29. [In another MS, A. Neubauer, "Documents Inédits,"*REJ* 12 (1886), p. 92, the incident is conveyed in the name of "a wise man who was a Sephardi." S.L.] Cf. Asheri, B. Yoma, chap. 8, 19; "And R. Hai said that the High Priest did not say *Ana Ha-Shem* [upon ministering in the temple on the Day of Atonement] but would say aloud the forty-two-letter name of God. This name still exists in the academy by tradition and is known to the sages." Cf. the statements of R. Hai in his responsum, *Ta'am Zekenim,* pp. 57 ff.: "Now there are men whose dreams are vivid and clear; when they are asked about the meaning of other people's dreams, sometimes their response is clear, sometimes ambiguous, and on other occasions no answer at all is given to the questioner. . . . . now that which has been said by you concerning a distinctive dream format which conveys the answer to the dream-master, whether in the guise of an old man or a young boy, we have heard that this is the case, but we ourselves have not seen it, nor have we had an eyewitness thereto." In these statements, R. Hai Gaon hints at the fact that he too was occupied with adducing answers through divinatory dreams. He merely denies that he actually saw the dream-master.

172. B. M. Lewin, *Oẓar ha-Ge'onim,* Sukkah, p. 28a. Cf. *Sha'arei Teshuvah,* Iyei ha-Yam, no. 74. *Ha-kotev le-Ein Ya'akov,* Sukkah, p. 28, in the name of Ritba; *Sefer ha-Eshkol,* ed. H. Albeck, p. 171a; *Arukh ha-Shalem,* no. 68. According to D. Friedmann and S. Löwinger, "Alpha Beta de-Ben Sira,"*Ve-Zot li-Yehuda, Koveẓ Ma'amarim . . . li-Kevod Yehuda Aryeh Blau* (Budapest, 1926), p. 256; J. D. Eisenstein, *Oẓar Midrashim* (New York, 1915), p. 45. Ben Sira, "when he was fifteen years old, had learned the language of the palm-trees, the ministering angels, the fables of the stars and foxes." Concerning Hillel and Shammai, it was claimed that they had mastered "the language of trees and grasses," *Masekhet Soferim* (New

The above-mentioned R. Joseph bar R. Abba was appointed Gaon of Pumbeditha because of a dream, despite the fact that prior right to this office should have been given to R. Aaron, the chief judge, who was "more learned and whose credentials were greater."[173]

York, 1937), ed. M. Higger, 17:7, p. 290. It was asserted that R. Johanan ben Zakkai knew the language of the ministering angels . . . and that of palm trees, the fables of fullers and foxes (B. Sukkah 28a). What is the language of palm trees? Rashi says: "the meaning of this is unknown to us." We have already mentioned the opinion of R. Hai Gaon in the body of the essay. An esoteric interpretation is to be found in the words of R. Gershom: "He knew how to mutter an incantation, so that the field would be filled with palm trees and they would then be uprooted." [Cf. B. Sanhedrin 68a.] Rashbam (B. Baba Batra 134a) sees a literary flair: "Because most men speak about palm trees, as Solomon has written: 'He discoursed about trees" [I Kings 5:13]." The author of a commentary to Genesis Rabbah attributed to Rashi sees in it a species of literary metaphor: "A man sows a *seah* of wheat with the expectation that he will reap just so many *se'ahs;* when the earth produces its fruit, it is as if the earth speaks with men, for she returns to men that which they have invested in her" (Genesis Rabah, chap. 13). According to R. Shem Tov ibn Shaprut, *Pardes Rimmonim* (Zhitomir, 1866), ed. E. Zweifel, p. 25, it means: "to know the nature of all vegetation, the trees and the grasses." And according to R. Ze'ev Wolf, "We recognize the wisdom of the Lord when one attends to these." Cf. also the explanation given by the author of *Be'er Mayyim Ḥayyim, Eẓ Yosef, Ein Ya'akov,* Sukkah 28; B. Ḥagigah 14b; *Zohar* III:228a. See L. Ginzberg, *Legends of the Jews* (Philadelphia, 1925), vol. 5, p. 61, n. 266; I. Loew, *Flora der Juden* (Vienna, 1924–34), vol. 2, p. 361. B. Gittin 45a recounts that in the days of Rav Ilish (a judge in Mehoza in the time of Rava) there was a man who "knew the language of the birds." This is the interpretation given to the phrase *be-lishna de-ẓippori* by the author of the *Arukh.* Rashi writes cautiously, "he understood birds." The author of *Seder ha-Dorot,* under the heading *Ilish,* attacks the interpretation of the *Arukh.* The *Halakhot Gedolot* (Berlin, 1888–92), ed. E. Hildesheimer, Hilkhot Gittin, p. 337, cites, in connection with the story of Samuel's father, that a Persian woman knew "the language of the birds." [This can be found in *Kiẓẓur Aggadot ha-Yerushalmi* published by L. Ginzberg in *Ginzei Schechter* (New York, 1928), vol. 1, p. 392, and cf. ibid., p. 389. S. L.] On this theme in folklore, cf. *Handwörterbuch des deutschen Aberglauben,* vol. 8, pp. 1683–1684.

173. *Iggeret Rav Sherira,* loc. cit.

According to R. Moses Ibn Ezra, R. Hai Gaon told R. Matzliach, the judge of Sicily who visited him in Baghdad, that he had found a word in "one of the problems" of Saadia Gaon "whose purport and meaning he did not understand." His mind was preoccupied with this until he fell asleep. In his dreams he saw R. Saadia and asked him the meaning of the Aramaic term used by him. R. Saadia answered him by hinting that he would find the meaning by reading a certain book. And, indeed, R. Saadia found the source for the correct meaning of the term in the book that was shown to him.[174]

Rabbenu Nissim Gaon wrote, "The elders of our generation told me that on the day of my circumcision, my father, the great rabbi, came to the synagogue cradling me in his arms. He sat down on the prepared chair and remained there for a while. He then arose and placed me on the other chair, viz., the one prepared for circumcision. Afterwards, he was asked the reason for his actions, since no one had ever witnessed this procedure before. He told them that the early sages had maintained that the first chair was prepared for Elijah, who was the angel appointed for circumcisions. He sat there with me that I might be blessed with wisdom through Elijah."[175]

The father of Rabbenu Nissim, R. Jacob b'rav Nissim, the recipient of a famous letter from R. Sherira Gaon, was one of the greatest savants of Kairouan and the head of its famous academy. According to the testimony of his son, he excelled in piety and reverence—a reverence which precedes wisdom.[176] The Geonim R. Sherira and R. Hai praised him greatly and called him "the holy chief."[177] A commentary on the *Sefer Yeẓirah,* only portions

---

174. *Shirat Yisrael,* trans. B. Z. Halper, p. 104.

175. *Oreḥot Ḥayyim,* pt. 2, Hilkhot Milah, sec. 9.

176. *Sefer ha-Mafteaḥ* (Vienna, 1847), ed. J. Goldenthal, introduction of Rabbenu Nissim, P. 8.

177. S. Poznanski, *Anshei Kairowan* (Berlin, 1909), p. 31; idem, "Inyanim Shonim le-Tekufat ha-Geonim," *Ha-Kedem* 2 (1908), p. 104.

of which have been published, has been attributed to him.[178] His disciples occupied themselves not only with esoteric wisdom, but with esoteric secrets of the Torah and wonder-working. They asked R. Hai Gaon questions concerning the divine name and the employment of holy names. In their writings we find the following:

> Many of our wise and pious men were adepts of dream interpretation. They were wont to fast several days, when they ate no bread (meat?) and drank no wine. They would rest in a place of purity, where they prayed and recited certain verses which contain a certain number of letters. They would then spend the night and see visions just the same as in prophecy. Some of these dreams we know; each had a distinctive style. For some, an old wise man, in others, a young man would be prominent. They would appear to the dreamer conveying information through the recitation of verses in answer to questions posed by the dreamer.[179]

The position of the Babylonian geonim was preeminent above that of all their contemporaries. From every corner of the Diaspora, Jews would turn to them with their problems, accepting their solutions, and deferring to their authority. No one dared question their rulings or their judgments; the people considered their responsa to be in the same category as those delivered by the Urim and Tumim. Just as the exilarchs deemed themselves the heirs apparent

---

178. *Kuntres ha-Masoret* (Tübingen, 1846), ed. L. Dukes, pp. 65 f. M. Steinschneider, *Hebräische Übersetzungen* (Berlin, 1893), p. 396. Cf. *Sha'arei Teshuvah,* sec. 71.

179. *Ta'am Zekenim* (Frankfurt a.M., 1855), pp. 54 ff. R. Judah Bargeloni, *Peirush le-Sefer Yeẓirah,* p. 104. The *yoredei merkavah* during the geonic period will not be discussed here.

to the Kingdom of the House of David,[180] so the geonim regarded themselves as the designated heirs of prophecy. R. Zemach bar R. Hayyim, gaon of Sura, of whom it was said that he knew secret lore,[181] expressed their claim in historical fashion: "When the nuclei of the wise and the prophets were exiled to Babylonia, they reestablished the Torah there by founding yeshivot on the Euphrates. From the days of Jehoiachin to this day, they have constituted the chain of wisdom and prophecy."[182] The authority of the geonim derived not alone from their abilities and competencies but from their office. "For their wisdom and reasoning constitute the word which the Lord commanded unto Moses . . . whoever disputes any judgment of theirs, it is as if he were disputing the mandate of God,"[183] "for they are all the words of the living God"; "even in the heavenly academy decisions are reached in accordance with their judgment," "even in the academy of Moses their rulings are secure."[184] Not only did the geonim constantly teach the people "what was permitted and what was prohibited, the difference between the profane and the holy, the fit and the flawed and all the minutiae of the Torah and its commandments," but they would "also pray for them and bless

---

180. Cf. S. Y. Rapoport, *Erekh Milin* (Warsaw, 1914), pp. 225–237.

181. "When he was sitting among the wise, he would address a question while awake and would receive an answer without anyone else sensing it." Quotation from *Megillat Setarim* of R. Hayyim Vital, in H. Y. D. Azulai, *Shem ha-Gedolim,* s.v. Rav Ẓemah Gaon.

182. *Eldad ha-Dani,* ed. A. Epstein, p. 8. Cf. the statement of Saadiah Gaon in A. Harkavy, *Zikhron la-Rishonim,* vol. 5, p. 158: "Just as the prophets were the leaders of Israel in their day, similarly the righteous lead the people today.

183. In a responsum attributed to Rav Sherira, printed after the title page in *Sefer Sha'arei Ẓedek.* Cf. *Teshuvot ha-Ge'onim,* Sha'arei Teshuvah, with the commentary *Iyyei ha-Yam,* sec. 187; D. Kahane, "Le-Toledot ha-Geonim," *Ha-Kedem* 3 (1909), pp. 124–127.

184. *Zikhron la-Rishonim,* mahberet 4, p. xi.

them at all times."[185] Nevertheless, their rulings were not issued in the name of the Holy Spirit but were grounded on the authority of tradition and reason.[186]

It was customary for the geonim to open and close their responsa with the following formulae, "So we have seen the matter," "thus it appears to me," "this is the law," "so our masters determined," "thus the matter appears," or "thus we see." Nevertheless, some of them, such as Rav Sar Shalom Gaon (whom R. Hayyim Vital considered to be a master Kabbalist), Rav Natronai (who, according to legend, was a miracle-worker),[187] R. Sherira and Rav Hai (both of whom according to later legendary tales were masters of secret lore and adepts at dream interpretation),[188] and R. Abraham ben David would write in a more elevated style, "Thus it has been shown to me by heaven,"[189] "for they have shown me from Heaven," or "thus it has

185. J. Mann, "The Responsa of the Babylonian Geonim as a Source of Jewish History,"*JQR*, N.S. 9 (1918–19), p. 150.

186. "If they were to be taken as the High Court, their opinions would be accepted only as judges; even if they were to be considered prophets, their opinions would not be accepted, except that which God had directed to them. They were only to be considered as teachers of the community." *Teshuvot ha-Geonim,* ed. A. Harkavy, sec. 214, p. 101.

187. Cf. *Ta'am Zekenim,* pp. 55 f.: "It was clear and well known to the people of Spain, and was a tradition from their ancestors, that R. Natronai Gaon came to them from Babylonia and returned by means of instantaneous travel [*kefiẓat ha-derekh*], because he did not travel in a caravan and was not seen on the way." R. Hai questioned the authenticity of this story. Cf. A. Harkavy, *Zikhron la-Rishonim ve-Gam la-Aḥronim,* vol. 4. p. xxiii.

188. See below, n. 193, and above, n. 7. "Instantaneous travel is not an impossibility," *Ta'am Zekenim,* p. 56.

189. [This expression is cited in *Arugat ha-Bosem* (Jerusalem, 1947), ed. E. E. Urbach, vol. 2, p. 25, in the name of the author of the *Halakhot Gedolot,* but is not found in our edition of the *Halakhot Gedolot.* It would seem that R. Abraham be-R. Azriel had before him an addendum to the responsa of the author of the *Halakhot Gedolot.* S.L.]

been shown me from above," [or in Aramaic] "for they showed us from Heaven," or "for so they showed us from Heaven."[190] This mode of expression was apparently based upon the dictum of the sages that "he who studies Torah for its own sake . . . the secrets of the Torah are revealed to him from heaven."[191] But this apothegm is insufficient warrant for investiture with prophetic inspiration or the comprehension of matter via visions or dreams, though this is a sign that the geonim believed, therefore, that a man could be worthy of heavenly aid in a natural manner[192] or merit an infusion of

---

190. Cf. the sources compiled by V. Aptowitzer, "Teshuvot Meyuḥasot le-Rav Hai," *Tarbiẓ* 1 (1930), pp. 82 f. Cf. L. Löw, *Gesammelte Schriften* (Szegedin, 1889–1900), vol. 5, pp. 47 f. Much can be added to Aptowitzer's list, e.g., Rashba, secs. 701, 706, 854. Cf. *Teshuvot Rashi* (New York, 1943), ed. I. Elfenbein, pp. 262, 272, 282.

191. Cf. above, n. 18.

192. It was in this sense that the term *bat kol* was used in the Amoraic period; cf. above, n. 4. Compare *Mekaḥ u-Mimkar* of R. Hai Gaon, sha'ar 52: "If the sender says to the messenger, use your discretion or follow the instructions of heaven, then the messenger is empowered to do whatever he deems best in selecting the merchandise from among the samples submitted to him in those lands to which he is sent." Here the intention is for heavenly assistance which reaches a person providentially and is disguised as a natural occurrence. B. M. Lewin, *Oẓar ha-Geonim,* Ketubot, p. 288, goes too far when he says that in every place that the geonim say, "So it was shown to me from heaven," it means, "So have we seen." Cf. B. M. Lewin, "Rabbanan Sabbora'ei ve-Talmidam" *Ezkerah . . . le-Nishmat . . . Rabbi Abraham Isaac ha-Kohen Kook* (Jerusalem, 1937), vol. 2, pt. 4, p. 197; B. M. Lewin, *Rav Sherirah Gaon* (Jaffa, 1916), p. 24; *Koveẓ Rav Sa'adiah Gaon,* p. 481. In fact, they sometimes used this expression to indicate divine illumination which comes to a person by means of a miracle or in a dream. Rabbenu Ḥananel (11th cent.) explains the statement of R. Simeon bar Yoḥai, "I have seen the elect and they are few in number," as meaning: I have seen with the aid of the Holy Spirit, as through a dream vision." He writes about himself, "What we have been shown by heaven, we have written down, and understand it." *Migdal Ḥananel* (Berlin, 1876), ed. D. Hoffmann, p. viii. Concerning the *yoredei merkavah* he says: "They do not ascend to heaven, but perceive and see through the understanding of their heart like a person who looks and sees through

a cloudy looking glass." Commentary to B. Hagigah 14b; *Migdal Ḥananel,* p. 45; Judah ben Bargeloni, *Peirush le-Sefer Yeẓirah,* p. 32.

In *Sefer Ḥasidim,* ed. R. Margulies, par. 18, we find: "It once happened that a Kohen recited the Priestly Blessing and said *Yishmedekha* ("may He destroy you") [instead of *Yishmerekha,* "may He guard you,"] a sage who was there removed him from before the Ark because he did not know how to properly recite the words of the Priestly Blessing. It was indicated from heaven to the sage that if he did not return him to his position, he would be punished for his actions." In the Parma MS, ed. Wistinetski, par. 424, the reading is: "The sage had a dream in which he was told that if he did not return him to his position, he would be expelled from Paradise." R. Barukh be-R. Isaac of Worms (12th–13th cent.), who compiled his book from the teachings of his master, Rabbi Isaac the Elder, the Tosafist, (*Hagahot Maimuniot,* Hilkhot Shabbat, chap. 3), of whom it was told that he ascended to heaven at night and received teachings from the angels (cf. above, n. 46), writes at the end of his book, *Sefer ha-Terumah:* "He decided as he had been instructed in heaven." This expression, at the end of the book, was no mere metaphor. Even Isaac Abrabanel, in his commentary to *Guide* II:36, uses a similar expression with regard to the teachings of the Holy Spirit: "The revelation which comes to the prophet and which is received by his intellect is not produced by him, but is in accord with that which has been taught to him by heaven." This expression was also utilized in later periods. Cf. R. Solomon Luria, *Yam shel Shelomo,* introduction 1; R. Joseph be-R. Eliezer ha-Sepharadi, *Ohel Yosef,* introduction; [commentary to] *Margaliyot Tovah* (Amsterdam, 1722); R. Moses Teitelbaum, *Heishiv Moshe,* Yoreh Deah, sec. 29; R. Ezekiel Landau, *Noda' bi-Yehudah,* Even ha-Ezer, sec. 31. [In addition to the statement of Rav Hai in *Sefer Mekaḥ u-Mimkar* mentioned at the beginning of this note, the following should be added, the responsa of Rav Sherira and Rav Hai (*Teshuvot ha-Ge'onim* [Jerusalem, 1929], ed. S. Assaf, vol. 1, sec. 59); S. Assaf, "Teshuvot ha-Geonim," *Mada'ei ha-Yahadut* 2 (1927), p. 77; *Eshkol* (Jerusalem, 1938), ed. S. and H. Albeck, vol. 2, p. 166): "the treasurers can withhold as they are instructed by heaven." The author of *Shibbolei ha-Leket,* vol. 2, p. 202, writes similarly (*Ha-Segulah,* ḥoveret, no. 69 [Jerusalem, 1940]): "Before a judgment is rendered, the parties can demur from submitting the case before him; they must first agree to accept the judgment in accordance with the decision heaven has imparted to the judge. Therefore, he who wants to assure himself that he will not be responsible if he errs, and wants his judgment to be accepted says to them: 'Are you willing to accept my judgment according to what is shown me by heaven?' " etc. S.L.]

knowledge emanating miraculously[193] from Above into his soul[194] without instruction or aid. "Know that the indwelling presence of God resides among the students and light dwells among them, that light which is called the Shekhinah . . . and wisdom is itself one of the Shekhinot."[195]

One cannot grasp the innermost thought of the holy men of Israel without remembering that in their eyes, prophetic inspiration hovered over human reason, and, at times, heaven and earth would meet and kiss. They believed that the divine voice which issued from Horeb was not stilled thereafter. "These commandments the Lord spoke in a great voice to your whole assembly on the mountain out of the fire, the cloud and the thick mist, then he said no more" (Deut 5:19). Onkelos translated (and so also Targum Jonathan), "it—the great voice—has not ceased from speaking."[196]

---

193. This belief underlies the statement of Rav Hai Gaon concerning the secrets of *Ma'aseh Bereshit* that "they are secrets and mysteries that are impossible to impart to every person, but only to those who have the prerequisites which have been handed down to us. . . . he is enlightened by heaven in the secret recesses of his heart . . . but we ask for God's mercy for you. May it be His will that whoever is deemed worthy by heaven, may he be enlightened." *Sha'arei Teshuvah,* sec. 122. This responsum is mentioned by Nahmanides in his commentary to Genesis 5:2; *Torat ha-Shem Temimah* (Leipzig, 1853), p. 26. Cf. *Oẓar ha-Ge'onim,* Ḥagigah, p. 12, n. 8. Graetz and others mistakenly thought this to be a forgery.

194. Cf. the statement of Rav Sherira and Rav Hai: "We have been directed by heaven, not through our own merits, but through the mercies of God and the merit of our ancestors; when we did so in this order, we have returned empty-handed; you do likewise. . . . I rely on heaven not to turn you away empty-handed and to perform miracles for you." *Ḥemdah Genuzah,* sec. 181; *Kevuẓat Ḥakhamim,* p. 108.

195. *Oẓar ha-Ge'onim,* Sotah 11a. Cf. ibid., Baba Kamma, p. 65; ibid., Ketubot, p. 103: "So too are the fines imposed by the sages, each one as they have been instructed by heaven."

196. Rashi adds: "Since his voice is mighty and exists forever." This explanation is found in B. Sanhedrin 17b, B. Sotah 10b.

Did Maimonides Believe That He Had Attained the Rank of Prophet?

I

Consider for a moment how Maimonides wearied himself all his days with the subject of prophecy.

It preoccupied him. When he was a young man, he was already preparing himself to deal with it. He intended to write a separate work that would be called the *Book of Prophecy.*[1] He even began writing it, but for various reasons the book was never finished.[2] Despite the fact that he never fully implemented his announced intent, the essence of his work, unblemished though perhaps incomplete, has been salvaged from the abyss of forgetfulness. In a number of chapters of the *Guide of the Perplexed* he deals with this subject. Many matters, great and small, which did not find their way into these chapters may be found scattered in other chapters throughout the work. This particular topic is a central one, around which the other subjects treated by Maimonides tend to cluster.

How does the subject of prophecy differ from all other topics? Why was he so preoccupied with it? Are not such matters as the concept and the problem of creation more compelling problems? We

---

1. "This matter needs a whole book by itself. Perhaps God will aid me with what is necessary in order to write about this matter." *Maimonides' Einleitung in die Mishna,* ed. B. Hamburger (Strassburg, 1902), p. 11.

"In the Book of Prophecy, which I am working on."*Mose Maimuni's Einleitung zu Chelek im arabischen Urtext und in der hebräischen Uebersetzung,* ed. J. Holzer (Berlin, 1901), Seventh Principle, p. 24. Cf. *Shemonah Perakim,* p. 7. "I shall complete this in the future, in the Book of Prophecy." Cf. ibid., p. 1.

2. *Guide* I:Introduction, p. 9.

may infer that his continual concern with this topic involved personal commitment rather than theoretical speculation alone. He maintained that those who merited the prophetic degree had opened before them the treasure house of wisdom, and that many of the persistent unsolved problems of philosophy which troubled him would find their resolution if one could peep behind the veil. Prophecy was considered by him a cognitive power, and whoever was master of that capacity could reach places where unaided reason faltered.

From hints in Maimonides' writings one suspects that this master rationalist and the teacher of all future generations, concerning whom modern scholars would claim that his soul recoiled from all taint of mystery-mongering obscurantism and would have totally rejected anything which lay beyond the bounds of the human intellect, was himself a seeker after prophecy.[3] We infer not from hypotheses or conjectures, but from clear and evident signs which combine into a solid proof. Do not think, however, that he flaunted his soul's desire in public. It is not the way of scholars to wear their hearts on their sleeves. The yearning for prophecy, moreover, is not something that one is obligated to proclaim in public. Nevertheless, it is worthwhile and proper for us to make his secret public. For in this light, both the personality and the doctrine of Maimonides will be further illuminated. One major assumption shall guide us. If you desire to truly know another man, look to his most impassioned commitments; from these you can learn the character of his soul and the source of his thoughts.

"The souls of the wise are the burial grounds of secrets." On many occasions Maimonides spoke of the need to conceal secrets; "the secrets of the Lord are delivered to those who truly revere Him." When he was still a young man, he wrote: "When the Holy One blessed be He, reveals something to a man, he should thereupon conceal it . . . and if he makes allusions to it, these should be directed

---

3. I broached this idea in my *Maimonides* (New York, 1982), pp. 25–32.

to someone whose intellect is already perfected and who has true knowledge already within his grasp."[4] He stood by this principle throughout his life.[5] His custom was to lay bare something and conceal much. He openly asserted in the introduction to the *Guide to the Perplexed* that he would not reveal any "secrets" beyond the citation of "chapter headings" alone.

> And even those [secrets] are not set down in order or arranged in a coherent fashion in this treatise, but rather are scattered and entangled with other subjects that are to be clarified. For my purpose is that the truth be glimpsed and then again concealed, so as not to oppose that divine purpose which one cannot possibly oppose and which has concealed from the vulgar among the people those truths especially requisite for His apprehension.[6]

Maimonides, who never used language loosely, says, "and as Heaven has informed me."[7] Moreover, he partially admits that he has reached "the beginning of the prophetic rungs." Without any circumlocution he claims to have benefited from "divine aid," an emanation from above, when he studied the Account of the Chariot [the first ten chapters of Ezekiel, which, according to Maimonides deal with metaphysics—Trans.][8] "Divine aid," according to the tenets of his doctrine, constitutes the "beginning of the prophetic rungs," a propaedeutic to prophecy, though a man who has reached this level cannot yet be counted among the ranks of the prophets.[9]

---

4. *Einleitung in die Mishna,* p. 46.

5. Cf. *Guide* III: introduction.

6. *Guide* I:introduction, pp. 6–7.

7. *Teshuvot ha-Rambam,* ed. A. Freimann (Jerusalem, 1934), sec. 371. I will deal with the meaning of this phrase elsewhere.

8. "Now rightly guided reflection and divine aid in this matter have moved me to a position which I shall describe." (וקד תרכתני אלפכר"ה אלמסדד"ה ואלמעונ"ה אלאלאהיי"ה) *Guide* III:introduction, p. 416.

9. *Guide* II:45.

But Maimonides was not content with this rung alone. On several occasions he hinted that he had reached the rung of prophecy.[10] It is for the discerning to understand truly the meaning and intent of these hints.

In the introduction to the *Guide* he says the following:

> You should not think that these great secrets are fully and completely known among us. They are not. But sometimes truth flashes out to us so that we think it is day, and then matter and habit in their various forms conceal it so that we find ourselves again in an obscure night, almost as we were at first. We are like someone in a very dark night over whom lightning flashes time and time again. Among us there is one for whom the lightning flashes continually so that he is always, as it were, in unceasing light. Thus night appears to him as day. That is the degree of the great one among prophets. . . . There are others between whose lightning flashes there are greater or shorter intervals. This is the level of the majority of the prophets.[11]

Here, unequivocally, we have testimony to the fact that he experienced in his own life that "flash of lightning." In his commentary, Abravanel gave voice to his concern that such was the case. "If the master [i.e., Maimonides] speaks personally here and is not a prophet, how is it possible that he would compare himself to prophets who see flashes of lightning?"[12] He endeavors to resolve the question, but his is a forced resolution. Concerning cases such

---

10. On the degrees of prophecy, cf. *Guide* II:45.

11. *Guide* I:introduction, p. 7. In the Arabic original, [ילוח לנא אלחק]. And in al-Ḥarizi's translation, "Occasionally, the truth will appear to us."

12. "One of the commentators has said that those who cleave to the Lord, blessed be He, will see some of that which appears to the prophets. That which appears to them will be similar to a lightning flash, which disappears almost at once, and then reappears either permanently or transiently. If it does have some degree of permanence, its duration will vary and its luminosity will be cast on either one or many objects." Falaquera, *Moreh ha-Moreh* (Pressburg, 1837), p. 9.

as these we are entitled to say: "There are many dicta which should have been burned, yet they remain essentials of the Torah." And if you persist in your objections, claiming that "one cannot make out a case from a single instance," know that this experience was incurred by Maimonides more than once. "Personal confession is equivalent to the testimony of a hundred witnesses." He himself attests, "The light which shines upon us is small and sporadic, but its luminosity which comes and goes, is equivalent to that of the swirling fiery sword" (cf. Gen 3:24).[13] From this we can see that Maimonides was beyond the stage of "one to whom the lightning flashes only once in the whole of his night" and of whom it is said, "they prophesied but they did so no more."[14]

When it came to explaining the account of the Works of the Chariot, which are considered to be 'secrets of the Torah' "that great and noble subject which constitutes the hinge upon which all hangs, and the pillar upon which everything rests," Maimonides emphasized that this knowledge has disappeared completely from the midst of the people "to such an extent that neither small nor large portions of it were to be found—neither a treatise nor a book." Concerning himself he said, "That which I have received has not been at the hands of any teacher." The question arises: How then did he reach the knowledge of these "secrets of the Torah"? He himself tells us, "No divine revelation has come to teach me that the intention of the matter in question was such and such . . . but rightly guided reflection and divine aid."[15] This sentence is astounding. We

13. There is the prophet who "perhaps achieves this high degree only once in his life and then is deprived of it." *Guide* II:45, p. 396.

14. *Aleinu* in all the MSS of Ibn Tibbon's translation to which Munck had access, and also in the JTS Sulzberger MS and in the first printed edition (before 1480). *'Alina'* in the Arabic original. In JTS MS Adler 308 and MS Jerusalem (cf. *Guide,* ed. R. Y. Even-Shmuel-Kaufmann): *alav.* This reading appears to be a scribal interpolation.

15. ולא אתאני בה וחי אלאהי יעלמני אן אלאמר הכד"ה קצד בה ולא תלקנת מא אעתקדה פי דלך ען מעלם *Guide* III:introduction, pp. 415–416. In the al-Harizi translation:

take for granted that a man does not deny the impossible. Only of him who is suspected of cultivating prophecy is it necessary to say that he did not reach his goal. This very rejection posits the possibility. Apparently he wanted to disabuse R. Joseph Ibn Aknin of the notion that his master might have reached the true exposition of the Account of the Chariot through the use of prophecy. After all, the prophet "does not continually prophesy all his days, but intermittently, for the spirit of prophecy leaves him periodically."[16] This denial is repeated in the *Letter on the Resurrection of the Dead:* "Know that these testimonies and others similar to them do not constitute a decree, since we have not received a divine revelation that is to be considered a metaphor, nor do we have a true tradition vouchsafed the sages by the prophets."[17] This expression is not to be found in traditional literature, nor was it the language spoken by Maimonides when he was younger.[18]

Maimonides explicitly states that he attained a kind of revelation in the understanding of the Book of Job. This book was a metaphor "whose contents were the repository of wonders and mysteries wherein many doubts were resolved; indeed, it made manifest sublime mysteries of the highest order." After explaining those sections of the book which deal with Satan, he made the following admission: "Note this matter well and understand how wondrous it is; observe that my exposition is akin (*ki-demut*) to prophecy."[19]

"The Holy Spirit did not come to me."Cf. ibid. I:10, p. 36, "to let some of us have knowledge deriving from Him and an overflow of prophetic inspiration."

16. *Guide* II:45, p. 396.

17. Ed. J. Finkel, *PAAJR* 9, pt. 2 (1939), p. 22 (Arabic), p. 22 (Hebrew).

18. "Know therefore that the statements I make in these chapters . . . are not my own invention, nor are they new explanations which I have devised. Indeed, they constitute matters which I have collected from Midrashim and the Talmud . . . and also from the words of the philosophers, both ancient and modern." *Shemoneh Perakim,* introduction. Cf. Falaquera, *Reshit Hokhmah* (Berlin, 1902), p. 9.

19. ואדי כיף תחצ״לת לי הד״ה אלמעני שבה אלוחי *Guide* III:22 (Munk ed., p. 46a; Pines ed., p. 488). Maimonides' note did not escape the eye of the translator:

Thus, from the very use of the expression "akin" we may infer that he did not receive a prophetic revelation per se, a revelation materially similar to it.[20] For us it is enough that he admitted this much. Let us not forget that "he who prophesies that which he did not hear through the medium of a prophetic vision . . . is a false prophet and is liable to death by strangulation."[21] It is obvious that Maimonides is not indulging in wordplay when he uses the words "akin to prophecy." "Akin to prophecy" is equivalent to prophecy.

Lest one ask how it is possible that Maimonides believed that he had attained the rung of prophecy, since prophecy ceased with the deaths of Haggai, Zechariah, and Malachi, let the claimant come forward and make his case. The testimony that Maimonides left to posterity is unmistakable in its intention, viz.,

> That which we say now is known to us as truth and we can pinpoint it exactly, since the event occurred not too long ago [1122]. A pious and noble individual, one of the sages of Israel, known by name as Moshe Al Dar'i . . . came to Andalus [Spain] . . . and the people gathered about him because of his piety, nobility, and knowledge. He informed them that the Messiah had appeared and that God had communicated this fact to him in a dream. He did not claim, however, that he was the Messiah. The people flocked around him and believed his every word, and my father, my master [Rabbi Maimon the Dayyan of Cordoba] (may his memory be for a blessing) tried to restrain the people from following this man and ordained that he leave the country. Most of the people did not heed his order, and most of them continued to follow Master Moses (may his memory be for a blessing). Soon afterwards he

---

"Those statements and allusions which our master alluded to in that chapter until the Introduction to Job which are truly akin to prophecy." R. Samuel ibn Tibbon in his letter to Maimonides, in Z. Diesendruck, "Samuel and Moses ibn Tibbon on Maimonides' Theory of Providence," *HUCA* 11 (1936), p. 354.

20. Cf. *Guide* III:7, I:1.

21. *M. T.,* Hilkhot 'Akum 5:8.

> began to make predictions which came true. It was his custom to inform the multitude, "Gather yourselves together on the morrow and such and such will occur." And so it happened. On one occasion he claimed that in the following week, the heavens would rain down blood, for this is a sign of the coming of the Messiah which God intended in the verse "And I will give portents in the heavens and on the earth, blood and fire and columns of smoke" [Joel 2:30]. This took place in the month of Marheshvan [October]. A hard and continuous rain fell the following week, and the waters were reddish and brackish as if they had been mixed with mud. This portent proved to everyone that he was undoubtedly a true prophet. Nevertheless, from the viewpoint of the Torah this matter is impossible. As I have explained to you in connection with prophecy, it will return to Israel before the coming of the Messiah . . . the land of Ishmael [Arabia] was no longer able to bear his presence, and he therefore left for the land of Israel, where he died (may his memory be for a blessing). As it has been related to me by those who observed him in the land of Israel, he there prophesied concerning what would happen to the Jews of the West in matters both great and small."

(This would be the persecution of the people by the Almohades beginning in the year 1140.)[22]

And why should we be astonished by such an occurrence? The rabbis of France saw nothing surprising in the appearance of a prophet in their own day. In the letter which they sent to Maimonides, they mentioned the fact that they had received a letter from the hands

---

22. *Iggeret Teiman,* trans. Jacob Mann, "Tenu'ot Meshiḥiot bi-Yemei Masaei ha-Zelav ha-Rishonim," *Ha-Tekufah,* 24 (1928), pp. 355–356. According to Maimonides, "Everyone who communicates knowledge as to something secret, whether this be with the help of soothsaying and divination or with the help of a veridical dream, is likewise called a prophet. For this reason prophets of Baal and prophets of Asherah are called prophets." *Guide* II:32, p. 363. However, the allusion here to the renewal of prophecy will prove that R. Moses Dar'i was a true and valid prophet in Maimonides' opinion. The identification of this prophet with the poet R. Moses Dar'i, who may have lived at that time, is not acceptable.

of men who had come a great distance to inform Maimonides that "in those parts a prophet had arisen and spoken of the coming of the redeemer."[23] Maimonides, moreover, was not building castles in the air when he spoke of wise men who hoped for prophecy and wondered "why it was that they did not prophesy since this power of prophecy was a natural power."[24] Many of the sages of Israel made use of prophetic inspiration during that period.[25] As for Maimonides, who stood head and shoulders above his contemporaries, he did not account their way as being superior to his, or in any way so exalted that it could not be attained.

Furthermore, a part of prophecy, and one greater than the conventional smidgin of "a sixtieth portion," was widespread in his generation. Maimonides believed in "soothsayers, augurs, dreamers of veridical dreams . . . whom we see eye to eye foretelling the future."[26] He explains that this power will accrue to a man if

---

23. A. Marx, "The Correspondence Between the Rabbis of Southern France and Maimonides About Astrology," *HUCA* 3 (1926), p. 349.

24. *Guide* II:36, p. 371. Compare the opinion of the philosophers that "a superior individual who is perfect with respect to his rational and moral qualities, his imaginative faculty is in its most perfect state, and when he has been prepared . . . he will certainly become a prophet." Ibid. II:32, p. 361.

25. I will discuss this topic in my essay "The Holy Spirit in the Middle Ages" [in this volume, pp. 1–67].

26. *Einleitung in die Mishna,* p. 12. Cf. *Guide* III:46, pp. 585–586: "[The Sabians] used to eat of it [blood], deeming that it was the food of the jinn, and that, consequently, whoever ate it fraternized with the jinn . . . . These jinn would come to them in dreams, inform them of secret things, and be useful to them." Cf. *M.T.,* Hilkhot 'Akum 11:6 "Who is a sorcerer? . . . Someone who performs an act in such a way that his thoughts are turned from ordinary matters completely and is able to predict future events. . . . Who is an astrologer? He who speaks in an unintelligible babbling manner and believes that such incantations are effective. . . . Those matters are completely lies and falsehood. . . . Whoever believes in these and similar matters and maintains in his heart that they are really true and matters of wisdom, even though the Torah has prohibited them, can only be considered a fool and ignoramus."

the divine overflow reaches his imaginative power alone without affecting the intellect. He establishes this capacity on the same footing as that of those who govern cities and legislators.[27] He thought that dreams too were a valid form of revelation. According to him, "veridical dreams and prophecy are of one species and differ from each other only in degree." He praised the metaphor of the sages who designate the dream as "the unripened fruit of prophecy"; "This is an extraordinary comparison . . . for unripe fruit (*novelet*) is the individual fruit itself, that has fallen before it was fully ripened and matured." Nevertheless, an "arousal,"[28] which is not prophecy at all, may descend upon man in a dream.[29] In prophecy the divine overflow reaches both the intellectual and the imaginative faculty. This is not true of dreams, "for in them only the imaginative power receives the efflux."[30]

Maimonides saw nothing amiss or impossible even in the prediction of future contingent events. On the contrary, everyone participates to some degree in the power of predicting the future.[31] This estimative power (*kaveh al-shi'ur*) or intuition is "found among all men,"[32] but in the case of prophets it is intensified because of the abundance of the efflux which descends upon them.[33] By means of

27. *Guide* II:37.

28. *He'arah* sometimes indicates spiritual awakening, the influence of heavenly wisdom. Cf. *Guide* II:41, p. 387, "An intimation came to that individual from God."

29. *Guide* II:41. Cf. J. Albo, *Ikkarim,* ed. I. Husik (Philadelphia, 1929), bk. 4, chap. 11.

30. *Guide* II:36.

31. "The estimative power is the name for the power whereby a person conjectures what will occur, without any reliable knowledge for such a projection." R. Samuel ibn Tibbon, *Peirush ha-Milim ha-Zarot.*

32. *Guide* II:38.

33. Ibid., p. 376. "You will find among people a man whose conjecturing and divination are very strong and habitually hit the mark, so that he hardly imagines that a thing comes to pass without its happening wholly or in part as he imagined it. The causes of this are many; they are various anterior, posterior, and present circumstances. But in virtue of the strength of this divination the mind goes over

this power it is possible to attain knowledge without the benefit of first principles or discursive searchings and by means of it "some men are enabled to foretell important future outcomes."[34]

II

Maimonides was quite careful not to disclose esoteric wisdom. He was careful to heed the warning "for the glory of God hide the matter" [cf. Prov. 25:2]; never did he publicly admit that he was preparing himself for prophecy. It is difficult to make this assertion and impossible to explain it fully. A soul as refined and noble as Maimonides' would not point to himself and say, "Behold, I am now fit and ready for the highest perfection." A man does not declare himself a prophet. Nevertheless, this secret, which was so well hidden in the folds of his personality, does peep forth in hints scattered throughout his writings, slight in some places and fuller in others. That which he refused to reveal in his works directed to a wider audience does appear in the exchange of correspondence between him and his disciple, R. Joseph ben Judah Ibn Aknin.[35] From these letters it is quite clear that the aspiration for prophecy burned within the breast of "his eminent disciple." And the master who could have reproved his disciple for his demands for enlightenment, not only did not protest, but actually encouraged him in the pursuit of his goal. Furthermore, he marked out the way to prophecy based

---

all of these premises and draws from the conclusions in the shortest time, so that it is thought to happen in no time at all. In virtue of this faculty, certain people give warnings concerning great future events."

34. Ibid. "These two faculties must necessarily be very strong in prophets, I mean the faculty of courage and that of divination. And when the intellect overflows towards them, these two faculties become very greatly strengthened."

35. Cf. M. Steinschneider, *Gesammelte Schriften* (Berlin, 1925) I, pp. 35 ff.

on his own experience of having already traversed the path and attained the goal.

Ibn Aknin was graced with intellectual and moral virtues. Richly endowed with Torah knowledge, he was already an author in his own right,[36] a philosopher and a physician, and he had composed poems full of a "strong yearning for philosophical speculation."[37] He had previously resided in Ceuta, Morocco, and studied philosophy with one of the great thinkers of that generation, Ibn Rushd. Because of difficult circumstances and the religious persecutions of that time, he fled from his homeland to Egypt, in order to study and serve Maimonides, whose fame had already reached Morocco.[38] His soul thirsted for esoteric wisdom and he did not hesitate to inquire and hungrily demand, "What lies behind and beyond all things?"; indeed his passion to know the nature of the immortal life never waned.[39] He desired not only to absorb the revealed doctrine of his teacher but to enter the hidden orchard of esoteric wisdom. In his own view, R. Joseph was no novice when it came to the investigation of esoteric wisdom. He already knew that many of his predecessors had interpreted the Song of Songs via the modes of

---

36. He had written books before he came to Maimonides. Cf. ibid., I, p. 47.

37. *Guide,* translator's introduction, p. 3a (Vilna 1904 ed.).

38. He called Maimonides "the wonder of the age" in his commentary to Avot, *Sefer Musar,* ed. W. Bacher (Berlin, 1910).

39. "I heard from our teacher, Rabbenu Nissim, that two hermits who were colleagues, one a Jew [Ibn Aknin] and the other a Muslim [Ibn al-Kifti], swore to one another that the first of them to die would appear to the other on the first night of his demise and tell him in a dream the truth concerning the world to come. It happened that the Muslim died first. That night he appeared in a dream to his Jewish colleague and told him in Arabic, 'Know that the whole remains whole and the part remains a part; it is impossible for me to reveal more than this.' What he meant was whoever binds his soul to the principle of the whole, i.e., God, may be cherished, and the 'part remains a part,' i.e., he whose soul cleaves to the vanities of this world . . . his soul cleaves to it permanently." M. Steinschneider and A. Neubauer, "Josef ibn Aknin, Analekten," *MWJ* 15 (1888), pp. 105–106.

its "plain and simple meaning," or homiletically. He prided himself, however, on being the first to give it an esoteric interpretation (*sirakh al-bat{aan*) and revealed that its true meaning was concerned with the yearning of the rational soul, portrayed as a bride, wife, and sister seeking her beloved, who was in reality the Active Intellect. He was convinced that he had thus uncovered secret "pearls" which could not be revealed except to initiates who had already reached the rung of perfection. Whoever revealed these secrets to those who were not ready for them, viz., who had not reached the rung of perfection, harmed his students. He opined that his commentary could be appreciated and understood by only a few people in his generation. He thought of himself as writing for posterity.[40] And R. Joseph aspired to even higher rungs of the spirit and sought prophecy.

See now the differences between the master and his student. The master is patient, circumspect, and cautious; the disciple is impatient, importunate, and impulsive. The master treads softly and slowly; the disciple rushes forward headlong. The disciple desires elevation to the rank of prophet and is certain that it does not lie beyond him; the master is insistent that he be restrained. The disciple finally bursts the bonds of his master's patience, and a swirling storm of complaints and demands fall upon the master's head.

From the time that he came "from the ends of the earth," the value and nature of this disciple grew in the eyes of Maimonides because of his diligence in the pursuit of wisdom. At first the master considered, "Perhaps his desire outstrips his capacity?" But after testing his abilities, studying astronomy and logic together with him, the master esteemed and loved him. Thus he wrote to him,

> My hopes fastened upon you, and I saw that you were one worthy to have the secrets of the prophetic books revealed to you so that you

40. Cf. A. Neubauer, "Josef ibn Aknin," *MGWJ* 19 (1871), pp. 348–355, 395–401, 445–448.

> would consider in them what perfect men ought to consider. Thereupon I began to let you see certain flashes and to give you certain indications. Then I saw that you demanded of me additional knowledge and asked me to make clear to you certain things pertaining to divine matters.[41]

Indeed, the disciple became so endeared to the master that he said of him, "You are my portion from all my toil."[42] And he enumerated his virtues in the following vein: "Behold, you are wise, prudent, and close to perfection."[43]

Not all times are equal. On one occasion the master refused to reveal the "secrets" to his disciple. Ibn Aknin, whom his master considered to be one of the "perfect ones," and whose spiritual strivings were boundless, was overwrought that his teacher would deny him the good that he sought. Out of bitterness he did not restrain his tongue, and he dared to send his teacher a letter composed in quatrains[44] in which he "spilled out his speech . . . and unravelled his spirit." His argument was that he had been betrothed "in all faithfulness, according to religion and law," and wed to wisdom, "the daughter" of Maimonides, and his soul was entwined and bound up with hers. Nevertheless, while standing under the wedding canopy the bride had gone awhoring and had abandoned him. Her father, Maimonides, had not prevented his daughter from departing—indeed he had perhaps encouraged her in her flight from her true beloved; now the student demands of the teacher that he return the wife to her master, "And now, I beseech you, return the wife, for the master is a prophet or will become one; he will pray on your behalf so that

41. *Guide,* translator's introduction, p. 3a (Vilna ed.).

42. *Kovez,* pt. II, 30a.

43. Ibid., 31b.

44. Z. H. Edelman, *Ḥemdah Genuzah* (Königsberg, 1855), pp. 17–18. S. Munck, *Notice sur Joseph ben Jehouda* (Paris, 1842), pp. 59–61. *Kovez,* pt. II, 29a–c.

you may live." He seals his letter with a verse taken from the Book of Daniel. "Blessed be he who waits for what shall come."[45]

It is as clear as the day that Ibn Aknin was certain that he would eventually become a prophet. A man does not withhold from another what he cannot himself attain. Taken together with all the various hints and allusions to the attainment of prophecy that we have found in the writings of Maimonides, we are forced to deduce the concealed from the revealed. If the student demands the prophetic mantle from the teacher, are we not then authorized to conclude that the master had already donned the garment? The entire matter constitutes a proof of sorts. Who gave the student title to such a demand? Did not the master do so? All of the powers of the disciple derive from those of the master, who was already showing him the "way of perfection." We have a principle that "designation is a valid act" [i.e., if the master designated the student, the goal was attainable].

Do not think, moreover, that Ibn Aknin's complaint was but the maundering of his pen or the blustering of his mouth. On the contrary, on the strength of this protest he challenged Maimonides' integrity and ethics. His teacher took it so seriously indeed that it constituted the burden of his reply and the target of his letter. In contrast to the abruptness of his disciple the master dealt at length with this matter. In his reply, Maimonides takes Ibn Aknin to task for saying, "For he is indeed a prophet . . . and prays on your behalf"; to this Maimonides says, "If he is a prophet, then he is a blind man peering through a window." And he continues in this vein: "Since you have become angry with me . . . and your heart has been lifted up, so as to account yourself one of the prophets . . . I would almost have crushed you with my reply . . . and moreover, my son, your thoughts are akin to those of a people devoid of counsel . . . here is your wife—take her and go!" Maimonides thus does not want

45. [Dan. 12:12] Does he mean by this the renaissance of prophecy in 1210? See below.

to uproot the profound desire of Ibn Aknin to attain prophecy, nor does he seek to weaken the latter's resolution or capacity so that he might say that he was unworthy of prophecy. He merely upbraids him for thinking that he has already attained this degree. This lack of achievement is due, furthermore, to the times: either the time for the reinstitution of prophecy had not yet arrived or the measures of preparation and perfection had not yet been fulfilled. Thus he says:

> Let not your heart vaunt itself so as to ascend the rungs of prophecy, nor let your eyes sweep upward in pride—not because these ascents are too steep for you, but because the time must be right. If you say that Samuel prophesied whenever he wished, therefore I in my strong firm wisdom will do likewise; nay, if you are truly wise in understanding and teaching your tasks are to teach and judge; you should have nothing to do with esotericism. Do not shore up your argument by quoting "a sage is deemed superior to a prophet," for not everyone who draws forth the sword is authorized to kill with it, and not everyone who assumes the title is entitled to it. Moreover, if Samuel did prophesy and work wonders, [remember that] Saul too is accounted among the prophets. Therefore be not wise too much nor overly proud. Rather observe the humility of the ancients in their designating the one who is today called prophet by the name of seer; do not seek greatness; in any case, may your like become many in Israel.

Our ancestors are worthy of praise for their efforts to preserve these letters, from whose contents we can observe the demand of the disciple for prophecy. In the light of these letters we may understand more fully many allusions in the writings of Maimonides.

It is well-known that he composed the *Guide to the Perplexed* for the benefit of his "beloved pupil"[46] who in the meantime had

---

46. *Guide,* translator's introduction, p. 3b (Vilna ed.). "Your absence aroused me to compose this treatise which I wrote for you and for others like you." Cf. also *Kovez̧,* pt. II, 30c; pt. III, 16d.

departed Cairo and settled in Syria.[47] Maimonides sent copies of the book to him there, chapter by chapter. It seems that the letters cited above were written during Ibn Aknin's stay in Egypt while he still had the opportunity to study with his master face to face. Echoes of the discussion concerning the pupil's desire for prophecy can be heard from the pages of the *Guide to the Perplexed*, especially when the master mentions to his disciple that it is possible that a man may prepare himself continually for prophecy, hoping for it but still not attaining it. Or when he quotes in this connection the word of the prophet Jeremiah which he cited in his letter to his pupil. "And, thou, do not seek greatness for thyself."[48] He therefore not only derogates those who pride themselves upon prophecy that is addressed to other people[49] but warns him as well to differentiate between true and seeming prophecy.

> You ought to attain knowledge of the true reality, which is that some people have—even while they are awake—extraordinary imaginings, dreams and amazed states, which are like the vision of prophecy so that they think that they are prophets. And they are very much pleased with what they apprehend in these imaginings and think that they have acquired sciences without instruction; and they bring great confusion into speculative matters of great import, true notions being strangely mixed up in their minds with imaginary ones."[50]

It was not for naught that Maimonides tried to set this matter straight in the mind of his disciple. Can you think that the pupil would dare to aspire to prophecy without some substance to this claim?! Undoubtedly he had a peg upon which he could hang his case. And perhaps he too was subject to "amazed states" which are "like the vision of prophecy."

47. *Koveẓ*, pt. II, 30a; pt. III, 16d.
48. *Guide* II:32, p. 362.
49. Ibid. II:40.
50. Ibid. II:37, p. 374.

There is a wheel of fortune that turns in our world. Maimonides did not always maintain the aforementioned opinion. After some time his attitude to his disciple's goal changed. From the letter which was appended to that important gift, i.e., the *Guide of the Perplexed*, which he sent to his disciple, we learn that he not only agreed with him but was supportive of his desire and tried to show him the way which would lead to the attainment of prophecy. Once again he uses the locution "to seek greatness" which Jeremiah had thrust at Baruch ben Neriah after the latter had been prepared and desirous for prophecy, but now the phrase is not used pejoratively but in praise. He praises him as follows:

> You are my portion from all my labor. . . . You are wise-hearted so that you might seek greatness and invoke a spirit of understanding so that you might ascend great heights and soaring monuments . . . may God reveal to you the innermost recesses of wisdom . . . and multiply and magnify your knowledge . . . and double your understanding of the secrets of the Torah. May the Lord open for you His goodly treasure from heaven and bring you into His chambers . . . and withal may you dwell upon the Book of Moses, and from it may you see the vision of the Lord . . . for this is the way trod by every seer, and this is the ladder of the vision.[51]

That it was Maimonides' desire that his spirit be poured forth upon his pupil, so that he might enter under the wings of prophecy, is seen clearly from what he says at the end of the *Guide of the Perplexed*. There in unmistakable terms he set forth and sets firmly down how "to attain that true worship which constitutes the final goal of man."[52] He turns directly to his disciple and says, "And now I shall begin to guide you towards that instruction and habits by whose aid you will reach this sublime goal."[53] How? By cleansing

51. *Kovez̧*, pt. II, 29d–30c.
52. *Guide* III:51, p. 618.
53. Ibid., p. 622.

his soul of mundane concerns during prayer and study, during that time when he is not preoccupied with earning a living, so "that he might draw close to the Lord and stand before him in the way and manner of truth." "Now my opinion is that this end may be achieved by those men of knowledge who have rendered their souls worthy of it by training of this kind."[54] Ultimately man should reach that stage where,

> through his apprehension of the true realities and his joy in what he has apprehended, [he] achieves a state in which he talks with people and is occupied with his bodily necessities while his intellect is wholly turned toward Him, may He be exalted, while outwardly he is with people. . . . I do not say that this is the level of all the prophets; but I do say that this is the level of Moses our Master. . . . This level is not one, with a view to the attainment of which, someone like myself may aspire to for guidance, but one may aspire to attain that which was mentioned before this one through the training we have described. One must beseech God that He remove the obstructions that separate us from Him, even though most of them come from us, as we have explained in certain chapters of this treatise.[55]

Here Maimonides excludes only the rank (level) of Moses from the possibility of attainment. "The level of the other prophets" is, however, open and available. It is towards that rank that he will direct his disciple.

Maimonides proposed the [following] parable.

> The ruler is in his place, and all his subjects are partly within the city and partly outside the city. Of those who are within the city, some have turned their backs upon the ruler's habitation, their faces being turned another way. Others seek to reach the ruler's habitation, turn towards it, and desire to enter it and to stand before him, but up to

54. Ibid., p. 623.
55. Ibid., p. 623–624.

> now they have not yet seen the wall of the habitation. Some of those who seek to reach it have come up to the habitation and walk around it, searching for its gate. Some of them have entered the gate and walked about the antechambers. Some of them have entered the inner court of the habitation and have come to be with the king, in one and the same place with him, namely, in the ruler's habitation. But having come into the inner part of the habitation does not mean that they see the ruler or speak to him. But their having come into the inner part of the habitation, it is indispensable that they should make another effort; then they will be in the presence of the ruler, see him from afar or from nearby, or hear the ruler's speech or speak to him.[56]

The following constitutes the proper interpretation of the parable. Those who are outside the city are all human individuals who have no doctrinal belief, neither one based on speculation nor one that acepts the authority of tradition.

Those who are within the city, but have turned their backs upon the ruler's habitation, are people who hold incorrect beliefs.

Those who seek to reach the ruler's habitation and to enter it but never see the ruler's habitation "are the multitude of the adherents of the law; I refer to the ignoramuses who observe the commandments."

Those who have come up to the habitation and walk around it are "the jurists who believe true opinions on the basis of traditional authority," but do not engage in speculation concerning the fundamental principles of religion.

"Those who have plunged into speculation concerning the fundamental principles of religion have entered into the antechambers. . . . He, however, who has achieved demonstration, to the extent that it is possible, of everything of divine matters that may be demonstrated . . . has come to be with the ruler in the inner part of the habitation." This rank constitutes that of the sages, and is close to that of the prophets, to which it leads. Nevertheless, in arriving at this rung, the

56. Ibid., p. 618.

sages do not exhaust either their possibilities or their strength. The power to rise from the rank of "those who are with the ruler in the inner part of his habitation" to the level of those who actually see the face of the king is correlative with the strength and capacity of the individual sage. To this rank "only those who set their thought to work after having attained perfection in the divine science, who turn wholly to God, may He be cherished and held sublime, renounce what is other than Him, and direct all the acts of their intellect toward an examination of created beings with a view to drawing from them proof with regard to Him, so as to know His governance of them in whatever way is possible."

In his desire to elevate his pupil to the rank of the prophets; [Maimonides] set forth the means of achieving this goal, viz., continuous intellectual concentration on divine science, and the arousal of his disciple's "thought towards God alone until he truly gains knowledge of Him" on the ground of "intellectual apprehension. Afterwards he can devote himself to His service and can endeavor though his nearness to the Lord to strengthen that attachment, i.e., reason." It is not the acquisition of concepts but the intense concentration of all one's thoughts upon God that is essential here: "To be totally devoted to Him and employ one's intellectual thought in constantly loving Him. Mostly this is achieved in solitude, and for this reason every pious person must separate and isolate himself and not meet anyone unless it is necessary."[57] The conclusion of the work is a proof for the goal of the entire book. Maimonides concludes the *Guide of the Perplexed* with the revelation that he placed in it: "It is a part of what I consider very useful to those like you. I hope for you that through sufficient reflection you will grasp all the intentions I have included therein, with the help of God."[58]

---

57. Ibid., pp. 620–621. According to the translations of Ibn Tibbon and al-Ḥarizi.
58. Ibid. III:54, p. 638.

Ibn Aknin was not alone in considering himself to be a prophet;[59] others took him to be one as well. R. Judah al-Ḥarizi, who knew him personally, relates in his *Taḥkemoni*: "And from thence I came to the blessed royal city of Aleppo . . . there is now resident within it for the past thirty years . . . the sage R. Joseph the Westerner . . . from whom all the wise learn wisdom, and if they are like Elisha he is in my eyes as Elijah the Tishbite . . . and his generation shall be the generation of prophecy; for the Lord has anointed him as a prophet of Israel."[60] This type of rare praise, seldom employed in Israel, goes far beyond convention and could never be construed as a literary conceit. A fortiori is this true of those verses which al-Ḥarizi composed regarding R. Joseph where he added to the aforementioned praises: "Behold, you are a mighty man, well known in the West, and in the East the Lord has anointed you as a prophet."[61] Here it is stated explicitly that R. Joseph attained the rank of prophecy after having left his native land, Morocco, and reached Egypt, or Aleppo, i.e., after he came into direct contact with Maimonides.[62]

59. It is noteworthy that in his commentary to the Song of Songs, *Hitgallut ha-Sodot ve-Hofa'at ha-Me'orot,* ed. A. Halkin (Jerusalem, 1964), Ibn Aknin utilizes the expression ממא פאץ מן נור אל בארי עלי which means, "from that which the Creator has caused to emanate upon me." Cf. Steinschneider, op. cit., vol. 1, p. 65.

60. *Taḥkemoni,* gate 46. Al-Ḥarizi here understood the term *bat kol* in the following way: "There are men (e.g., Hillel and Samuel Ha-Katan) who were worthy of prophetic inspiration, but their generation was unworthy." Cf. t. Sotah 13:3–4. Prof. Spiegel has directed my attention to something similar in R. Judah Ha-Levi's poem in honor of Rabbi Nathan, the registrar of the Egyptian academy: "Were his generation worthy of prophecy, he would prophesy and be called a man of delights." *Diwan,* ed. H. Brody (Berlin, 1901), pt. I, pp. 113, 192.

61. *Taḥkemoni,* gate 50. Similarly in JTS MS 1791, p. 262a; JTS MS 90a, p. 144a.

62. Occasionally al-Ḥarizi uses the word "prophecy" when he praises certain Hebrew poets. Even concerning himself he says the following: "And reason put forth its hand . . . and said to me . . . and in the vision of a poem declared: I have made you a prophet for the nations"(*Taḥkemoni,* introduction). He says of the Spanish

Two witnesses are necessary for the establishment of a case. There has come into our hands a "Lamentation for a Wise Man" excerpted from the prayerbook of Aleppo, which was evidently written on the occasion of R. Joseph's death. There it says, "This bright day has now been darkened, because the sage and prophet has departed from our midst. The light of the West has been snuffed out, and the sanctuary of truth has been destroyed."[63]

---

poets: "This was a generation of wondrous poets, a band of poets of whom R. Judah Ha-Levi was one"(gate 18, 1; cf. gate 18, 4; 3, 6). Nevertheless, the metaphor is apparent. It is easy to differentiate between this species of poetic exaggeration and his depiction of Ibn Aknin, where his language is both unmistakable and specific. Not only did al-Ḥarizi call him a prophet but he gave precise details so as to ground this claim, e.g., that "he was anointed as a prophet," and he mentions where this happened. These details attest to the fact that Alḥarizi was not engaging in poetic exaggeration when he called Ibn Aknin a prophet. Moreover, it is easy enough to understand how it was possible for him to be caught by a metaphor and compare the poets to prophets. But it was not for his poetry that al-Ḥarizi labeled Ibn Aknin a prophet. It is worthy of note that al-Ḥarizi's language is more circumspect when he is speaking of the poetry of R. Judah Ha-Levi: "It may be likened to a descent of one of the stars on high or an emanation of the Holy Spirit" (3, 6). In one poem Maimonides is called "a prophet of wisdom." Cf. H. Brody, "Mikhtavim al ha-Rambam," *Moznayim,* 1935, p. 407.

63. S.Z. Halberstam, *Koveẓ al Yad* vol. 9, year 15 (1899). The metaphorical expression "and the prayer on behalf of all his prophets" which Ibn Aknin cites at the beginning of his treatise *Bi-Meḥuyyav ha-Meẓ'iut* (ed. J. Magnes [Berlin, 1904], p. 3), and which M. Löwy (*Drei Abhandlungen von Josef ben Jehuda* [Berlin, 1879] p. 2 n. 2) found problematic, was customary among Jewish authors who wrote in Arabic and also translators of books from Arabic to Hebrew. It was a circumlocutory way of avoiding the blessing of Muhammad with which Muslims would normally begin their works.

III

The further we probe into this important chapter of Maimonides' life, the better we see his yearning for prophetic rank, discovering proofs for this yearning on his part. A personal testament to this effect and one which enables us to pierce the veil, has fallen into our hands. We refer to the *Chapters Concerning Felicity,* which in the opinion of most scholars was authored by Maimonides.[64] This book, known as the "Seal of the Treatise" (viz., the *Guide of the Perplexed*) since it includes everything treated by the author in the *Guide of the Perplexed* in its "term and completion" was written for "his noble pupil," Joseph Ibn Aknin.[65]

In this book Maimonides does not hesitate to admit that he has reached the "ultimate felicity," i.e., prophecy. This admission is clear and explicit. He sets up the principle that the man who has attained such perfection is in duty bound to influence other persons as he has been influenced by the divine efflux. What is the nature of this "perfection"? This is the rank of "whoever has been permanently and thoroughly influenced without interruption by God," the rank of that person "to whom are revealed the secrets of the Torah from Heaven."[66] In the course of his exposition he relates additionally that he counseled and prepared another man—evidently his disciple, Ibn

64. Elsewhere, I shall attempt to buttress the opinion of Steinschneider and Bacher that *Pirke Hazlaḥah* is a product of the Maimonidean spirit.

65. "And now, my brother, hearken and incline your ear to understand everything involved in this matter, since I have deliberately set it as the seal of the *Guide* and [it] includes everything contained there as its proper term and completion." *Perakim be-Hazlaḥah,* ed. S. Z. Dawidowicz (Jerusalem, 1939), pp. 13 f.

66. "Therefore the man who has attained such perfection must impart to others from that which God has imparted to him. . . . this influence is permanent, thorough, and without interruption, so that of him who receives it, it may be said that the secrets of the Torah are revealed to him from heaven." Ibid., p. 10.

Aknin—for "the attainment of such a rank."[67] With this there is an open admission of the fact that he had already achieved such a rank.

A fiery blast seems to issue from his mouth when he speaks of the prophetic vision. He describes this state in the fiery colors that only a man who has undergone the experience could invoke. He reiterates to his disciple that prophecy can only be acquired through purification of the soul, i.e., the utmost refinement of the senses, the intellect, and the imagination.[68] Prophecy is a vital need and a permanent state. Just as the individual perishes if he ceases breathing for one instant, so will he perish if the holy spirit, or prophecy, abandons him.[69] On the other hand, if a person is properly prepared, he will merit the indwelling presence of the Shekhinah[70] and his soul will receive unceasingly the divine emanation and will be infused with a divine light and with angelic glory.[71]

He can attain through prayer a divestiture of corporeality and the ascent of the soul to a higher world, the world of "intelligences"

---

67. "And to the attainment of this rank, which is reserved for whomever will be perfected in the principles and fundamental doctrines, and will have done that which I directed him." Ibid., p. 11.

68. "Noble student, when your heart has been purified and you are separated from mundane matters, it will then become clear to you, as it has to all the pious, what it means to be numbered among the separate intelligences." Ibid., p. 6. Cf. W. Bacher, "The Treatise on Eternal Bliss Attributed to Moses Maimuni," *JQR,* O.S. 9 (1897), p. 271, n. 5.

69. " 'Spirit' is an ambiguous term. Sometimes it may be defined as 'breath,' and at other times as 'prophecy.' Just as the vital spirit in the body is cooled through breathing, which if it stops but for an instant would cause death, so, too, if the prophetic inspiration should flag and cease from his heart, this would bring about his death." Ibid., p. 2.

70. "Then your noble soul shall be freed from the domination of many possessions and artificial acquisitions." Ibid., p. 14.

71. "Since wise inquiry leads to prophetic apprehension . . . and when one attains awe of the Lord, which is the purpose of the Torah, his awe will lead him to the wisdom of the holy ones, so that he will be influenced by the angels." Ibid., p. 12. Cf. p. 3.

where, with the aid of the imagination, he will discern the future with the same certainty that he knows the past. He will predict events prior to their occurrence, viz., wars, famine, death, or life. In brief, nothing in the world will be hidden from him.[72] All of this occurs within the mind of a man when prophecy is bestowed upon him without any sensory component and without a voice being heard.[73] Prophecy will descend upon his tongue, independently of his cognition and counsel "other than that which is uttered by his lips." Man is neither the cause nor the initiator of that which "descends upon him"—he is the subject and the recipient.[74]

Man's nature is to keep private the precious inwardness of his spirit. Maimonides was wont to conceal what lay in the recesses of his heart and to muzzle his lips. What caused him to reveal the secret? His love for his "noble disciple" who implored him persistently and continuously until he introduced the latter into the secret grove. Love overcame inhibition.

Maimonides' desire for prophecy was not born of an intention to utilize or manipulate its high status, i.e., to work miracles and wonders.[75] After wrestling with the problems and riddles which

---

72. "His soul is subjugated and abstracted from sensibilia . . . and he shall discern through the imaginative faculty and see and hear that which is indubitable. Since contingents and past events are on the same plane, due to their compresence before him in all their clarity and distinctiveness, he will view the future just as he inspects the past." Ibid., pp. 7–8.

73. Ibid., p. 11.

74. "What occurs within my soul, and this is indeed a sublime metaphor concerning prophecy which descends upon him unuttered, unspoken and unheard, other than the movement of his lips, which is sent to him by God without his cognition or counsel concerning that which descends upon him. Ibid., p. 13.

75. "Any prophet who arises and says that God has sent him will not have to perform a miracle . . . that changes the course of nature. His sign will be that he predicts the future and his words will be confirmed. *M.T.,* Yesodei ha-Torah 10:1 (cf. Ibid. 7:7, 5:2). A prophet will arise "not to found a religion, but to warn us against transgressing the prescriptions of the Torah." Ibid. 9:2.

stood "at the apex of the world" and concluding that their solution lay beyond the bounds of the human intellect, he thereupon sought to cross the boundary line.

Maimonides prized prophecy more than any of the modes of knowledge. He was a veritable lion among his fellows; the sovereign master of many disciplines sensed that not all of the gates of wisdom were open to him—that many treasures were hidden from the gaze of logic and that "the human intellect had set its bounds."[76] He knew that vis-à-vis many problems, human cognition was stumbling blindly in the dark.[77] "Human knowledge has its limits, and so long as the soul is within the body it cannot know what transcends nature. Since the soul is part of the order of nature, it is impossible that it envision what is Above."[78] There are matters to which human cognition is inadequate, "there are some subjects which human reason cannot grasp, nor does it have the means to [grasp them] and thought wearies itself with that which it cannot comprehend and for the understanding of which it does not have the means . . . it is either an intrinsic flaw of the rational power or a species of insanity."[79] There exists therefore "a level in knowledge higher than that of the philosophers and that level is—prophecy."[80] With its aid man can

76. *Guide* I:32, p. 70.

77. "This means that you should let your intellect move about only within the domain of things that man is able to grasp. For in regard to matters that it is not in the nature of man to grasp, it is very harmful to occupy oneself with them." *Guide* I:32, pp. 69 f. "If, however, your eyes are forced to do something they are reluctant to do—if they are made to gaze fixedly and are set the task of looking over a long distance, too great for you to see . . . your sight will weaken and you shall not be able to apprehend what you could apprehend before having gazed fixedly and before having been given this task." Ibid., p. 68. Cf. *Ma'amar ha-Yiḥud* (Berlin, 1846), ed. M. Steinschneider, p. 17.

78. Maimonides' letter to R. Hasdai in Alexandria. *Koveẓ,* pt. II, 23b.

79. *Guide* II:24, p. 327.

80. *Koveẓ,* pt. II, 23c.

grasp that which eludes the power of rationality.[81] A philosopher, no matter how perfect, cannot occupy the position held by a prophet. Even Aristotle, the "perfect exemplar of human knowledge," is of inferior worth by comparison with those "influenced by the heavenly overflow to the extent that they have attained the prophetic rank, than which there is no higher rung."[82]

What drove Maimonides to compare prophecy with philosophy? What has Aristotle to do with Sinai? The analogy was neither originated by nor forged in the school of Maimonides. He did not draw forth this comparison in and of himself. The interpenetration of these two realms was the product of an ancient polemical confrontation, one which stemmed from Hellenistic times. When the descendants of Japhet invaded the tents of Shem, the latter promptly preempted the territory of the former.

When the times were in joint and Israel was domiciled in its own land—to what may this be compared? To a deep well filled with water, clear, sweet, and nourishing. To this well there came all the residents of the city, both young and old, drawing forth its refreshing contents. Such was the situation until there came to the city a wine merchant eager to sell his wares. When his customers' palates tasted his wine, and when its effects could be felt in their every limb, then their hearts were indeed gladdened. So anxious were they to partake of the wine that they would not desist from importuning the wine merchant until their pitchers, originally intended for water, overflowed with the more intoxicating liquid. So

---

81. *Guide* II:24, 38. Cf. R. Shem Tov ibn Falaquera: "Because when the authentic sage will consider the truth of the words of the prophets, he will have clarified thereby divine secrets and true opinions which are too elevated for those who are expert in philosophical research." H. Malter, "Shem Tov ben Joseph Palquera. II. His Treatise on the Dream," *JQR*, N.S. 1 (1911), p. 489. Cf. J. Guttmann, *Philosophies of Judaism* (New York, 1964), p. 431, n. 64.

82. Maimonides' letter to R. Samuel ibn Tibbon. *Kovez̤*, pt. II, 28d. Cf. H. Malter, op. cit., p. 492.

it was in antiquity—"the anointed days" of the prophet. Once again the prophet had been transformed into another kind of person. The man of spirit had been changed into an intellectual—a master of abstract ideas.

A man sees only that to which his heart inclines. Maimonides, who combined within himself Torah and philosophy, deliberated, inquired and proposed many metaphors and similes aimed at a peaceful settlement between the domains and claims of Torah and of theoretical speculation. He spoke in complete innocence when he designated prophecy as equivalent to human perfection, as being the power to grasp noble concepts beyond the reach of human reason. "True prophets are able to grasp theoretical concepts which are indubitably beyond man's theoretical powers alone. These cannot account for or produce the causes from which these ideas flow." They provide information "which no amount of hypothesis or conjecture" can yield.[83] They (i.e., the prophets) comprehend that which man is incapable of comprehending through "principles and deductions and cogitation."[84] For prophecy "constitutes another world and is not susceptible to dialectical argumentation. Once [an insight] is discerned as prophetic, there is no longer any room left for dialectical argument . . . for prophecy is superior to such arguments . . . dialectic cannot attain to that which prophecy attains."[85]

Maimonides customarily enunciated the following principle as central. Man's final end is the perfection of his soul. This constitutes the true goal of the Torah.[86] He gave the following advice to all. "Never be satisfied with your spiritual attainment; attempt always to rise higher than your present estate." And this urging of his was not a vain pronouncement. He was certain that every man had "the

83. *Guide* II:38, p. 377; "The Torah has given us knowledge of a matter the grasp of which is not within our power." Ibid. II:25, p. 329.

84. Ibid. II:38, p. 377. Cf. II:45.

85. *Kovez̧*, pt. II, 23c.

86. *Guide* III:33.

power to be as righteous as Moses our Teacher."[87] It is easy for us to imagine how Maimonides could set forth this doctrine when every one of his auditors was conscious of the fact that he practiced in his own life what he was preaching to others. A sage who seeks to guide others must exemplify in his own life that which he demands of others. Maimonides' behavior throughout his life is witness and warrant for his striving always to attain higher and higher rungs on the ladder of the spirit—the object of his yearning was always perfection. And what is perfection? "To know everything that man can know of existing things."[88] To comprehend "true theological ideas."[89] Indeed "the highest of the rungs attainable by man and the goal of perfection available to the human species" is prophecy.[90] Evidence abounds for the fact that many of the discourses in the *Guide of the Perplexed* were addressed exclusively to that individual who had attempted to scale this ladder of human perfection.[91] And of whom was he speaking, when he mentioned in this book "that man who chooses human perfection [as his goal] and truly seeks to become a man of God," if not of himself?

Many were the occasions on which he confronted the boundaries of unaided human reason. More than once he observed and felt that human understanding was in need of help from prophetic intuition. The gourd is known by its stalk. In his youth, he had grappled with questions of purpose, the purpose of existence and that of every particular being. He was certain that "everything must have a purpose which justified its existence."[92] But he became perplexed

87. *M.T.,* Hilkhot Teshuvah 5:2.

88. *Guide* III:27, p. 511.

89. Ibid. III:54.

90. Ibid. II:36, p. 369.

91. "Concerning this matter . . . it behooves to explain the matter to those whose souls grasp at human perfection." *Guide* I:26, pp. 56 f.

92. *Einleitung in die Mishna,* p. 50. He retracted this opinion in his old age. Cf. *Guide* III:13.

when he tested this principle and sought to determine the nature of particular beings or individuals. Although he could fix a purpose for existence as a whole, a question remained unanswered: What is the purpose of particular individuals? Why did nature produce some insects with wings and some without? Why were some worms many-footed and others not? Beyond this, what is the purpose of this individual and that particular worm? In disappointment he was forced to admit the following truth: "Their purpose is concealed in mystery—not to be apprehended by human reason, since it lies beyond its capacity, but only to be revealed by prophecy or that power which is capable of discerning the future."[93]

But simple despair concerning the power of human understanding gains one nothing. Here, however, despair and hope are intertwined. Prophecy may have ceased from the midst of Israel, but hope for the resumption of prophecy has not ceased. Under what conditions, then, will prophecy recur? According to Maimonides, prophecy died out, not because of our sins or because the Ark of the Covenant was hidden away,[94] but because "we were exiled," "indubitably" because

93. Ibid., p. 50.

94. According to the Sifre (ed. M. Friedman, p. 107b), Deut. 18:11, prophetic inspiration does not rest upon us because of our sins. According to R. Solomon ibn Adret (*Teshuvot ha-Rashba,* pt. I, resp. 94), "The wells of wisdom have been stopped up because of sin and the consequent destruction of the Temple, from whence prophecy and wisdom were sent to flow to the prophets and to the sages." According to R. Meir Ibn Gabbai (*Avodat ha-Kodesh* IV:24), "The proximate cause of prophecy and the reason for the decent of the Holy Spirit and the indwelling presence of God upon those worthy of receiving it was the Ark of the Covenant and the Cherubim atop it; this happened during the time of the First Temple, and from that place the light and the efflux would be diffused . . . because the Ark and the Cherubim represented the interweaving of the strands of God's glory similar to the interweaving of lights in a leaping flame which is bound to the wick and from there grows ever stronger and higher; from thence it diffuses light to those worthy of it. The Temple therefore was the proximate cause of the descent of prophecy, and for this reason, when the Temple was destroyed and the Ark was hidden, there were no longer any prophets." The Talmudic sages distinguished between the

the Israelites were now "depressed and melancholic [in their exile]." As long as Israel remains in exile it is comparable to "a slave sold to fools and evil masters, whose entire existence is therefore bereft of truth, and is given over to the free play of animal desires and who has no power of mastering them."[95] Nevertheless, redemption will refine us from the dross of evil desires and will prepare our souls

---

indwelling of the Holy Spirit on a few individuals and the nesting of the glory of the indwelling presence in the Holy of Holies within the Ark. ("What is the function of the Ark? The Twin Tablets of the Law were contained therein and God's indwelling presence was domiciled there." Cf. *Yalkut Shimoni,* Beha'alotekha, no. 729; cf. also Tosafot, Baba Batra 25a, s.v. "the host of heaven"). The indwelling presence was continuous and permanent (B. Baba Batra 25a, s.v. "fixed within the Shekhinah"; cf. L. Ginzberg, *Peirushim ve-Ḥiddushim bi-Yerushalmi* [New York, 1941–61], vol. III, pp. 383 and 397). Apparently this served as the source for the opinion cited above ("The Ark . . . from which light spread to the entire world"; Bereshit Rabah 55:3; J. Berakhot 4:8, 3), the investiture of individuals with the Holy Spirit. When R. Yoḥanan was told of Rabbah Bar Ḥanna's statement to Resh Lakish, that if the Babylonian [Jews] had emigrated to the Holy Land during the days of Ezra, the Holy Spirit would then have descended upon those living during the Second Temple era, he replied: even if "they all had migrated to the Holy Land in the days of Ezra, the Holy Spirit would still not have rested over the Second Temple, for it is written, 'God shall enlarge Japheth and He shall dwell in the tents of Shem' [Gen. 9:27]: i.e., although God has enlarged Japheth, the Holy Spirit rests only in the tents of Shem."(B. Yoma 9b–10a). It is possible that R. Yoḥanan differentiated between the Shekhinah and the Holy Spirit. "Five things were missing in the Second Temple: the Ark, the Kaporet, Cherubim [Rashi: they are all one thing], fire, Shekhinah, Holy Spirit, and Urim ve-Tumim [Rashi: The Shekhinah did not rest (on the Second Temple)and the prophets of that period did not have the Holy Spirit]."In J. Ta'anit 2:1 the text is: "Fire, the Ark, Urim ve-Tumim, the anointing oil, and the Holy Spirit, and [R. Yoḥanan] believes that all depended on each other; i.e., the Holy Spirit did not end during the Second Temple as a result of the Babylonian Jews' errors, but because the Shekhinah had departed.

95. *Guide* II:36, p. 373. R. Isaac ben R. Jacob de Lattes, *Sha'arei Ẓion* (Premysl, 1885), ed. S. Buber, p. 14. He sees the reason for the cessation of prophecy in "our many troubles and wars."

for the reception of the light of prophecy.[96] Then prophets will arise and profound mysteries will be revealed.

For prophecy is pertinent to the Messianic era. The doctrine that in the end of days the indwelling presence of God will return to the people as in days of old, and all of the children of Israel will be prophets, was well known.[97] Many of the sages viewed this spiritual phenomenon not as a consequence but as the essence of redemption. For them, the Messianic hope was a consequence of the "revival of the Holy Spirit," a yearning for the day when "the righteous will sit with crowned heads, basking in the radiance of the divine presence."[98] Why was all of Israel, sages as well as prophets, enamored of the Messianic days? "Not that they might exercise political sovereignty over the other nations of the world"; rather, says Maimonides, "that they might find respite from those foreign governments, which [now] prevent them from being occupied with [the study of] Torah and [the practice of the] commandments in the proper manner, and that they might find leisure [so to do] and increase their wisdom,"[99] . . . "since in those days knowledge and

96. Depression negatively influences the imaginative faculty, since it is a bodily faculty, which "sometimes grows tired, is weakened, and at other times is in a healthy state." *Guide* II:36, p. 372. Perfection of the imaginative faculty is a prerequisite for the receipt of prophecy.

97. Concerning this belief, see my article, "The Descent of the Holy Spirit in the Days of the Talmudic Sages" [It was never published; however, this theme is dealt with in Heschel's *Torah Min ha-Shammayin,* 2 vols. (London, 1962–1965), ed.].

98. Kallah Rabbati (New York, 1936), ed. M. Higger, chap. 2, pp. 194 ff. From the continuation of the discussion it is clear that the statements refer to the Messianic age. Cf. *Zohar* I:135a (*Midrash ha-Ne'elam*); M. Higger, "Yarhi's Commentary on Kallah Rabbati," *JQR*, N.S. 24 (1934), pp. 342 ff.; Naḥmanides, *Ḥeshbon Keẓ ha-Ge'ulah* (New York, 1904), p. 20: "Since we long for it . . . that we will soon experience proximity to the Lord . . . this is the primary reason for our desire and yearning for the days of the Messiah."

99. *M.T.,* Hilkhot Melakhim 12:4.

understanding will be increased,"[100] and the Israelites "will be very wise, knowing sublime and profound mysteries and living the life intended for them by their Creator, insofar as this is possible for human beings."[101] And it was Saadia Gaon who described the days of the Messiah as that time "when prophecy will rest upon every Israelite so that even our children and servants will prophesy . . . [and] when an Israelite travels abroad and announces his country of origin, they will say to him, 'Tell us what will happen tomorrow or what happened yesterday'—if these matters were concealed from them. When he answers their request, they will truly know him to be an Israelite."[102]

Maimonides knew that even upon its resumption, prophecy would rest only upon a properly trained recipient. To claim that "the simpletons among ordinary people" could prophesy would be equivalent to claiming that "it [will] be possible for an ass or a frog to prophesy."[103] Only that man who "is wise and faithful, whose passions are completely controlled, intelligent and preeminent in his character traits"[104] is worthy of prophecy. If such spiritual heroes existed in his generation, viz., men worthy of having the divine spirit rest on them, it is certain that he counted himself among them. It is not to be taken lightly that even in the days of his youth he had not forgetten that it was impossible for a man to learn esoteric wisdom from a teacher or by the exertion of independent effort. Rather it could be grasped only if the Holy One, blessed be He, removed "the

---

100. Ibid., Hilkhot Teshuvah 9:2.

101. Ibid., Hilkhot Melakhim 12:5.

102. *Emunot ve-De'ot* (Warsaw, 1864), ed. D. Slutzki, p. 125. After the dead are resurrected, "all Israelites will be prophets." Cf. B. M. Lewin, *Oẓar ha-Ge'onim* (Haifa and Jerusalem, 1929–42), Sukkah, p. 74. We find a similar doctrine in the Mutaẓilite Ibn Manus; cf. *Abu-'l Fath' Muh'ammed asch-Schahrastani's Religionsparteien und Philosophenschulen* (Halle, 1850), ed. T. Haarbrücker, pt. I, p. 63.

103. *Guide* II:32.

104. *Einleitung in die Mishna,* p. 10.

veil of sense-perception from the heart."[105] For man has no choice, when it comes to matters of wisdom and speculative inquiry, but "that he seek after and pray to his Creator that He enlighten his understanding and lead him in the right path and reveal to him those secrets which are hidden in the text."[106] Apparently only the master of events can penetrate their innermost nature. Try to anticipate that future time when prophecy will recur!

Maimonides' doctrine of prophecy is reminiscent of a container without handles. We hypothesize that Maimonides prepared himself to receive prophecy as if it had handles attached. In the main, Torah spoke in the language of philosophers—a refined and theoretical tongue, abstracted from the mundane world of the practical. Nevertheless when it comes to prophecy Maimonides treats the matter, in terms of the need of his generation, as something which will come to pass in the near future. How can a man prepare himself to receive that cherished treasure to which no object of human desire is to be compared? Here Maimonides' theory becomes practice: as a sage and as a prudent man of wise experience he offers us both speculative wisdom and practical counsel.

IV

Ordinarily it is not the method of men to inquire into methods. Nevertheless, one must take heed of the unique approach of Maimonides to prophecy. His is not the way trodden by most men. He does not ask, as Saadia does, What is the purpose of prophecy?[107] He

105. Compare the expression "the eyes of the soul,"*M.T.*, Hilkhot Yesodei ha-Torah 4:7: "Those forms which have no shape are not visible to the naked eye; they are apprehended by the eye of the soul." Cf. Steinschneider's note, *Ma'amar ha-Yiḥud*, p. 17.

106. *Einleitung in die Mishna*, p. 45.

107. *Emunot ve-De'ot* (ed. Slutski), treatise 8, p. 125.

asks rather: What is the nature of prophecy? What happens when a man receives the prophetic efflux? What are the preconditions which ready the soul for prophecy? The object of his inquiry is the place of the Holy Spirit in the life of the prophet and not its function in the life of the people. He paid no attention to demonstrating its truth or showing its beauty and greatness to the nations or to heretics, but turned his attention to another aspect of prophecy, viz., teaching how one could attain it. Indeed, Maimonides did not allow himself entree into the subject matter of prophecy until he had annulled the opinion of the "host of fools" for whom prophecy was a miracle ordained by heaven, which phenomenon could occur to any man upon whom the Lord desired to rest His spirit, whether or not the individual in question was prepared or should prepare himself to receive it.[108] It is of no small moment that Maimonides begins his treatment of prophecy in this way. The problem of preparation for prophecy, which was despised by the "simpletons," was the keystone of his doctrinal arch. In order to change the minds of the masses he emphasized man's capacity to prepare himself for the attainment of that status. It is a valid presumption that no man arranges a feast unless there be diners in the offing. Undoubtedly, he was "preoccupied with himself." And if you say that his concern was solely for others—he who seeks a boon for his fellow man while in need of it himself is answered first.

He taught openly that prophecy was the goal of all right action. When he came to praise the tractate Abot, concerning which the sages had said, "Whoever seeks to become a saint, let him seek to fulfill the words of Abot," he deemed it praiseworthy because "it leads to perfect felicity and true bliss . . . for we have no greater rank of sainthood than that of prophecy, the former being conducive to the latter, as it is said, 'sainthood brings one to the Holy Spirit'; it

108. *Guide* II:32.

is thus clear from their words that the performance of the words of this tractate leads one to the rank of prophecy."[109]

Maimonides invested many measures of wisdom in his doctrine of prophecy. Most of them were concerned with the problem of preparation: what are the conditions precedent to the attainment of prophecy? It was not arbitrary on his part to devote the best part of his intellectual energies to this area. His theory was first and foremost propounded for himself. He originated the doctrine of prophecy to adorn first himself and then others. We cannot evaluate it properly unless we first see that it was oriented primarily to his own person. Neverthless, his yearning for prophecy remained Maimonides' secret. But if we listen closely we can infer one truth from another. The words of the wise must be taken conjointly, since what one word locks the other opens. Suddenly, we find a hint once, twice, a third time in his writings, that he was personally concerned in this matter.

Theory becomes significant if it issues from practice. The following definition is advanced for prophecy: "an overflow [from the Holy Spirit][110] overflowing from God, may He be cherished and honored, through the intermediation of the active intellect towards the rational faculty in the first place and thereafter towards the imaginative faculty."[111] The reception of the overflow "occurs in a vision or in a dream."[112] In order to receive this overflow, a man must first have attained (1) perfection of the intellect, (2) perfection of the imaginative power, and (3) perfection of character.[113] Let

---

109. *Shemoneh Perakim* (New York, 1912), ed. J. Gorfinkle, p. 6.

110. "Air [*ru'aḥ*] . . . is also a term denoting the divine intellectual overflow that overflows to the prophets and in virtue of which they prophesy." *Guide* I:40, p. 90.

111. Ibid. II:36.

112. Ibid. II:44.

113. There is another trait of character which, though it does not constitute a prerequisite for prophecy, is necessary if the prophet is to sustain his mission, viz., courage, by means of it, the prophet overcomes all obstacles and does not fear any

us now see whether Maimonides believed that he had himself met all three of these preconditions. Perfection in theoretical sciences[114] is constitutive of intellectual perfection, which is reached through arduous learning.[115] This perfection is a precondition for prophecy, since the prophet must comprehend the noblest subject-matters.[116] Maimonides, whose like has not arisen either before or after in Israel, never gloried in his intellectual powers, but certainly their range and depth were no secret to him. The moral vision inheres in a man to the extent that he has "human traits that are refined and well-proportioned."[117] A man such as this "will have his thought detached from, and will have abolished his desire for, bestial things, viz., the preference for the pleasures of eating, drinking, and sexual intercourse."[118] This perfection is prerequisite to prophecy, since "the moral virtues are precedent to and conducive towards superiority in theoretical matters," and one cannot reach intellectual prefection unless one be "morally virtuous, dispassionate, and deliberative."[119] Once a man, however, becomes preoccupied with bodily matters, "he will find that his theoretical desires have grown weak, and decline. . . . He accordingly would not grasp things that otherwise would have been within his power to grasp."[120] Maimonides knew that he had achieved perfection in the realms enumerated. On the basis of his epistle to R. Samuel Ibn Tibbon we can see to what extent he dedicated himself in his later years to the cure of the sick—gentiles as well as Jews—even to the point of self-sacrifice.

---

man (ibid. II:38). Maimonides knew indeed that he had this trait (ibid., translator's Introduction, p. 9b [Vilna ed.]). Concerning the estimative faculty, cf. above, n. 33.

114. Ibid. II:36.

115. Ibid.

116. Cf. above, n. 83.

117. *Guide* II:36, p. 371.

118. Ibid.

119. Ibid. I:34, p. 77.

120. Ibid., p. 79.

Despite his professed "yearning and longing" to see the face of the translator of his *Guide of the Perplexed*, and the statement that he would have been "overjoyed and effervescently happy" to have seen him, nevertheless he advised him not to come to him, since he knew that he would have "no opportunity to sit alone and quietly" even for one hour.[121] "And, in general, I desire you, if indeed you are my disciple," he writes to R. Joseph Ibn Aknin, "that you follow in my footsteps and imitate my ways."[122] So, too, he testifies concerning himself,

> Know too that I intend to practice the utmost degree of humility, even though this harms me much in the eyes of the multitude. And to everyone who seeks to magnify his own greatness by picking fault in my character, even if he is the merest of disciples, we forgive him for doing so. . . . Even if I see with my own eyes and hear with my own ears someone who assaults the dignity of my person in my presence, I will not suspect him [of ill-will]; on the contrary, I will subject myself to him and will respond in cordial and pleasant tones, or I will remain silent or answer in a manner that is charming and congruent with the circumstances of that particular subject and time."[123]

> Now, thank God, even if I hear it with my own ears and know for a certainty that an individual is advancing himself at my expense . . . I pay no attention to it nor am I severe [with him] regarding this; rather I forgive and pardon that individual.[124]

---

121. *Kovez̩,* pt. II, 28b–c.

122. Ibid. 31b.

123. Letter to Joseph Ibn Aknin, *Kovez̩,* pt. II, 29d, 31a. Cf. his letter to R. Joseph ben Jabir, ibid., 16a: "There are persons who speak evil of us and desire to achieve prominence through our downfall. . . . we, however, forgive whoever acts in this manner because of his foolishness." Even Maimonides' opponent R. Samuel Ha-Levi of Bagdad wrote: "We have heard of the excellence of his character . . . and his humility." *Kovez̩,* pt. I, 32d, no. 155.

124. Letter to R. Pinehas bar Meshullam, *Kovez̩,* pt. I, p. 25a. "Your honor knows that the pomp and circumstance of our Jewish contemporaries do not

The notion that perfection of the imagination is prerequisite to reception of the prophetic overflow is at first blush a self-contradictory notion. The conjoining of imagination with intellection is a *mésalliance*. According to Maimonides' opinion, "the power of imagination is also, in true reality, the evil impulse, for every deficiency of reason or character is due to the action of the imagination or consequent upon its action."[125] It is "without doubt a bodily power"[126] that is the common property of both men and animals, and in terms of its functioning is the enemy and contradiction to rationality.[127] But a power which in science is inimical, in prophecy becomes helpful. Prophets will pursue it, while theoreticians will find in it a stumbling block. Prophecy is the conjoining of the rational and the irrational; an open road stretching from one end of the world to the other, embracing the abstract and the concrete, genus and species, universal and particular.[128] The perfection of the imaginative power is rooted in the nature of the individual. It is not acquired through habituation or learning but is dependent on the temperament of the individual.[129] When the prophetic overflow reaches the imagination, the prophet begins to see things—whether awake or in a vision—as if they existed extramentally.[130] On the

---

constitute success or felicity in my eyes; indeed, it is not a minor evil." *Kovez,* pt. II, 31d.

125. *Guide* II:12, p. 280.

126. Ibid. II:36, p. 372.

127. Ibid. I:73, p. 209. "The act of imagination is not the act of the intellect, but rather its contrary."

128. Ibid. I:73. Cf. Z. Diesendruck, "Maimonides' Lehre von der Prophetie,"*Jewish Studies in Memory of Israel Abrahams* (New York, 1927), pp. 99 ff. Perhaps it is Maimonides' opinion that the prophet is enabled to apprehend the purpose of the particular individual by virtue of his power of imagination. Cf. above, n. 93.

129. *Guide* II:36.

130. Ibid.

basis of his imaginative power, the prophet is enabled to discern the future and apprehends matters "as if they were things that had been perceived by the senses."[131] It happens that through an allusion we can determine that Maimonides considered his own imagination to be fully perfected. This we learn from a Genizah fragment found in Egypt. There it is told that Maimonides claimed of himself, "The forgetfulness which afflicts man did not affect me in the days of my youth."[132] It sufficed him to read a book once for its contents to be inscribed on his memory. The faculty of memory is, according to Aristotle, dependent upon the imaginative faculty,[133] and it was so understood by Maimonides.[134] And if his memory was so highly developed, it is certain that this was true of his imaginative faculty as well. His intellect, imagination, and character towered above those of his contemporaries. Is it possible that he forgot himself when writing of prophecy? Is it possible that he thought himself free of the burden of prophecy?

Maimonides authored the opinion that prophecy was a natural phenomenon.[135] Nature decrees that whoever is worthy of prophecy

---

131. Ibid. II:38, p. 377.

132. וכאן יקול מן לפטה אן אלנסיאן אלדי יעתרי אלנאס מא כאן יעתריני פי זמאן שביבתי בל לם יכון יחתאג אן יקף עלי אלכתאב סוי שפעה ואחדה וקד ארתסמת אנראצה E. Mittwoch, "Ein Geniza Fragment," *ZDMG* 57 (1903), p. 63.

133. *De Memoria,* I.

134. "Imagination recalls impressions made on the senses long after the objects apprehended by the senses have disappeared." *Shemoneh Perakim,* chap. 1. "You know, too, the actions of the imaginative faculty that are in its nature, such as retaining things perceived by the senses, combining these things, and imitating them." *Guide* II:36, p. 370. "Traces have remained impressed upon their imaginings." Ibid. II:38, p. 378.

135. All intellectual operations are the product of the influences exerted by the Active Intellect, for it activates the human intellect by bringing it from potentiality to actuality (*Guide* II:4). Now, when the overflow of the Active Intellect affects only the human intellect, its product is a sage; when it affects the imagination alone, the product is a statesman, a diviner, or a dreamer of veridicial dreams (ibid., II:37), and when it affects both the power of speech and imagination, the product is

will prophesy. It would be more miraculous if such a person did *not* prophesy. Attaining prophecy is a purely natural process. Only God can intervene so as to prevent a man from becoming a prophet.[136] This doctrine exceeds all bounds. The disciples of Maimonides were astounded that their master dared to pronounce it.[137] It was in the nature of a "contrary opinion"; not the attainment of prophecy, but its lack of attainment, was truly wondrous. This is further evidence for the fact that it was conceived in the innermost recesses of Maimonides' personality, in his reflections on his own fate and destiny. He considers prophecy in terms of himself and utilizes his own person as its proper norm. Who else was destined, prepared, and readied for prophecy, if not he? Despite this, God's indwelling presence did not come to rest upon him. This in itself was a sign from heaven.

On the other hand, one should never rely on miracles. He who prepares himself for prophecy should, in truth, wait and hope for its attainment. Because of this, he taught with complete certainty that prophecy remained within human ken.

> You should know that the case to be taken into consideration is that of a human individual, the substance of whose brain at the origin of his natural disposition is extremely well-proportioned, [who] would obtain knowledge and wisdom until he passes from potentiality to actuality

---

a prophet. On Maimonides' doctrine of prophecy, cf. H. A. Wolfson, "Hallevi and Maimonides on Prophecy," *JQR* 32 (1942), pp. 349 f.; ibid. 33 (1942), pp. 70 f. Cf. L. Strauss, *Philosophie und Gesetz* (Berlin, 1935), pp. 87 f.

136. "For we believe it may happen that one who is fit for prophecy and prepared for it may not become a prophet, on account of the divine will. To my mind this is like all the miracles and takes the same course as they. For it is a natural thing that everyone who according to his natural disposition is fit for prophecy and who has been trained in his education and study should become a prophet." *Guide* II:32, p. 361.

137. Cf. Efodi, Shem Tov, and others.

> and acquires a perfect and accomplished human intellect and pure and well-tempered human moral habits. Then all his desires will be directed toward acquiring the science of the secrets of what exists and knowledge of its causes. His thoughts will always go towards noble matters, and he will be interested only in knowledge of the Deity and in reflection on His works and on what ought to be believed in regard to that. By then he will have detached his thoughts from, and abolished his desire for, bestial things. . . . An individual of this description . . . will only apprehend divine matters of the most extraordinary nature, will see only God and His angels and will only be aware and achieve knowledge of matters that constitute true opinions and general directives for the well-being of men in their relations with one another.[138]

Maimonides treats of prophecy in full detail in the *Mishneh Torah* as something ubiquitous in all places and times, without once mentioning that it is no longer operative in Israel.[139] Did his silence concerning its disappearance allude to the opinion that prophecy was attainable, or was it reminiscent of the doctrine that prophecy would

---

138. *Guide* II:36, pp. 371 f. "He who prepares himself for prophecy, separates himself from everything that is mundane and purifies his soul . . . there is no doubt that angelic beings will hover over this person's soul and he will cleave to prophetic inspiration. Upon reaching this rank, there is no doubt that he has thereby attained the most exalted rank, i.e., that of the angels." M. Steinschneider, ed., *Ma'amar ha-Yiḥud* (Berlin, 1846), pp. 18–19.

139. This matter is only alluded to in passing in the *Mishneh Torah.* "They made the Urim ve-Tumim during the Second Temple in order to complete the eight garments, but they did not ask questions of them. Why didn't they ask questions of them? Because the Holy Spirit was not there, and any priest who does not speak through the Holy Spirit and the Shekhinah does not rest on him, one does not ask him." Cf. M.T., Hilkhot Klei ha-Mikdash 10:10. The Babylonian Talmud mentions that during the Second Temple period, sages sought gems for the ephod (B. Kiddushin 31a), and that any priest who does not speak through the Holy Spirit is not asked questions with them (B. Yoma 73b). Maimonides utilizes these two traditions in speaking of the demise of prophecy.

someday return to Israel? He speaks of it as something which one could acquire: "A man who is perfected in all these traits . . . the Holy Spirit will immediately rest upon him."[140] The word "immediately" sparkles in this context. The Maimonideans had great difficulty in explaining it.[141]

V

Maimonides too looked forward to that time when prophecy would in future days be restored to Israel. His opinion in this matter varies from that of other sages, since he limits the range of its recipients and advances the time of its recurrence. He maintains, as we have noted above, that in the future, as in the past, prophecy will be allotted only to those who are properly prepared for it.[142] In addition, he "precipitates the end" and asserts that the return of prophecy will precede the promised Messiah. In opposition to those who averred

140. The source of this opinion can possibly be found in *Seder Eliyahu Zuta,* chap. 15 (ed. M. Ish-Shalom, p. 167), "If a man studies Torah, let him then study the Prophets; if he studies the Prophets, then let him study the Writings. Afterwards he should study Mishnah, Halakhot, Midrash Halakhah, and Midrash Aggadah. Let him study much and lessen his preoccupation with commerce. The Holy Spirit will then immediately rest upon him."

141. "That which our master said, viz., that the Holy Spirit will immediately rest upon him, at first glance implies that prophecy will be his once he is prepared for it; yet he did not write this [in the *Guide*] . . . but there maintained that God's will was the necessary factor involved. It seems, therefore, that what is meant here is that the spirit of prophecy will immediately rest upon him if he is prepared and God acquiesces. But it is possible that he may be prepared and not be invested with prophecy, despite the fact that Maimonides' commentators there explained his words as being in complete agreement with those of the Philosopher. Nevertheless, their plain sense does not signify this." Cf. *Leḥem Mishnah.* Cf. also *Migdal Oz,* "This entire chapter is a composite of secular wisdom and the words of our sages, may their memory be for a blessing."

142. Cf. *Guide* II:32.

that in the generation prior to the arrival of the Messiah irrationality would abound and truth would be in such short supply that "heads of academies, faithful shepherds, pietists, and men of renown" would be unknown,[143] Maimonides believed that even before the Messiah the wisdom of humankind would grow enormously and "their intrinsic merit and yearning for God and the Torah would be multiplied."[144] He asserted also that one of the thirteen principles of faith was to believe that the Messiah will come and not to think that he will tarry.[145] This article of faith he held steadfastly before him when he saw the troubles of his contemporaries, who "were afflicted with religious persecution and enforced apostasy to the very ends of the earth from east to west." When the troubled Jews of Yemen turned to him in their hour of trial, a time when "their hearts were confused and halting, when doubts weakened their religious opinions," he consoled them by saying "that these days were the birthpangs of the Messiah, which the sages of old prayed that they would not see [but that the coming of the Messiah would follow]."[146] Yet, at the very time that the hearts of the children of Israel were filled with hope that the time of the redemption was approaching[147] and the Lord would effect their ingathering from all their habitations to Jerusalem, as had been promised by his servants the prophets, and many of

143. *Otiyot ha-Mashiaḥ, Bet ha-Midrash,* ed. A. Jellinek (Jerusalem, 1938), vol. 2, p. 58. Cf. also B. Sanhedrin 90a. "The Son of David will not come until the number of students has dwindled."

144. *M.T.,* Hilkhot Sanhedrin 1:3. The opinion that the renewal of prophecy would signal the beginning of redemption was also maintained by him in *M.T.,* Hilkhot Melakhim 12:2: "The war of Gog and Magog will occur at the beginning of the days of the Messiah. Before this war, a prophet will arise in Israel to direct the people and to prepare their hearts." Cf. Neubauer, *MJC,* vol. 2, p. 179: היהודים וסביבותיה פיץ יישר" and also the Ishamelites will ask, what are you, a prophet or the Messiah?"

145. *Maimuni's Einleitung zu Chelek,* twelfth principle.

146. *Koveẓ,* pt. II, lc.

147. On Messianic expectations in Maimonides' generation, see F. Baer, "Eine Jüdische Messiasprophetie auf das Jahr 1186, und der dritte Kreuzzug," *MGWJ* 70

them had already been led astray by false Messiahs, Maimonides demurred from supporting the claims of those who would calculate the precise time of the Messiah's arrival, because "the masses will stumble when they see the promised time at hand and the Messiah has not appeared."[148] Instead, he predicted the return of prophecy.

There can be no doubt as to Maimonides' consistency or sincerity. He believed that with the return of prophecy his proposed guides for Jewish conduct would have a practical implementation. He considered it his clear and present duty to compose a manual of Jewish law which people would use because they were in need of it. He was careful not to waste his own time with irrelevancies, however attractive it might be to dig and delve speculatively. Those matters which were "wasters of time" and practically inapplicable "did not concern him."[149] He was no historian seeking to consider prophecy from an historical standpoint. Matters whose day had passed did not concern him. He would never sow seed upon stones nor cast his wisdom to the winds. It is no accident that he entitled his opinions concerning this matter "education for prophecy."[150]

(1926), pp. 113 ff.; S. Zeitlin, *Maimonides: A Biography* (New York, 1935), pp. 84 ff.

148. *Kovez̧* pt. II, 5b. According to R. Moses ibn Ezra, *Shirat Yisrael* (Leipzig, 1924), trans. B. Z. Halper, p. 166, "There is no doubt that God will reveal the end-time first to those who are well versed in wisdom, as it is written, 'And the wise of the people will understand.'"

149. Apparently Maimonides felt that the renewal of prophecy was a function of time, for if not, why would Ezekiel mention the month, year, and day when he saw his vision? (Cf. *Guide* III:7.) Cf. also Efodi and Shem Tov. It is strange that he did not explain this further despite his own statement that "the matter requires an explanation."

150. Cf. *Guide* II:38, "This is the true reality of prophecy, and these are the opinions that are peculiar to the prophetic teaching."

Prophecy was, therefore, neither remote nor inaccessibly sequestered in the heavens nor hidden in the islands of the sea, for redemption was truly nigh. So he wrote to the Jews of Yemen:

> We have a great and wonderful tradition which I have received from the hands of my father, which he in turn received from his fathers extending back to the exile from Jerusalem . . . that in the prophecy of Balaam there is an allusion to the return of prophecy to Israel after its [temporary] cessation . . . for what Balaam said, "Now it shall be said of Jacob and Israel, 'What has God wrought' " [Num. 23:23], hints at the secret, viz., concerning that time one is to calculate its arrival on the basis of the same amount of time that occurred from the six days of creation until then; it is then that the prophets will exclaim, "What has God wrought." . . . according to this analogy and this explanation, prophecy is to return to Israel in the year 4970 after the creation [1210]. There is no doubt that the return of prophecy is the forerunner of the Messiah."[151]

---

151. כן ענדנא רואיה̈ גריבה̈ ארויהא ען אבי ען גדי ען אביה ען גדה זצ״ל הכד̇א אלי אול גלותנא מן ירושלם כמא שהד אלאנביא וקאל ונלו ירושלים אשר בספרד והי אן פי נצוץ נבוה̈ בלעם נץ פיה אלאשארה̈ אלי רג̇וע אלנבוה̈ פי ישראל בעד אנקטאעהא לכן קד ג̇א פי אלתורה נצוץ ואן כאן אלג̇רץ̇ בהא מעני מא יכון פיהא אשארה̈ למעני אכ̇ר נחו קול יעקב לאולאדה רדו שמה לאנא אקמנא פי מצר מנין רדו מאיתין ועשר סנין. וכדלך קול משה רבי׳ כי תוליד בנים ובני בנים וגו׳. אקמנא פי ארץ ישראל מן יום דכלנאהא אלי גלות המלך יהויכין עדד ונושנתם והי ת̇מאן מאיה וארבעין סנה ומת̇ל הד̇א כת̇יר. כדלך קיל לנא אן קולה אעני בלעם כעת יאמר ליעקב פיה סר אן מן דלך אלוקת יעני מת̇ל מא מן ששת ימי בראשית אלי ד̇לך אלוקת ותרג̇ע אלנבואה לישראל ויקולון להם אלאנביא מה פעל אל. והד̇א אלקול כאן פי אלסנה אלת̇אמאנה ות̇לאת̇ין מן כרוג̇הם מן מצר ירון מן אול אלתאריך אלי ד̇לך אליום אלפין וארבע מאיה וכמסה ותמאנין סנה לאן פי אול סנה תמאניה וארבעין כאנת אלג אולה פעלי הד̇א אלקיאס והד̇א אלתאויל תרג̇ע אלנבוה לישראל פי סנה סבעין ותסע מאיה וארבע אלאף ליצירה (4970-1210) ולא שך אן רג̇וע אלנבוה לישראל הי מן מקדמאת אלמשיח כמא קאל ינבאו בניכם ובנותיכם. This is Maimonides' language in the Arabic source according to MS Deinhard 625, which I compared with British Museum MS add. 27542, which Dr. Finkel copied for me. In both of them the date for the restoration of prophecy is 4970 (1210).

In Ibn Tibbon's translation (Vienna, 1873), ed. D. Holub, p. 46, the date is 4972 (1212); in the translation of R. Naḥum ha-Ma'aravi (*Koveẓ*, pt. II, 6c): 4976 (1216). In R. Judah be Barzilai al-Bargeloni's *Peirush le-Sefer Yeẓirah*, ed. S. Z.

Maimonides was born in 1135 and died in 1205. He could have hoped to reach his eighties and thus actually see the reinstitution of prophecy. After all, was he not the person who had promised that a man who comported himself in terms of medical science would live long; "whoever behaves in the ways that we have set forth, will, I promise, not be sick during his lifetime and will live to a ripe old age and will then die without ever having need of a physician; indeed will be hale and hearty throughout his lifetime."[152] It is inconceivable that a soul such as his, thirsting for perfection, would postpone this state or willingly relinquish the opportunity to seize the day. It is almost certain that this hoped-for consummation was before him always. Whoever was the medium for conveying the message would himself look forward to salvation; "Let him who dictates the letter be the courier," i.e., let him who gives the advice be its executor.

Maimonides was not alone in his faith. There were many among his contemporaries who shared it. The tradition that prophecy would be renewed in 1210 or 1212 was an ancient one; an allusion to

---

Halberstam (Berlin, 1885), p. 239: 4972 (1212). There were those who questioned the authorship of this passage (D. Kaufmann, "Une Falsification dans la Lettre Envoyée par Maïmonide aux Juifs du Yemen," *REJ* 24 [1892], p. 112; I. Levi, Une Falsification dans le Lettre de Maimonide," *REJ,* 33 [1896], p. 144). At present no one doubts that Maimonides authored it. Cf. W. Bacher, "Le Passage Relatif un Messie dans le Lettre de Maimonide aux Juifs du Yemen," *REJ* 34 (1897), p. 101, and S. Poznanski, "Miscellen über Saadya," *MGWJ* 44 (1900), p. 401.

152. *M.T.,* Hilkhot Deot 4:20. "Indeed, that a man will live long if he abides by correct rules and if his temperament is well balanced has been affirmed by many philosophers and physicians." Z. Schwarz, "Reshit *Sefer ha-Zikharon* shel ha-Ritba," *Ha-Ẓofeh* 7 (1923), p. 303. "One of the ancients thought that a man could so comport himself that he could live forever. Galen mocked him for claiming that a man could live forever. He did admit, however, that if a man comported himself properly, he could live a long time, provided that he has the correct temperament." *Sha'ar ha-Shammayim* (Rödelheim, 1901), treatise 4, p. 22a. Cf. Nahmanides, Commentary to Genesis 5:4, who criticizes Maimonides' opinion concerning the long lives of the first generations.

it is found in the Jerusalem Talmud[153] and is cited by R. Judah Bargeloni.[154] Great was the value of this tradition because it did not remain a tradition of hope alone, but led to actions of great consequence. In the year 1211 the rabbis of France and England were aroused "to go up to the Holy Land."[155] That very year, a rabbinical assembly was convened in London concerning the return

---

153. J. Shabbat 6.9: "Now it will be said to Jacob and to Israel, what has God wrought." R. Hanina the son of R. Abahu said, "At the midpoint of historical time that evil one will arise.'" The authors of *Korban Ha-Edah* and *Seder Ha-Dorot* (4972 = 1212) explained this passage according to *Iggeret Teiman.* Cf. R. Azariah de Rossi's *Meor Einaiyim,* chap. 43; R. Abraham bar Ḥiyya's *Megillat Ha-Megalleh,* ed. A. Poznanski, with intro. and notes by J. Guttmann (Berlin, 1924), p. 36, and the statement of J. Gutmann in his introduction, p. xii; S. Lieberman, *Yerushalmi Kifshuto* (Jerusalem, 1934), vol. 1, pp. 116–117; A. Marx, "Ma'amar al Shenat ha-Ge'ulah," *Ha-Ẓofeh* 5 (1921), p. 198.

Addendum

Prof. A. Marx has kindly drawn my attention to the section which he published in *Ha-Ẓofeh* 5 (1921), p. 195, drawn from a commentary to Avot written sometime between 1220 and 1235 and whose author lived in France or Germany. I quote: "An Arab wanted to write to Rabbi Moses ben Maimon, but he [i.e., the Arab] died, and immediately after his death came to him [i.e., Maimonides] in a dream and told him: 'The redemption will occur when a time elapses equal to that of the era from the Revelation at Sinai to the birth of Jesus the Nazarene. Now, that lapse of time is equivalent to 1310 years. This is when the Messiah will come after the birth of Jesus.' . . . the Arab who told this to Maimonides was directed through divine intervention. For in olden times, there was a book in the possession of Nicodemus ben Gurion which contained all the calculations concerning redemptions. This book fell into the hands of the Arabs; Nicodemus ben Gurion had himself inherited the book from the ancients, such as Adam, Enoch, and Methuselah . . . and Isaiah, Ezekiel, and Jeremiah, who transmitted it through the rest of the prophets until it fell into Nicodemus' hands." Despite the fact that one should not draw conclusions from such a bizarre bit of fanciful legend, it illustrates a tendency.

154. *Peirush le-Sefer Yeẓirah,* p. 239.

155. "The king accorded them great honor and built them synagogues and study houses there. . . . a miracle was performed for them; they prayed for rain, they were answered, and the name of God was sanctified through them." *Shevet Yehudah* (Hannover, 1855), ed. M. Wiener, p. 113. Cf. *Mikhtav ha-Masa' me-Aḥad ha-Olim, R. Shmuel ben R. Shimson,* in Carmoly, *Itineraires de la Terre Sainte*

to Zion, and more than three hundred spiritual leaders left their native lands for Jerusalem. Among them were "Our Rabbi, the High Priest," Rabbi Johanan the priest of Lunel,[156] Maimonides' great admirer, and Rabbi Samson the Tosafist, who was one of Maimonides' opponents. The immigration of such a large and important group to the Holy Land had not taken place since antiquity and betokens a signal occurrence in the life of our people. These rabbis were the forerunners and founders of the return to Zion, which continues to this day.[157] What caused this sudden migration? Why was it precisely these rabbis, "masters of wisdom, understanding, and reverence,"[158] who uprooted themselves, and not the masses, the merchants, and the artisans? The only reasonable surmise is that this migration was linked to the hoped-for renewal of prophecy.[159] This was Zunz's

---

(Brussels, 1847), pp. 121–122; "Mikhtav mi-R. Shmuel bar Shimshon," *Oẓar Tov,* 1878, pp. 35–38; A. Kaminka, "Olei Golah be-Sof ha-Elef ha-Ḥamishi," *Knesset Yisrael* (ed. S. P. Rabinowitz), 2 (1878), pp. 127–132; A. Harkavy, in his addenda to H. Graetz, *Geschichte der Juden von Altesten Zeiten bis auf die Gegenwart* (Leipzig, 1897–1911) (4th ed.), vol. 5, p. 12, questions the exact date.

156. R. Jonathan of Lunel was an ascetic, divorced from the cares and preoccupations of the outside world. "All day he would meditate, humming a low song from sunrise to sunset. . . . he rejected temporal pleasures . . . he earned only that which was sufficient to sustain his life; this was his habit from earliest childhood through old age." N. Wieder, "Sifro ha-Nisraf shel Yehudah ibn Shabbtai," *Meẓudah* 3 (1943), p. 124.

157. Bar Tuviah, "Shenei Alafim Yemot ha-Mashi'aḥ," *He-Atid* 5 (1913), p. 182.

158. *Milḥamot Adonai* of R. Abraham, son of Maimonides. *Koveẓ,* pt. III, 16c. R. Menahem Verdimas may have been among the migrants. During his pilgrimage wonders were performed, as is recounted in *Shalshelet ha-Kabbalah* (Amsterdam, 1697), p. 40. Cf. also L. Zunz, *Literaturgeschichte der synagogalen Poesie* (Berlin, 1865), p. 328; idem, *Gesammelte Schriften* (Berlin, 1875–76), vol. 1, p. 168.

159. The hypothesis of Graetz, *Geschichte,* vol. 7, p. 11, and H. Gross, "Étude sur Simson ben Abraham de Sens," *REJ* 6 (1882), p. 176, that the worsening situation in France and R. Judah ha-Levi's love of Zion were the causes of the migration, and that of S. Krauss, "L'émigration de 300 Rabbins en Palestine en l'An

hypothesis though he spoke vaguely and offered neither proof nor source for it.[160] Nevertheless, there is one item which sheds light on this matter. Some of these immigrants did not proceed at once to their desired goal, but went first to Egypt, apparently to Alexandria and from there to Fostat—a journey of several days—to meet R. Abraham, the son of Maimonides.[161] They did not go directly from France to Acre. What persuaded these sages to interrupt their trip in order to first visit Rabbi Abraham? It could only have been to hear from his lips Maimonides' opinion as to the promised forthcoming renewal of prophecy. He had already proclaimed its imminence in the *Letter to Yemen,* and perhaps he is to be considered the ultimate cause for migration. This may explain why the ordinary Jew did not participate. Prophecy is not a merchandise in which everyone can invest.

VI

"The son is the issue of his father." Many were the admirers of Maimonides and his doctrine, but the greatest among them, in faith and feeling, was his own son, Abraham, who followed his father as head of the community and of its academy. All his days he fought with energy and discretion to defend the honor of Maimonides. Loyal

---

1211," *REJ* 82 (1926), pp. 333–352, esp. p. 337, that the goal of the migration was to investigate Maimonides' writings (cf. C. Roth, *A History of the Jews in England* [Oxford, 1941], p. 35) have nothing to support them. Cf. H. J. Zimmels, "Erez Israel in der Responsenliteratur des späten Mittelalters," *MGWJ* 74 (1930), pp. 46–48; E. N. Adler, "Note sur l'émigration en Palestine de 1211," *REJ* 85 (1928), pp. 70–71; J. Mann, "A Second Supplement to *The Jews in Egypt and in Palestine under the Fatimid Caliphs,*" *HUCA* 3 (1926), p. 299.

160. *Gesammelte Schriften,* vol. 3, p. 227.

161. *Kovez̤,* pt. III, 16c. Except R. Samson, who migrated directly to Acre; "we did not see him since he did not follow our route."

as he was to the doctrines of his father, he would not have allowed any alien interpretation of Maimonides' position. Is it possible that something which Maimonides prohibited would have been permitted by his son?

The Islamic mystical sect of the Sufis was very powerful in the days of R. Abraham, and deeply influenced both the trend and content of his thought. He esteemed them highly and praised their holy qualities. Other sages of Israel did not hesitate to recount tales of the Sufi saints, so that Jews would learn from them and imitate their example. But R. Abraham was so unstinting and lavish in his praises that were it not for the fact that we have them in writing, we would be loathe to believe that they had been uttered. In his opinion, the Sufis were true disciples of the prophets in that they despised their bodily desires, subjugated their evil inclination, and isolated themselves from ordinary human community. Their own conventicles he considered in the same light as those of "the sons of the prophets," and he claimed that the characteristics previously prevalent in Israel had been removed from our midst and transferred to the Sufis. He regrets that Jews have abandoned the prophetic path which was the characteristic trait of their ancestors and in this connection, he quotes the rabbinic interpretation of Jeremiah 13:17: "For if you will not give heed my inmost self must weep because of your pride." What does "because of your pride" signify? Because that which constitutes the pride of Israel has been taken away from Israel and given to the nations of the world" (Hagigah 5b).[162]

The Sufis mortified themselves only as a means to achieve "illuminations" from above.[163] They lived a life of poverty, and spent their time in the study of the Koran and devotional prayer. They endeavored to refine their souls so as "to receive fully and

---

162. R. Abraham ben Maimonides, *The High Way to Perfection,* ed. S. Rosenblatt (Baltimore, 1938), p. 321 (MS fol. 91b, line 7), p. 323 (fol. 92a15).

163. Cf. R. A. Nicholson, *Hastings' Encyclopedia of Religion and Ethics,* vol. 12, p. 14.

whole-heartedly the indwelling presence of God."[164] Despite their belief, shared by the Muslim community, that their prophet was indeed "the seal of the prophets," they thought themselves enabled to reach a penultimate stage of prophecy.[165] Al-Ghazali relates that he heard "one of the Sufi teachers proclaim: O ye sons of men, know that who seeks the Lord in the life to come already has Him present in this life; divine paradise resides within his own breast seeking only for him to enter therein. The way thereto is to divest himself of the vanities of time and to strive with all his might to think of heavenly matters until he receives a heavenly illumination revealing their secrets. Attaining this state is true bliss."[166]

One fundamental principle of Sufi doctrine is that of the twin sources of knowledge, one inferential and the product of training, the other transmitted by divine illumination (*al-ham*). The two are not in opposition. There are untutored individuals who receive knowledge through divine infusion. How is this possible? No man knows how or from whence or why he has been permeated with divine grace. The Sufis prized the knowledge acquired through divine infusion more highly than the knowledge acquired through study. With the aid of the former one can, through a single and singular illumination, know that which cannot be acquired through discursive reasoning. But not everyone merits this "arousal from Above." Only saints and holy men merit revelations from on high. Whether awake or dreaming, when the veil of the senses is removed, a man is then empowered to grasp esoteric matters which ordinary human reason

164. Al-Ghazali, *Moznei Ẓedek* (Leipzig and Paris, 1834–39), p. 48.

165. Cf. R. A. Nicholson, *The Mystics of Islam* (London, 1914), p. 51. Cf. also J. Obermann, *Der Philosphie und Religiöse Subjektivismus Ghazali's* (Vienna, 1921), p. 99.

166. *Moznai Ẓedek,* p. 26. Cf. R. Moses Ibn Ezra's statement, *Arugat ha-Bosem, Ẓion* (Frankfurt a.M., 1842), vol. 2, pp. 120 ff.

cannot.[167] Occasionally, not only do the saints attain elevation of their souls,[168] but in an ecstatic state where all bodily affects are transcended they attain the prophetic state.[169] According to the Sufis there are two types of prophecy: the revelation vouchsafed to the few for transmission to the many (*wahy*), and those revelations which are granted to and intended for the few alone (*al-ham*). The latter type may denote "personal" prophecy, viz., it has no function to perform in the life of the nation.[170] As an illustration, I cite one of the great Muslim mystics, Ibn Al-Arabi (b. Murria, 1165), a contemporary of Maimonides, who lived for a time in Ceuta and in Egypt. He was accustomed to say that the source of religious ideas lay in divine illumination and not in discursive human reason. He believed that divinely inscribed texts were made manifest to the worthy man. He too maintained that the Sufis were prophets, since God revealed His secrets to them without mediation of any sort. Nevertheless, their prophetic revelations do not constitute a new canon of scripture. In effect, they draw Muhammad's teachings from the same font from which he himself had drawn.[171] He admits that he too was witness to divine apparitions and was the recipient of angelic communications. He was far-famed in his own lifetime and numerous admirers flocked to him.[172] Even in Egypt, Maimonides' dwelling place, he was renowned.

---

167. R. A. Nicholson, *Studies in Islamic Mysticism* (Cambridge 1921), pp. 77 ff.

168. E. Brögelman, *Die religösen Erlebnisse der Persischen Mystiker* (Hannover, 1932), p. 40.

169. R. A. Nicholson, *The Mystics of Islam*, pp. 122 ff.

170. D. B. McDonald, *EI*, s.v. "ilham." Cf. idem, *Religious Attitude and Life in Islam* (Chicago, 1909), pp. 252 ff. and 275 ff.

171. A. E. Affifi, *The Mystical Philosophy of Muḥyid Din Ibnul Arabi* (Cambridge, 1939), pp. 96 ff.

172. Schreiner, *ZDMG*, 52, pp. 516–525; A. von Kremer, *Geschichte der herrschenden Ideen des Islams* (Leipzig, 1868), pp. 100–108; R. A. Nicholson, trans., *Tarjuman al-Ashwaq* (London, 1911). Cf. E. Jabra Jurji, *Illumination in*

R. Abraham, the son of Maimonides, is very close to Sufi thought in his ethical doctrine.[173] The essential thrust of his *Kitab Kiffiyyah Al-Abadin* [A Comprehensive Guide for the Servants of God] is to show that man's purpose is to attain perfection, the highest good. And what is this ultimate perfection? It is prophecy defined as man's union with God. It is possible to attain this level only after a long and arduous spiritual regime. What does this regime consist of? Similar to R. Phineas b. Yair in his time, Maimonides sets before his readers

---

Islamic Mysticism (Princeton, 1938), introduction; Massignon, *EI,* vol. 4, pp. 681, 685; R. A. Nicholson, *Kashf al-Maḥjub* (Leiden, 1911), p. 271.

173. There are many instances where Sufi expressions and sentiments seem to issue from Maimonides himself. Compare, for example, his opinion that "the first idea of the intellect is that the soul is destroyed by undue concentration upon the body, while it is improved by the diminution of bodily desires" (*Einleitung in die Mishna,* p. 53) and that mortification of the body and its isolation from social concerns constitute the preconditions for the attainment of felicity. There are many parallels between Maimonides and Sufi doctrine. In a future essay we hope to provide evidence for this claim. As an illustration we cite the parable of the lightning in the *Guide* (I:introduction, p. 7; cf. above, n. 11), which can also be found in Al-Ghazali (*Moznei Ẓedek,* p. 50). In his words concerning the Sufis, Al-Ghazali states that those who cleave to God can envision "something of that which appeared to the prophets, such as a flash of lightning, which is momentary and then may or may not reappear. If it does reappear, its brightness may be brief or sustained. It may cast its illumination upon one or many objects . . . these are the ways of the Sufis." It is worth noting that Maimonides himself practiced reclusiveness. Cf. R. Eleazar Azkari's *Sefer Ḥaredim* (Venice, 1601), p. 10a; "I have found . . . in a manuscript of Rabbi Moses, the great light of the Exile: 'One night I set sail . . . and on the Sabbath . . . a violent storm arose which might have drowned us. I took it upon myself that these two days would in the future be devoted to fasting for myself and my household and all those associated with me; I would command my descendants to do likewise even to the end of time. . . . On the tenth day of Iyyar I will sit alone, not seeing the face of any man, but praying and studying the entire day by myself. For since on that day, in the midst of the seas, I found no one but the Holy One, blessed be He, on the anniversary of that day, I see no man unless I am absolutely forced to do so.' "

a ladder of virtuous traits by means of which a man ascends from outer distractions via isolation until he reaches an inner isolation and from there to union with the life of God even unto prophetic union. Many saints of various generations were very close to the level of the prophetic, e.g., R. Simeon b. Yohai and his son R. Eleazer. However, a person should not pursue this path without a guide. Many obstacles and snares lie along the way of the saint; it is very easy to be misled or to deviate from the high road to perfection. Occasionally a man will think that he has reached union with the divine, only to be mistaken.[174]

Maimonides was his son's only exemplar also when it came to concealing esoteric matters from the eyes of the multitude;[175] "and in the stages of prophecy," writes Rabbi Abraham, "there are secrets which are not understood, and for those which are amenable to understanding, how they occur it is forbidden to reveal—-for they must be concealed for the glory of God."[176] To which events and secrets is he referring? Apparently, he knew how they occurred, but he placed his hand over his mouth. That which the son did reflected his father's practice!

Not only the greatest of this group of spiritual descendants of their master, viz., Abraham Maimonides, but many others known to have been close to the spirit of Maimonides hoped to become prophets. In addition to his foremost disciple and his only son there was R. Samuel ibn Tibbon, who translated the *Guide* into Hebrew.

---

174. *The High Way to Perfection,* p. 403 (fol. 112a), p. 415 (fol. 115a), p. 421 (fol. 116b), p. 423 (fol. 117a, line 7), p. 325 (fol. 92b, 1.4). At the end of the treatise he remarks that the teaching of this "way" was not given to him but to others. Did he thereby refer to the Sufis in general, or was it a specific reference to R. Joseph Ibn Aknin, whom Maimonides had instructed in the path to prophecy? R. Abraham was nineteen years old when Maimonides died.

175. "Now this is a secret"—referring to prophecy. Cf. *Responsa of R. Abraham ben Maimonides,* no. 24; cf. also nos. 16, 43.

176. Ibid., no. 30, p. 39.

Of him Maimonides said, "he has plumbed the secrets of the *Guide of the Perplexed* and the rest of my works, and he has discerned their intent."[177] And when R. Samuel felt that he knew all the allusions "of the secrets of creation and its ambiguities," he said concerning this, "it is as if they came to me via the Holy Spirit."[178] Maimonides' grandson, R. David Ha-Nagid, was preoccupied with esoteric matters as well. He was the author of a commentary on the apocalyptic work "The prophecy of the child which Nahman of Katofa foresaw" after the sages of Barcelona had written him "as to whether he had any clear information to tell them about the secret of the End."[179]

It is no accident that it was R. Abraham b. Samuel Abulafia (b. 1240) who set forth the doctrine of prophetic Kabbalism so close to the Maimonidean era.[180] It is axiomatic that doctrines fit their times. It is plausible to assume that Abulafia endeavored to fill a desideratum. His approach satisfied a widespread yearning. We have knowledge of a number of names of wise and pious men of Germany and France who were seized by the topic of prophecy. There is no doubt that these were the few known who betokened the many unknown, and that many of the names were forgotten in the course of time and in the wake of persecution.

Abulafia was thirty-one years old when it seemed to him that he merited receiving prophecy. He continued to prophesy and to write down his prophecies.[181] Moreover he taught how one could learn to

---

177. *Kovez̧,* pt. III, p. 16c.

178. *Ma'amar Yikavu ha-Mayyim* (Pressburg, 1837), p. 9.

179. R. Joseph Sambari, quoted in *MJC,* vol. 1, p. 135. Cf. M. Steinschneider, *Polemische und Apologetische Literatur in Arabische Sprache* (Leipzig, 1877), p. 367.

180. Cf. G. Scholem, *Major Trends in Jewish Mysticism* (Jerusalem, 1941), pp. 119–152.

181. Cf. A. Jellinek, "*Sefer ha-Ot,*" in *Jubelschrift zum Siebzigsten Geburtstage des Prof. Dr. H. Graetz* (Breslau, 1887), pp. 65–88, Hebrew sec. "Ve-Zot li-Yehudah," the letter sent by R. Abraham Abulafia against R. Solomon ben Adret, *Ginzei Ḥokhmat ha-Kabbalah* (Leipzig, 1853), ed. A. Jellinek, p. 16.

be a prophet. He intended to teach prophecy and raise up prophets. And like a mystery encased in an enigma, there is this wondrous trait in this astonishing man, viz., his relationship to Maimonides. He too claimed doctrinal derivation and descent from Maimonides. Was he being completely arbitrary when he declared that the *Guide* and the *Sefer Yeẓirah* were the sole guides to esoteric wisdom?[182] Perhaps such a statement is not without special significance. Or perhaps a secret was revealed to him that is hidden from our view. The answer is God's.

---

182. Cf. Scholem, op. cit., p. 124. Abulafia wrote a commentary to the *Guide* (*Peirush Sodot Moreh ha-Nebukhim, Sitre Torah,* JTS MS 24, Kabbalah). He looked upon Maimonides' doctrine of prophecy as a manual for the attainment of prophecy. "If you seek to walk in this way, so as to merit the investiture of the Holy Spirit and perhaps prophecy as well, accept first the yoke of the kingship of God," etc., p. 49b. On Maimonides himself he writes, "One must recognize the oath of our master not to reveal that which was revealed by God to him, as he hinted at the beginning of the third part of the *Guide,*" p. 7b.

Bibliography

Adler, E.N. "Note sur l'émigration en Palestine de 1211." *REJ* 85 (1928): 70–71.

Aeshcoli, A. "Al ha-Tenu'ah ha-Meshiḥit be-Sicilia." *Tarbiẓ* 11 (1940): 207–217.

Affifi, A. *The Mystical Philosophy of Muḥyid Din Ibnul Arabi*. Cambridge, 1939.

Al-Ghazali, *Moznei Ẓedek he'etiko mi-Leshon Higri le-Ivri Avraham ben Hasda*. Leipzig, 1839.

Albeck H., ed. *Ha-Eshkol*. Jerusalem: Mass, 1935–38.

Anon., "Hora'ah al She'elat ha-Malachim." *Kerem Ḥemed* 9 (1856): 141–8.

Aptowitzer, V. *Sefer Ravyah*. Berlin/Jerusalem: Mekitzei Nirdamim, 1913–38.

—. *Meḥkarim be-Sifrut ha-Geonim*. Jerusalem: Mosad Ha-Rav Kook, 1941.

—. "Teshuvot Meyuḥasot le-Rav Hai ve-eynan lo." *Tarbiẓ* 1, no. 4 (1930): 63–105.

Ashkenazi, E. *Ta'am Zeḳenim*. Frankfurt, 1854.

Assaf, S. "Mi-ginzei Ha-Sefarim." *Kiryat Sefer* 2 (1924): 117–139.

—. "Teshuvot ha-Geonim." *Mada'ei ha-Yahadut* 2 (1927): 9–146.

—., ed. *Teshuvot ha-Geonim mi-tokh ha-Genizah*. Jerusalem, 1929.

—. "Teudot Ḥadashot al Gerim ve-al Tenu'ot Meshiḥiyot." *Ẓion* 5 (1940): 112–124.

Azulai, H. Y. D. *Shem ha-Gedolim*. Vienna, 1864.

Bacher, W. *Die Bibelexegese Moses Maimunis*. Budapest, 1897.

Bacher, W. "Le Passage Relatif un Messie dans le Lettre de Maïmonide aux Juifs du Yémen." *REJ* 34 (1897): 101–105.

Bacher, W. *Leben und Werke des Abulwalid Merwan Ibn Ganaḥ und die Quellen seiner Schrifterklärung*. Budapest: Athenaum, 1885.

Bacher, W. "The Treatise on Eternal Bliss Attributed to Moses Maimuni." *JQR*, O.S. 9 (1897): 270–289.

Bacher, W., ed. *Sefer Musar* (ibn Janah). Berlin: Itskowski, 1910.

Bacher, W., ed. *Sefer ha-Shorashim* (ibn Janah). Berlin, 1893–96.

Bachtold-Staubli, H. *Handwörterbuch des deutschen Aberglaubens*. Berlin/Leipzig, 1987.

Baer, F. "Eine jüdische Messiasprophetie auf das Jahr 1186 und der dritte Kreuzzug." *MGWJ* 70 (1926): 113–122, 155–165.

Baer, F. "Ha-Maẓav ha-Politi shel Yehudei Sefarad be-Doro shel R. Yehuda ha-Levi." *Ẓion* 1 (1935): 6–23.

Baer, Y. *Toledot ha-Yehudim be-Sefarad ha-Noẓrit*. Tel Aviv: Am Oved, 1945.

Bar Tuviah. "Shenei Alafim Yemot ha-Mashiaḥ." *He-Atid* 5 (1973): 172–199.

Berliner, A. and D. Hoffman. "Mikhtav mi-R. Shmuel bar Shimshon." *Oẓar Tov* 1 (1878): 35–38.

Bialik H.N. and Y. Ravnitzky, *Shirei Shelomo ben Yehudah ibn Gabirol*. Berlin, 1924.

Bislikhes, M., ed. *Moreh ha-Moreh (*Falaquera*)*. Pressburg, 1837.

Brody H. "Einzelschriften." *ZfHB* 1 (1896): 76–16.

—. *Diwan vehu Sefer Kollel Shirei Yehuda ha-Levi*. Berlin, 1901.

—. art. Dari, Moses. *JE* 3 (1903): 440–441.

—. art. Avila, der Prophet von. *EJ* 3 (1927): 788–789.

—. "Mikhtamim al ha-Rambam u-Sefarav." *Moznayim* 3 (1935): 402–413.

Brögelman, E. *Die religösen Erlebnisse der Persischen Mystiker*. Hannover, 1932.

Brüll, N. "Beiträge zur jüdischen Sagen und Sprachkunde im Mittelalter," JJGL 9 (1889): 1–71.

Buber, S., ed. *Sha'arei Ẓion (*R. Isaac ben R. Jacob de Lattes*)*. Premysl, 1885.

—., ed. *Shibbolei ha-Leket ha-Shalem*. Vilna, 1887.

Carmoly, E. *Itinéraires de la Terre Sainte*. Brussels, 1847.

Cohen, B. *Kuntres ha-Teshuvot*. Budapest, 1930.

Davidson, I. *Oẓar ha-Shirah ve-ha-Piyyut*. New York, 1924–33.

Davidson, I., ed. *Milḥamot ha-Shem* (Suleiman ben Yeruḥam). New York, 1934.

Davidson, I., ed. *Sefer Sha'ashu'im* (ibn Zabara). New York, 1914.

Dawidowicz, H. S., ed. *Perakim be-Haẓlaḥah*. Jerusalem: Mekiẓei Nirdamim, 1939.

Dembitzer, H.N. *Kelilat Yofi*. Cracow, 1888–93.

de Rossi, J.B. *Manuscripti codices hebraici* . . . Parma, 1803.

Derenbourg, H. *Abou'lwalid Merwan Ibn Djanah, Takrīb wa-Tashīl, Opuscules et Traités* . . . Paris, 1880.

Diesendruck, Z. "Maimonides Lehre von der Prophetie." In *Jewish Studies in Memory of Israel Abrahams*. New York, 1927, pp. 74–134.

—. "Samuel and Moses ibn Tibbon on Maimonides Theory of Providence." *HUCA* 11 (1936): 341–366.

Dinaburg, B.Z. "Aliyato shel R. Judah Ha-Levi le-Ereẓ Yisrael," In *Minḥah le-David: Le-Yovel ha-Shiveim shel R. David Yellin*. Jerusalem. 1935, pp. 157–182.

Dukes, L. *Kuntres ha-Masoret*. Tübingen, 1846.

Edelman, Z.H. *Ḥemdah Genuzah*. Königsberg, 1857.

Egers, J. "Shirei R. Shelomo ibn Gabirol." In *Jubelschrift zum neunzigsten Geburtstag des Dr. L. Zunz*. Berlin: Gerschel, 1884. pp. 193–196.

Eisenstein, J.D. *Oẓar Yisrael*. New York, 1907–13.

—. *Oẓar Midrashim*. New York, 1915.

Elbogen, I. *Der jüdische Gottesdienst in seiner geschichtlichen Entwicklung*. Frankfurt a.M.: J. Kauffmann, 1931.

Elfenbein, I., ed. *Teshuvot Rashi*. New York, 1943.

Epstein, A. *Eldad ha-Dani*. Pressburg, 1891.

—. "R. Shmuel ha-Ḥasid be-R. Kalonymous ha-Zaken." Ha-Goren 4 (1903): 81–101.

Epstein, Y.N. "Perishat Rabbenu Eliyah Menachem b"r Moshe mi-Londres." *Madda'ei ha-Yahadut* I (1926): 51–71.

—. "Toratah shel Ereẓ Yisrael." *Tarbiẓ* 2 (1931): 308–327.

Even Shmuel (Kaufmann), Y. *Moreh ha-Nevukhim*. Jerusalem. 1959.

Filipowski, Z., ed. *Sefer Yuḥasin*. London, 1857.

Finkel, J. "Maimonides' Treatise on Resurrection." *PAAJR* 9 (1939): 57–105 א־מב.

Frankel, Z. "Ein handschriftliches Schreiben des Scheschet Benveniste über Maimunis Wirksamheit." *MGWJ* 25 (1876): 509–513.

Frazer, J.G. *Pausanias' Description of Greece*. London, Macmillan: 1898.

Freimann, A. "Annalen der Hebräischen Druckerei in Wilhermsdorff." In *Festschrift zum siebzigsten Geburtstage A. Berliners*. Frankfurt: Kauffmann, 1903. pp. 100–115.

Fried, N. "Od al Nevi'uto shel R. Ezra mi-Montcontour." *Tarbiẓ* 2 (1931): 514.

Friedlaender, M. *The Commentary of Ibn Ezra on Isaiah*. London, 1873–77.

Friedlander, I. "The Arabic Original of the Report of R. Nathan Hababli." *JQR*, O.S. 17 (1905): 747–761.

Friedmann D. and S. Löwinger, S. "Alpha Beta de-Ben Sira." In *Ve-Zot li-Yehudah, Koveẓ Maamarim . . . li-Kevod he-Hacham Yehuda Aryeh Blau*. Budapest, 1926), pp. 250–81.

Ginzberg, L. *Geonica*. New York: JTS, 1909.

—. *The Legends of the Jews*. Philadelphia: JPS, 1909–1938.

—. "Haggadot Ketu'ot." *Ha-Goren* 9 (1922): 31–68.

—. *Ginzei Schechter*. New York: JTS, 1928.

—. *Peirushim ve-Ḥiddushim bi-Yerushalmi*. New York: JTS, 1941–61.

Goitein, S.D. "Inyanim Yehudim be-Sefer Ansab el Ashraf shel el Bladri." *Ẓion* 1 (1935): 75–81.

Goldenthal, J., ed. *Sefer ha-Mafteaḥ*. Vienna, 1847.

Gorfinkle, J., ed. *Shemoneh Perakim*. New York, Columbia University Press: 1912.

Gottheil, R. art. Egypt in Medieval and Modern Times. *JE* 5 (1903), pp. 60–73.

Graetz, H. "Ein Pseudo-Messias im 14. Jahrhundert." *MGWJ* 28 (1879): 78–83.

—. *Geschichte der Juden von Altesten Zeiten bis auf die Gegenwart.* 4th ed. Leipzig, 1897–1911.

Greenhut, A. *Sibbuv R. Petaḥiah.* Jerusalem, 1905.

Gross, H. "Zur Geschichte der Juden in Arles." *MGWJ* 31 (1882): 465–471, 496–523.

—. "Étude sur Simson ben Abraham de Sens." *REJ* 6 (1882): 167–186; 7 (1883) 40–77.

—. "Das Handschriftliche Werk Assufot." *MWJ* 10 (1883): 64–87.

— *Gallia Judaica.* Paris: Cerf, 1897.

—. "Zwei kabbalistische Traditionsketten des R. Eleazar aus Worms." *MGWJ* 49 (1905): 692–700.

Grossberg, M., ed. *Sefer Yeẓirah with the Commentary of Abu-Saḥal Dunash ben Tamim.* London, 1902.

Grossberg, M., ed. *Megillat Ta'anit.* Lwów, 1906.

Guttmann, J. "Über Abraham bar Chijjas Buch der Enthüllung." *MGWJ* 47 (1903): 446–468, 545–569.

—. *Philosophies of Judaism.* New York: Holt, Rinehart and Winston, 1964.

Haarbrücker, T. *Abu-l Fath Muhammed asch-Schahrastanis Religionsparteien und Philosophenschulen.* Halle, 1850.

Halberstam, S.Z. *Kehilat Shelomo.* Vienna, 1890.

—. "Kinah al Rabbenu Avraham b'ha-Rambam, zal, ve-Kinah al Ḥakham (lo Nizkar Shemo) ve-od Kinah Aḥeret." *Koveẓ al Yad* 9, year 15 (1899).

—., ed. *Peirush le-Sefer Yeẓirah* (Bargeloni). Berlin, 1885.

Halkin, A., ed. *Hitgallut ha-Sodot ve-Hofa'at ha-Me'orot* (ibn Aknin). Jerusalem, 1964.

Halper, B. Z., ed. *Shirat Yisra'el.* Leipzig, 1924.

Halperin, M. *Ha-notarikon ha-Simanim ve-ha-Kinu'im.* Tel Aviv, 1930.

Hamburger, B., ed. *Maimonides Einleitung in die Mishna.* Strassburg, 1902.

Harkavy, A., ed. *Teshuvot ha-Geonim.* 1887.

—. *Zikhron la-Rishonim.* Vilna, 1879-.

Heilprin Y. *Seder ha-Dorot.* Warsaw, 1882.

Heller, C. *Peshitta in Hebrew Characters*. Berlin, 1928.

Heschel, A.J. *Die Prophetie*. Warsaw, 1936.

—. "Perush al ha-Tefillot." In *Koveẓ Mada'i le-Zekher Moshe Schorr*. New York, 1944.

—. *Torah Min ha-Shammayim ba-Aspeklariah shel ḥa-Dorot*, 2 vols. London, 1962–1965.

—. *Maimonides: A Biography*. New York: Farrer, Strauss and Groux, 1982.

Higger, M. "Yarḥi's Commentary on Kallah Rabbati," *JQR*, N.S. 24 (1934): 331–348.

—., ed. *Kallah Rabbati*. New York, 1936.

—., ed. *Masekhet Soferim*. New York, 1937.

Hildesheimer, E., ed. *Halakhot Gedolot*. Berlin, 1888–92.

Hirschberg, H.Z. "Ikvot ha-Mashiaḥ be-Ereẓ Arav be-Mei'ah ha-Ḥamishit ve-ha-Shishit aḥar Ḥurban Bayit Sheni." In *Sefer ha-Zikaron le-Vet ha-Midrash le-Rabbanim be-Vina*. Jerusalem, 1946. pp. 112–124.

Hoffman, D., ed. *Migdal Ḥananel*. Berlin, 1876.

—., ed. *Midrash Tannaim*. Berlin, 1908–9.

Holzer, J., ed. *Mose Maimunis Einleitung zu Chelek im arabischen Urtext und in der hebräischen Uebersetzung*. Berlin, 1901.

Holub, D., ed. *Iggeret Teman, oder Sendschreiben des Rabbi Moses ben Maimon an die jüdische Gemeinde Jemens*. Vienna, 1873.

Horowitz, S. H., ed. *Seder Olam Katan*. Breslau, 1903.

Hurwitz, S. *Maḥzor Vitry*. Berlin, 1889–97.

Husik, I., ed. *Sefer ha-Ikkarim le-Rabbi Yosef Albo*. Philadelphia, 1929.

Magnes, J., ed. *Bi-Meḥuyyav ha-Meẓi'ut* (ibn Aknin). Berlin, 1904.

Ish Shalom (Friedmann), M., ed. *Sifrei de-Vei Rav*. Vilna, 1864.

—. *Seder Eliyahu Rabbah*. Vienna, 1901.

—., ed. *Seder Eliyahu Zuta*. Vienna, 1904.

Jurji, E. *Illumination in Islamic Mysticism*. Princeton, 1938.

Jellinek, A. "Die Kabbalistenfamilie R. Sherira Gaon, R. Elija ha-Saken, R. Haja Gaon, R. Jekutiel und deren Anhänger R. Salomo Ibn Gebirol." *Der Orient, Literaturblatt* 12 (1851): 545–560.

—., ed. *Ginzei Ḥokhmat ha-Kabbalah*. Leipzig: Colditz, 1853.
—. "Sefer ha-Ot." In *Jubelschrift zum Siebzigsten Geburtstage des Prof. Dr. H. Graetz*. Breslau, 1887, pp. 65–88, Hebrew sec.
—. *Bet ha-Midrasch*. Jerusalem, 1938.
Joel, I. *Reshimat Kitve Yad Ivri'im be-Veit ha-Sefarim he-Leumi veha-Universita'i bi-Yrushalim*. Jerusalem, 1934.
Kahane, D. "Le-Toledot ha-Geonim" *Ha-Kedem* 3 (1909): 115–128.
Kamelhar, Y. *Ḥasidim ha-Rishonim*. Vac, 1917.
Kamelhar, Y., ed. *Sodei Razayya* (R. Eleazar Rokeach). Bilgoraj, 1936.
Kaminka, A. "Olei Golah be-Sof ha-Elef ha-Ḥamishi." *Knesset Yisrael* 2 (1887): 128–132.
—., ed. Taḥkemoni. Warsaw: Ahiasaf, 1899.
—. *Kovez̧ Ḥochmat ha-Ra'avah*. Warsaw: Ahiasaf, 1894
Kaufmann, D. "La Discussion sur le Phylactères." *REJ* 5 (1882): 273–277.
—. "Une Falsification dans la Lettre Envoyée par Maïmonide aux Juifs du Yémen." *REJ* 24 (1892): 112–117.
—. "Lettres de Scheschet b. Isaac b. Joseph Benveniste de Saragosse aux princes Kalonymos et Levi de Narbonne." *REJ* 39 (1899): 62–75, 217–225.
—. *Gesammmelte Schriften*. Frankfurt: Kaufmann, 1908–1915.
Kircheim, R. "Sefer Ketav Tamim le-R. Moshe Taku." *Oz̧ar Neḥmad* 3 (1860): 54–99.
Kobak, J. "Likkutei batar Likkutei." *Ginzei Nistarot* 3. Bamberg, 1872.
Krauss, S. "L'émigration de 300 Rabbins en Palestine en l'An 1211." *REJ* 82 (1926): 333–352.
Kristianpoler, A. *Traum und Traumdeutung* (=*Monumenta Talmudica*, IV, 2, 1). Vienna, 1923.
Lambert, M., ed. *Commentaire sur le Séfer Yesirah . . . par la Gaon Saadya de Fayyoum*. Paris: Bouillon, 1891.
Lévi, I. "Une Falsification dans le Lettre de Maïmonide aux juifs du Yémen." *REJ*, 33 (1896): 144–146.
Levy, A. J. *Rashi's Commentary on Ezekiel 40–48*. Philadelphia, 1931.
Levy, J. *Chaldäisches Wörterbuch*. Leipzig, 1867–68.

Lewin, B. M. *Rav Sherira Gaon*. Jaffa, 1916.

—., ed. *Iggeret Rav Sherira Gaon*. Haifa, 1921.

—. *Oẓar ha-Ge'onim*. Haifa and Jerusalem, 1928–42.

—. *Rabbanan Sabbora'ei ve-Talmidam*. Jerusalem, 1937.

—. "Esa Meshali le-Rasag." In *Rav Saadiah Gaon Koveẓ Turani-Madai* (Y.L. Fishman, ed.). Jerusalem, 1943, pp. 481–532.

Lewy, Y. (H.) "A dream on Mandulis." *Annales du Service des Antiquites de l'Égypte* 44 (1946), pp. 227–234.

Lichtenberg, A. *Koveẓ Teshuvot ha-Rambam*. Leipzig, 1859.

Lieberman, H. *Ohel Raḥel*. Brooklyn, 1980.

Lieberman, S. *Yerushalmi Kifshuto*. Jerusalem, 1934.

Löw, I. *Die Flora der Juden*. Vienna, 1924–34.

Löw, L. *Gesammelte Schriften*. Szegedin, 1889–1900.

Lowenthal, A., ed. *Musarei ha-Filosofim*. Cracow, 1896.

Löwy, M. *Drei Abhandlungen von Josef ben Jehuda*. Berlin, 1879.

Mainz, M., ed. *Yosef Omeẓ* (R. Juspa Hahn). Frankfurt, 1928.

Malter, H. "Shem Tov ben Joseph Palquera. II. His Treatise on the Dream." *JQR*, N.S. 1 (1911): 451–501.

Malter, H. "Dreams as a Cause of Literary Composition." In *Studies in Jewish Literature in Honor of Professor Kaufmann Kohler, Ph.D.* Berlin, 1913. pp. 199–203.

Mann, J. "The Responsa of the Babylonian Geonim as a Source of Jewish History." *JQR*, N.S. 9 (1918–19): 139–79.

—. Ha-Tenu'ot ha-Meshiḥiot bi-Ymei Masa'ei ha-Ẓelav ha-Rishonim, *Ha-Tekufah* 23 (1925): 243–261; 24 (1928): 335–358.

—. "A Second Supplement to The Jews in Egypt and in Palestine under the Fatimid Caliphs." *HUCA* 3 (1926): 257–308.

—. A Messianic Excitement in Sicily and Other Parts of Southern Europe, Texts and Studies. Cincinnati, 1931. vol. 1, pp. 39ff.

Marcus, A. *Keset ha-Sofer*. Cracow, 1912.

Margaliot, R., ed. *She'elot u-Teshuvot min ha-Shammayim by Jacob ha-Levi he-Ḥasid*. Lvov: 1929.

Margulies, R., ed. *Sefer Ḥasidim*. Lwów, 1920?

Markon, I. art. Judges, *EJ* 9 (1932): 548–550.

Marx, A. "A New Collection of Manuscripts." *PAAJR* 4 (1933): 125–167.

Marx, A. "Ma'amar al Shenat Ge'ulah." *Ha-Ẓofeh* 5 (1921): 194–202.

Marx, A. "The Correspondence Between the Rabbis of Southern France and Maimonides about Astrology." *HUCA* 3 (1926): 311–358.

Massignon, L., art. Tasawwuf. *Encyclopedia of Islam* 4 (1934), pp. 681–85.

McDonald, D.B. *Religion Attitude and Life in Islam*. Chicago, 1909.

—. art. Ilham, *Encyclopedia of Islam* 2 (1927): 467–68.

Michael, H. *Or ha-Ḥayyim*. Frankfurt: Kaufmann, 1891.

Mittwoch, E. "Ein Geniza Fragment." *ZDMG* 57 (1903): 61–66.

Moritz, D., ed. *Reshit Hokhmah* (Falaquera). Berlin, 1902.

Müller, J. *Teshuvot Ḥakhmei Ẓarfat ve-Lotir*. Vienna, 1881.

Munk, S. *Notice sur Joseph ben Iehouda*. Paris, 1842.

—. *Notice sur Aboul-Walid Merwan ibn Djanah et d'autres grammariens hébreux du X et du XIme siècle*. Paris, 1851.

—. *Le Guide des Égarés*. Paris, 1856–66.

Neubauer, A. "Josef ibn Aknin." *MGWJ* 19 (1871): 348–355, 395–401, 445–448.

—. "Documents Inédits." *REJ* 10 (1885): 79–107.

—. "Documents Inédits." *REJ* 12 (1886): 80–94.

—. *Medieval Jewish Chronicles and Chronological Notes*. Oxford: Clarendon, 1887–1895.

Neubauer, A. and Cowley, A. E. *Catalogue of the Hebrew Manuscripts in the Bodleian Library*. Oxford, 1886–1906.

Nicholson, R. A. art. Sufis. *Hastings Encyclopedia of Religion and Ethics* 12 (1958): 10–17.

—. *The Kashf al-Maḥjub. The oldest Persian Treatise on Sufism by Ali b. Uthman al-Jullabi al-Hujwiri*. Leiden, 1911.

—. *The Mystics of Islam*. London: Bell, 1914.

—., trans., *The Tarjuman al-Ashwaq. A Collection of Mystical Odes by Muhyiddin ibn al Arabi*. London, 1911.

—. *Studies in Islamic Mysticism*. Cambridge: CUP, 1921.

Obermann, J. *Der Philosophie und Reliögese Subjektivismus Ghazalis.* Vienna, 1921.

Pines, S. *The Guide of the Perplexed.* Chicago, 1963.

Poznanski, S. "Miscellen über Saadja." *MGWJ* 44 (1900): 400–46.

—. *Schiloh. Ein Beitrag zur Geschichte der Messiaslehre.* Leipzig: Hinrichs 1904.

—. "Inyanim Shonim ha-Nog'im li-Tekufat ha-Geonim." *Ha-Kedem* 2 (1908): 91–113.

—. *Anshei Kairowan.* Berlin, 1909.

—., ed. Peirush al Yeḥezkel u-Trei Asar (R. Eliezer of Beaugency). Warsaw, 1913.

—. *Babylonische Geonim im nachgaonäischen Zeitalter.* Berlin, 1914.

—. "Meyassedei Kitot be-Yisrael bi-Tekufat ha-Geonim." *Reshumot* 1 (1920): 207–216.

—. *Sefer Megillat ha-Megalle von Abraham bar Chija*, with intro. and notes by J. Guttmann, Berlin: Itskowski, 1924.

Rapoport, S.Y. *Erekh Milin.* Warsaw, 1914.

Ratner, B., ed. *Seder Olam.* Vilna, 1894–97.

Recanati, R. Menahem, Perush al ha-Torah, Naso.

Reifman, J. "He'arot al Sefer: Ḥukei ha-Torah." *Bet Talmud* 1 (1881): 248–9.

Rosenberg, H. "Ḥibburei Rav H. Y. D. Azulai u-Ketavav she-lo Rau adayin or ha-Defus." *Kiryat Sefer* 5 (1928).

Rosenberg, J. *Kovez̧ Ma'asei Yedei Geonim.* Berlin, 1856.

Rosenblatt , S., ed. *The High Ways to Perfection of Abraham Maimonides.* Baltimore, 1938.

Rosenthal, S., ed. *Sefer ha-Yashar.* Berlin, 1898.

Rosin, D. "Die Religionsphilosophie Abraham Ibn Esras." *MGWJ* 42 (1898): 17–33, 58–73, 108–115, 154–161, 200–214, 241–252, 305–315, 345–362, 394–407, 444–457, 481–503.

Roth, C. *A History of the Jews in England.* Oxford, 1941.

Sambari, J. *Likkutim mi-Sefer Divrei Yosef.* Frankfurt/Berlin, 1896.

Sassoon, D.S. *Ohel David. Catalogue of the Hebrew and Samaritan Manuscripts in the Sassoon Library.* London, 1932.

Schechter S. "Notes on Hebrew Mss. in the University Library at Cambridge." *JQR*, O.S. 4 (1892): 90–101.

—. "Notes on a Hebrew Commentary to the Pentateuch in a Parma Manuscript." In *Semitic Studies in Memory of Rev. Dr. Alexander Kohut*. Berlin: Calvary, 1897. pp. 485–494.

—. *Midrash ha-Gadol*. Cambridge, 1902.

Scholem, G. "Ha-Mekubbal R. Abraham ben Eliezer ha-Levi." *Kiryat Sefer* 2 (1925): 101–141.

—. *Kitvei Yad be-Kabbalah*. Jerusalem, 1930.

—. "Al Nevi'uto shel R. Ezra mi-Montcontour." *Tarbiẓ*, 2 (1931): 244–245.

—. "Od al Nevi'uto shel R. Ezra mi-Montcontour." *Tarbiẓ* 2 (1931): 514.

—. *Major Trends in Jewish Mysticism*. Jerusalem, 1941.

—. "Sidrei de-Shimusha Rabah." *Tarbiẓ* 16 (1945): 196–209.

—. "Hatḥalot ha-Kabbalah" *Knesset* 10 (1947): 179–228.

Schreiner, M. "Le Kitab al-Mouhadara wa-l-Moudhakara de Moïse b. Ezra et ses sources." *REJ* 21 (1890): 98–117; 22 (1891): 62–81, 236–249.

—. "Beiträge zur Geschichte der theologischen Bewegungeng in Islam." *ZDMG* 52 (1898): 463–563.

Schröter, R. "Bar-Hebraeus Scholien zu Gen. 49.50. Ex. 14.15 Deut. 32–34 u. Jud. 5." *ZDMG* 24 (1870): 495–562.

Schwarz, Z. "Reshit Sefer ha-Zikharon shel ha-Ritba." *Ha-Ẓofeh* 7 (1923): 299–304.

Slutzki, D., ed. *Emunot ve-Deot* (Saadia/ibn Tibbon). Leipzig, 1864.

Steinschneider, M., ed. *Shenei ha-Me'orot*. Berlin, 1846.

—. *Catalogus Librorum Hebraeorum in Bibliotheca Bodleiana*. Oxford, 1852–60.

—. "Zur Pseudepigraphischen Literatur." *HB* 3 (1860): 117–20, *HB* 4 (1861): 20–24.

—. "Miscellen." *HB*, 9 (1869): 115–17.

—. "Poeten und Polemiker in Nordspanien um 1400." *HB* 14 (1874): 95–99, *HB* 15 (1875): 54–60.

—. "Jacob aus Marvège der Himmelscorrespondent." *HB* 14 (1874): 122–4.

—. *Polemische und Apologetische Literatur in Arabische Sprache.* Leipzig, 1877.

—. "Zur Geschichte der Uebersetzungen aus dem Indischen ins Arabische." *ZDMG* 24 (1870): 325–392.

—. "Zur kabbalistischen Literatur: IV. Isak Kohen." *HB* 18 (1878): 18–22.

—. *Hebräische Übersetzungen des Mittelalters und die Juden als Dolmetscher.* Berlin: Verlag des bibliographischen Bureaus, 1893.

—. *Gesammelte Schriften.* Berlin, Poppelauer, 1925.

Steinschneider, M. and A. Neubauer. "Josef ibn Aknin, Analekten." *MWJ* 15 (1888): 105–112.

Strauss (Ashtor), A. *Toledot ha-Yehudim be-Miẓrayim ve-Suriya tachat Shilton ha-Mamlukim.* Jerusalem, 1944.

Strauss, L. *Philosophie und Gesetz.* Berlin, 1935.

Urbach, E.E. "Halakhah u-Nevuah." *Tarbiẓ* 18 (1946): 1–27.

—., ed. *Arugat ha-Bosem.* Jerusalem, 1947.

von Kremer, A. *Geschichte der herrschenden Ideen des Islams.* Leipzig, 1868.

Weiss, I.H. "Iggeret Bikoret." *Bet Talmud* 5 (1889): 257–59.

—., ed. *Sifra.* Vienna, 1862.

—. "Toledot Rabbenu Yaakov Tam." *Bet Talmud* 3 (1883): 33–36, 129–38, 161–69, 193–201, 225–233, 257–61, 289–95, 321–23.

Weiss, M.Z. "Ha-Navi." *Ha-Ẓofeh,* 5 (1921): 46–47.

Werner, A., ed. Nachmanides, *Ḥeshbon Keẓ ha-Ge'ulah.* New York, 1904.

Wieder, N. "Sifro ha-Nisraf shel Yehudah ibn Shabbtai." *Meẓudah* 3 (1943): 122–31.

Wiener, M., ed. *Shevet Yehudah.* Hannover, 1855.

Wilenski, M., ed. *Sefer ha-Rikmah.* Berlin, 1929.

Wistinetski, ed. *Sefer Ḥasidim.* Frankfurt, 1924.

Wolfson, H.A. "Hallevi and Maimonides on Prophecy." *JQR* 32 (1942): 345–370; 33 (1942): 49–82.

Yaakov, Y. "Das Sefer Amarkol al hilchot yen nesech." In *Festschrift zum siebzigsten Geburtstage David Hoffmans*. Berlin, 1914, 421–434; heb. sec. 12–13.

Zeitlin, S. *Maimonides: A Biography*. New York: Bloch, 1935.

Zimmels, B. "Zur Geschichte der Exegese," MWJ 17 (1890), p. 152–165, 177–197.

Zimmels, H.J. "Erez Israel in der Responsenliteratur des späten Mittelalters." *MGWJ* 74 (1930): 44–64.

Zuckermandel, M., ed. *Tosefta*. Jerusalem, 1937.

Zunz, L. *Zur Geschichte und Literatur*. Berlin: Veit u. Co., 1845.

—. *Literaturgeschichte der synagogalen Poesie*. Berlin: Gerschel, 1865.

—. *Gesammelte Schriften*. Berlin: Gerschel, 1875–76.

Zunz, Y.M. *Ir ha-Ẓedek*. Lwów, 1874.

Zweifel, E. Z., ed. *Pardes Rimmonim*. Zhitomir, 1866.

Index of References

Bible

Genesis
3:24 73
5:2 67
9:27 100
37:19 5
49:10 11

Exodus
3:9 33
14:19 16
28:4 38
28:30 3

Numbers
12:8 5
23:23 115

Deuteronomy
3:2 33
5:19 67
8:11 45
18:11 99
18:13 26
18:19 11
30:12 1
31:16 15
31:18 3
33:8 3

I Samuel
10:5 40
28:6 4

I Kings
5:13 60
17:6 21

II Kings
9:11 28

Isaiah
30:21 3
44:25 33
59:21 11

Jeremiah
13:17 120

Ezekiel
1:1 54
29:21 38
42:3 38

Joel 2:30 76

Psalms
25:14 9
97:11 44

Proverbs
25:2 79

Job
4:16 2
6:6 5

Daniel
12:12 83

Esther
4:1 5

Talmudim, Mishnah and Tosefta

Berakhot
10b 5
25b 5
28b. 23
4:8, 3 (Jer.) 100

Maaser Sheni
5:9 (Jer.) 4
55b (Jer.) 4

Shabbat
12b 18
39b 10
6:7 (Tos.) 4
6:3 (Jer.) 3
6.9 (Jer.) 117

Erubin
43a-b 6
60b 9, 10

Pesaḥim
36a 25

Yoma
73b 111
9b-10a 100

Taanit
2:1 (Jer.) 100

Megillah
14a 7
32a 2

Ḥagigah
5b 3, 120
11b 16
14b 60

Yevamot
16b 16
16:6 (Mishnah) 3

Ketubot
103b 15

Nedarim
22b 1
32a 10

Sotah
10b 67
33a 2, 5
13:2 (Tos.) 2
13:3–4 (Tos.) 90
24b (Jer.) 2

Gittin
7b 9
36b 12
45a 60
88a 19
89a 3

Kiddushin
31a 111
71a 16

Baba Kamma
23b 19
30a 12

Baba Meẓia
59b 12
102a 36
107b 4

Baba Batra
11a 9
12a 9, 10
12 9
25a 100
134a 60

Sanhedrin
101b 16
11a 2
17b 67
30a 4, 5
44b 16
67b 39
68a 60
90a. 113
62b 39

Shevuot
25a 19

Avodah Zarah
17b 16
34a 17

Avot 12
6:1 10

Avot de Rabbi Nathan A,
17 4

Bekhorot
45a 9, 10

Menaḥot
110a 23
41a 6

Midrashim

Bereshit Rabbah
13 60
55.3 100

Bamidbar Rabbah
14.37 23

Esther Rabbah
7.18 5

Shir ha-Shirim Rabbah
8.11 2

Sifre Deuteronomy
103 23
Sifre Deuteronomy
172 99

Pirkei de R. Eliezer
8 27
21 14
29 6

Yalkut Shimoni
Beha'alotekha, no. 729 100

Guide of the Perplexed 92

Translator's Introduction
3a 80, 82
3b 84
9b 106
I: Introduction 69, 71, 72, 123
I:1 75
I:10 74
I:26 98
I:32 95
I:34 106
I:40 105
I:73 108
II:4 109
II:12 108

II:24 95, 96
II:25 97
II:32 76, 77, 85, 102, 104, 110, 112
II:36 66, 77, 78, 98, 100, 105, 106, 108, 109, 111
II:37 78, 85, 109
II:38 78, 96, 97, 114, 109
II:40 85
II:41 78
II:44 105
II:45 71, 72, 73, 74, 97
III: Introduction 71, 73
III:7 75, 114
III:13 98
III:22 74
III:27 98
III:33 97
III:46 77
III:51 86
III:54 89, 98

Mishneh Torah

Yesodei ha-Torah 4:7 103
Yesodei ha-Torah 5:2 94
Yesodei ha-Torah 7:2 27
Yesodei ha-Torah 7:2 27
Yesodei ha-Torah 7:7 94
Yesodei ha-Torah 9:2 94
Yesodei ha-Torah 10:1 94
Deot 4:20 116
Teshuvah 5:2 98
Teshuvah 9:2 102
Lulav 8:5 36
Klei ha-Mikdash 10:10 111
Akum 5:8 75
Akum 11:6 77
Mitamei Mishkav u-Moshav 7:7 36
Sanhedrin 1:3 113
Melakhim 12:2 113
Melakhim 12:4 101
Melakhim 12:5 102

Kovez̦ Iggerot ha-Rambam

I, 25a 107
I, 32d 107
II, 1c 113
II, 5b 114
II, 16a 107
II, 23b 95
II, 23c 95, 97
II, 28b-c 107
II, 28d 96
II, 29a-c 82
II, 29d 107
II, 29d-30c 86
II, 30a 82
II, 30a 85
II, 30c 84
II, 31a 107
II, 31b 82
II, 31d 108
III, 16c 119, 125
III, 16d. 84, 85

Zohar

I:93a 6
I:135a 101
I:149b 5
I:171a 27
I:183a 5

II:154a 11
III:228a 60
III:268b 27
Tikkunei Zohar 19 3

Manuscripts

Bodleian 1816 20
Bodleian 2644 21
British Museum add. 27542 1115
Deinhard 625 115
Halberstam 388 34
Jerusalem (Guide of the Perplexed) 73
JNUL 90 52
JTS 24 126
JTS 90a 90
JTS 346 38
JTS 1340 34
JTS 1791 90
JTS 877 33
JTS 878 33
JTS Adler 308 73
JTS Adler 1161 20
JTS Adler 2503 35
JTS Enelow 682 52
JTS Sulzberger (Guide of the Perplexed) 73
Sassoon 290 35
Sasson 349 21

General Index

Aaron 55, 56
Aaron the son of R. Samuel, R. 56
Aaron, R. (chief judge of Pumbeditha) 60
Abiathar, R. 9
Abot 104
Abrabanel, R. Isaac 1, 66, 72
Abraham 44
Abraham be-R. Azriel, R. 64
Abraham ben David, R. (Rabad) 14, 21, 33, 34, 35, 36, 37, 38, 39, 40, 56, 64
Abraham ben R. Isaac, R. 35
Abraham ben R. Samuel the prophet, R. 21
Abraham, the son of R. Samuel the Prophet, R. 48
Abraham Gaon Kabassi, R. 59
Abraham Maimonides 124
Abraham of Posquières, R. 35
Abraham the Pious, R. 34
Abraham, the son of Maimonides, R. 119, 120, 123, 124
Abraham bar Ḥiyya, R. 39, 117
Abraham ben Maimonides, R. 120, 124
Abulafia , Abraham b. Samuel, R. 125, 126
Abravanel, *see* Abrabanel
Abu Issa of Isfahan 31
active intellect 81, 105, 109
Adam 117
Agudat Shmuel 25
Aha, R. 3
Ahimaaz, Book of 37
Akiva, R. 44
Albo, J 1, 78
Al Dari, R. Moshe, *see* Dar'i, R. Moses
Al-Ghazali 121, 123
al-Ḥarizi 22, 40, 72, 73, 89, 90, 91
al-Zafah (Arab king mentioned by Ibn Ezra) 55
Aleppo 90, 91
Alexandria 30, 95, 119
Alfasi, R. Isaac 37, 38
Almohades 76
Amnon, R. 46
Amoraim 2, 6, 49
Amudei Golah 51
Amudei Shelomo (R. Solomon Luria) 45
Andalusia 29, 75
angel 5, 6, 10, 14, 15, 16, 18, 19, 23, 26, 29, 31, 37, 51, 53, 54, 58, 59, 60, 61, 66, 93, 111, 122
Arab 55, 117
Arabia 25, 28, 76
Arabic 32, 55, 80, 91, 115
Arabs 29
Aristotle 23, 96, 109
Ark of the Covenant 66, 99

Artemidorus 4
Arugat ha-Bosem 28, 64, 121
Asher, Rabbenu 36
Ashkenaz 13, 25
astrologer 77
astronomy 81
Avdimi of Haifa, R. 9
Avodat ha-Kodesh (R. Meir ibn Gabbai) 35, 99
Azkari, R. Eleazar 123
Azriel, R. 35

B

baal ḥalom 4, 5, *see also* dream master
Baalei ha-Nefesh 36
Babylonia 55, 56, 57, 62, 63, 64, 100
Bagdad 47, 56, 61, 107
Baḥya ben Asher , R. 3
Balaam 115
Bar Hebraeus 11
Bargeloni, R. Judah 4, 62, 66, 115–116, 117
Baruch ben Neriah 86
Baruch, R. 12
Barukh be-R. Isaac of Worms, R. 66
bat kol 2, 3, 6, 18, 65, 90
Beer Mayyim Ḥayyim 60
Bet ha-Beḥirah (Meiri) 37
bet midrash 12, 36
Birkei Yosef 52
Book of Prophecy 69
Botarel, R. Moses 19, 22, 55, 56, 58
Bruzak (person in Bagdad) 47

C

Cairo 85
Catania 30
Ceuta, Morocco 80, 122
chair of Elijah 6
Chapters Concerning Felicity see *Pirke Haẓlaḥah*
Chariot mysticism 10, 71, 73, 74, *see also* merkabah mystic
Cherubim 99, 100
Christian Church 11
Cicero 40
circumcision 6, 44
Colon, R. Joseph (Maharik) 25
conjecture(s) and conjecturing 70, 78, 97
Constantinople 48
Cordoba 75
Crusades 29, 48

D

Daat Zekenim 20
Daniel 5
Daniel, Book of 83
Dar'i, R. Moses 29, 30, 75
Darkei Moshe (R. Moses Isserles) 28
Darkei Teshuvah (R. Eleazar Rokeach) 13
David ben Zakkai 57
David ha-Nagid, R. 125
David Reubeni 26
David the Chief Judge, R. 35
Day of Atonement 35, 59, 109
de Rossi, R. Azariah 117
Delmegido, R. Joseph Shelomo of Candia 1, 35
demon 5, 51, 54
demonic rites 26
Derekh Emunah 35
dialectical argumentation 97
diaspora 46, 62
divination 76, 78, 79

divine infusion (efflux) 92, 121
divine name 26, 51, 52, 53, 57, 58, 62
Divrei Navi (R. Nehemiah ben R. Abraham) 12
Donolo, R. Sabbatai 42
dream divination 55
dream inquiries 4, 15, 16, 29, 47, 48, 51, 52, 53, 55, 58, 59
dream master (adept) 4, 5, 15, 16, 44, 55, 59
dreams 3, 4, 5, 6, 8, 12, 14, 15, 18, 23, 26, 28, 29, 39, 42, 43, 44, 45, 46, 47, 48, 50, 51, 52, 53, 54, 55, 58, 59, 60, 61, 62, 64, 65, 66, 75, 77, 78, 80, 85, 105, 109, 117, 121
Duran, R. Simon ben Zemach 24, 54

E

Edels, R. Samuel 3, 25
Efodi, 110, 114
Egypt 80, 85, 90, 109, 119, 122
Egyptian academy 90
Egyptian rabbinic authorities 47
Ein Yaakov 60
Einleitung in der Mishna 69, 71, 77, 98, 99, 102, 103, 123
Einleitung zu Chelek (ed. Holzer) 28, 69, 113
Eleazer, R. 124
Eleazer, R., the author of Rokeaḥ 3, 6, 49, 56
Eliakim ben R. Joseph of Mainz, R. 43
Eliezer ben Nathan 43
Eliezer ben R. Solomon, R. 15
Eliezer of Beaugency, R. 45, 46
Eliezer of Worms, R. 21
Eliezer, R. (Tanra) 6
Eliezer, the son of R. Judah the son of R. Eliezer the Great, R.48
Elijah 5, 6, 7, 8, 21, 22, 30, 33, 34, 35, 48, 49, 50, 55, 56, 61, 90
Elijah of Londres [London], R. 45
Elijah the Elder, the son of R. Menahem of Le Mans, R. 22
Elisha 90
Emunah Ramah (R. Abraham ben David,) 39
Emunot ve-Deot (Saadiah) 102, 103
England 54, 117
Enoch 5, 117
Ephraem the Syrian of Edessa 11
Ephraim bar Samson, R. 15
Ephraim ben R. Jacob of Bonn, R. 46
Ephraim ha-Gevir from Regensburg (Ratisbon), R. 17, 25, 49
Ephraim, Rabbenu 50
esoteric wisdom 19, 62, 79, 80, 102, 126
estimative faculty 106
Euphrates 63
Even ha-Ezer (R. Eliezer b. Nathan) 43
exilarch 57, 62
Eẓ Yosef 60
Ezekiel 38, 71
Ezra 37, 100
Ezra, R. (of Gerona) 35
Ezra, R., the prophet of Montcontour (Tosafist) 19, 20, 30

F

Falaquera, Shem Tov ben Joseph 72, 74
Folush (city) 47

forty-two-letter name of God 15, 16, 53, 59
France 19, 30, 38, 76, 117, 118, 119, 125
France, rabbis of 76
Franco-German Jewry 13

G

Gabriel 5, 16
Galen 116
Garden of Eden 51
Gavison, R. Abraham 40
Genizah fragment 109
Geonic Circles 48, 55
geonim 40, 55, 56, 58, 61, 62, 63, 64, 65
German pietists 51
Germany 117
Gerondi, R. Jonah 15
Gershom, Rabbenu 10, 22, 60
Gersonides 26
Gilyon Mordechai 43
Ginzberg, Louis 16
Ginzei Ḥokhmat ha-Kabbalah 125
Gog and Magog 113
Guide of the Perplexed 69, 71, 84, 85, 86, 89, 92, 98, 107, 124, 125

H

Ha-Kotev (commentary on *Ein Yaakov*) 9, 59
Ha-Segulah 66
Ha-Terumah 19
Hagahot Asheri 46, 50, 59
Hagahot Maimuniot 37, 66
Hahn, R. Yuspa 16
Hai Gaon, Rav 8, 14, 16, 32, 42, 55, 56, 58, 59, 60, 61, 62, 64, 65, 66, 67
halakhah 6, 7, 43, 52, 112
Halakhot Gedolot 60, 64
Hamburg 2
Hananel, Rabbenu 4, 10, 12, 65
Hanina, R. 39
Hasdai Ibn Crescas, R. 26
ḥasid 49
Ḥasidei Ashkenaz 16, 24, 28, 51, 125
Hayyat, R. Judah 34
Hayyim ha-Kohen, R. 15
Hayyim, R. 10
Hebrew language 25, 28, 40, 41, 43, 44, 46 58, 91, 124
Heishiv Moshe (R. Moses Teitelbaum) 66
Hellenistic times 96
Ḥemdah Genuzah 67
Hesiod 40
Hillel 12, 59, 90
Hisda, R. 9
Hitgallut ha-Sodot ve-Hofa'at ha-Me'orot (Ibn Aknin) 90
Holy Land 24, 100, 117, 118
holy men 67, 121
Name of forty-two letters *see* forty-two letter name of God
Holy of Holies 100
Holy Spirit 1, 2, 3, 5, 6, 10, 17, 22–23, 27, 32, 33, 36, 37, 38, 40, 41, 45, 53, 54, 58, 64, 65, 66, 74, 77, 91, 93, 99, 100, 101, 104, 105, 111, 112, 1125, 26
Homer 40
Horeb, Mount 67
Hoshana Rabah 55
House of David 28, 63
Ḥovot ha-Levavot 1

Hurwitz, Pinehas 24
hypothesis 97, 119

I

Ibn Aknin, R. Joseph 74, 79, 80, 81, 82, 83, 84, 85, 90, 91, 93, 107
Ibn Al-Arabi 122
Ibn al-Kifti 80
Ibn Aryeh 29, 30
Ibn Ezra, R. Abraham (Biblical commentary of) 6, 11, 15, 19, 28, 33, 54
Ibn Ezra, R. Moses 1, 28, 40, 41, 42, 61, 114
Ibn Gabbai, R. Meir 35, 99
Ibn Gabirol, R. Solomon 42–43
Ibn Habib, R. Moshe 37
Ibn Janah, R. Jonah 41
Ibn Migash, R. Joseph 9
Ibn Rushd 80
Ibn Shaprut (R. Shem Tov) 6, 60
Ibn Shueib, R. Joshua 34, 56
Ibn Tibbon, R. Judah 28
Ibn Tibbon, R. Samuel 73, 78, 89, 106, 115
Ibn Zabara, R. Joseph 22
Iggeret Rav Sherira 60
Iggeret Teiman 29, 30, 31, 76, 119
Ilish, Rav 60
imaginative power 78, 108
indwelling presence 5, 67, 93, 99, 100, 101, 110, 121
intellectual apprehension 89
Isaac ben Giyyat, R. 42
Isaac ben R. Jacob de Lattes, R. 100
Isaac ben R. Samuel, R. 19
Isaac of Acre, R. 32, 33, 34
Isaac of Corbeille, R. 51
Isaac of Dampierre, R. 38
Isaac of Rome, R. 52
Isaac the Blind, R. 33, 34, 35
Isaac the Elder, R. 10, 19, 66
Isaac the Nazirite, R. 34, 35
Isaac the son of R. Moses of Vienna, R. 44
Isaac the Tosafist, R. 38
Isaac, son of the master, R. 33
Isaiah 117
Isaiah the Elder of Trani, R. 50
Ishmael 76
Ishmael the High Priest, R. 4
Israel 115, 120
Israel, land of 76
Issa'ites 31
Isserles, R. Moses 28

J

Jacob 115
Jacob b'rav Nissim, R. 61
Jacob Baal ha-Turim, R. 27
Jacob ha-Levi the Zaddik of Marvège, R. 51, 52, 53
Jacob ha-Levi, R. 16
Jacob the Nazirite, R. 34, 35
Jacob the Prophet-Gaon, ben R. Moshe ben R. Abun, R. 21, 22
Jacob, Rabbenu 15, *see also* Tam, Rabbenu
Jaffe, R. Mordecai 35
Japhet 96, 100
Jeremiah 85, 86, 117
Jerusalem 4, 30, 37, 55, 113, 115, 118
Jesus the Nazarene 117
Jews of the West 76
Job, book of 74

Johanan ben Zakkai 60
Johanan the priest of Lunel, R. 118
Johanan, R. 2
Jonah the Pious of Gerona, R. 27
Jonah, R. 3
Jonathan of Lunel, R. 37, 118
Jose, R. 3
Joseph bar R. Abba, R. 55–56, 60
R. Joseph be-R. Eliezer ha-Sepharadi 66
Joseph ben R. Isaac, R. 52
Joseph of Marseilles, R. 20
Joshua, R. 10
Judah al-Botini, R. 33
Judah ben Schneur, R. 48
Judah Ha-Levi 41. 90, 91, 118
Judah the Pious, R. 13, 14, 21, 48, 49, 51
Judah, R. (scribe of R. Joseph) 56
Judah, son of R. Samuel the Prophet 48
Judah, the son of Rabbenu Asher, R. 38

K

Kabbalah 14, 32, 33, 35, 39, 55
Kabbalism 125
Kabbalist 13, 16, 21, 22, 32, 33, 34, 35, 64
Kairouan 61
Kalir, R. Eleazar 17, 18
Kallah Rabbati 101
Kalonymos ben R. Meshullam, R. 46
Kalonymos of Lucca ben R. Moshe ben R. Kalonymos, Rabbenu 23
Kaporet 100
Katina, R. 6
Katofa, Nahman (of) 31, 125
Keter Shem Tov (R. Shem Tov Gaon) 33
Kevuẓat Ḥakhamim 67
Kimḥi, R. David 4
Kiẓẓur Aggadot ha-Yerushalmi 60
Kiẓẓur Zekher Ẓaddiq 1, 56
knowledge of the Deity 111
Kohen-Zedek, R. 57
Kol Bo 17
Koran 120
Korban ha-Edah 117
Koreit, R. Judah 33
Koveẓ Shirei R. Abraham ibn Ezra 15
Kuntres ha-Masoret 62
Kuzari 1

L

Landau, R. Ezekiel 66
Lekaḥ Tov 48
Leḥem Mishnah 112
Leon d'Moreal, R. 17
Letter on the Resurrection of the Dead 74
Letter to Yemen see *Iggeret Teiman*
Levush ha-Orah 18
Levush ha-Tekhelet 18
Levush Ir-Shushan 18
Levush Or Yikrat (R. Mordecai Jaffe) 35
Lieberman, R. Hayyim 25
Likkutei ha-Shulḥan Arukh shel ha-Ari 58
Likkutim (R. Joseph of Marseilles) 20
Likkutim mi-Divrei R. Yosef Sambari 38, 58
Loewe, R. Judah 6
logic 81, 95
London 45, 117

Lorraine 17
Lucca 56
Lucena 42
Lunel 29, 35, 118
Luria, R. David 6
Luria, R. Solomon 45, 60

M

Ma'amar Eẓ Ḥayyim (R. Isaiah b. Joseph of Tabriz) 54
Ma'amar ha-Yiḥud 95, 103, 111
Ma'amar Yikavu ha-Mayyim 125
Ma'arekhet ha-Elohut 34
Ma'aseh Bereshit 10, 16, 67
Ma'aseh Merkavah, see Chariot Mysticism.
Magen Avot (Meiri) 36
Magen Avot (Duran) 24, 54
Maharsha 3, 25
Maharshal 25
Maimon the Dayyan, R. 75
Maimonideans 112
Maimonides 1, 14, 23, 27, 28, 29,31, 35, 36, 40, 45, 46, 47, 58, 69, 70, 71, 72, 73, 74, 75, 76, 77, 78, 79, 80, 81, 82, 83, 84, 85, 86, 87, 89, 90, 91, 92, 94, 95, 96, 97, 98, 99, 101, 102, 103, 104, 105, 106, 108, 109, 110, 111, 112, 113, 114, 115, 116, 117, 118, 119, 120, 122, 123, 124, 125, 126
Makhiri on Psalms 14
Malachi 1, 6, 19, 75
Manot ha-Levi 5
Maḥberet ha-Arukh 41
Maḥzor Vitry 10, 17
Margaliyot Tovah 66
Masekhet Soferim 59–60
master of dreams, *see* dream master
Master of the Divine Name 48
Matzliach, R. (Sicily) 61
medieval Jewish philosophers 39
medieval sages 7, 8
Megillat Aḥimaaẓ 57
Megillat ha-Megalleh (R. Abraham bar Ḥiyya) 1, 39, 117
Megillat Setarim (R. Hayyim Vital) 63
Megillat Taanit 3
Meir, R. 10
Meirat Einayim (Isaac of Acre) 32, 33, 34
Meiri, R. Menachem 36, 37
Menahem ben R. Jacob of Worms, R. 44
Menahem ben Zeraḥ, R. 38
Menahem Hordimsi, R. 14
Menasseh ben Israel, R. 58
Mendel, Zechariah 24
Menorat Zechariah 24
Meor Einaiyim (R. Azariah de Rossi) 117
Me'ora'ot Ẓvi (Warsaw, 1838) 26
Merkabah mystic 11, 19, *see also* chariot mysticism
Messiah 26, 29, 30, 48, 55, 58, 75, 76, 101, 102, 112, 113, 114, 115, 117
Messiah, birthpangs of 113
Messianic days 101
Messianic excitement 28
Messianic hope 101
Metatron 14
Methuselah 117

mezuzah 45
Meẓaref le-Kesef 13
Meẓaref le-Ḥokhmah (R. Joseph Shelomo Delmegido of Candia) 1, 35
Michael 16
Michael the Angel, R. 53, 54
Middle Ages 1, 13, 40, 77
Midrash Aggadah 112
Midrash ha-Gadol 9, 11
Midrash Halakhah 112
Midrash Tannaim 4
Migdal Ḥananel 65, 66
Migdal Oz 14, 32, 112
Mikhtav ha-Masa mi-eḥad ha-Olim (R. Shmuel ben R. Shimson) 117–118
Milḥamot Adonai (Gersonides) 26
Milḥamot Adonai (Abraham son of Maimonides) 118
Milḥamot ha-Shem (Suleiman ben Yeruḥam) 1
Minḥat Kenaot (Rashba) 40, 51
Minḥat Yehudah al ha-Torah 20
miracle 17, 29, 43, 56, 57, 64, 65, 67, 94, 104, 110, 117
Mishnah 112
Mishneh Torah 36, 46, 111
Mizrahi, R. Elijah 11
Mordecai 5
Mordecai 19
Moreh ha-Moreh (Falaquera) 72
Morocco 80, 90
Moses 3, 5, 9, 14, 17, 26, 27, 31, 46, 50, 63, 87, 98
Moses Al Dar'i, R., *see* Dar'i, R. Moses
Moses ben Jacob, R. (of Coucy) 44
Moses of Lugatch, R. 25
Moshe ben Kalonymos, R. 57
Mount of Olives 55
Muhammad 28, 91, 122
Musarei ha-Filosofim 39
Mushka (follower of Abu Issa of Isfahan) 31
Muslims 80, 91, 121, 122

N

Nahman of Katofa 31, 125
Nachmias, R. Joseph 5
Nahmanides 3, 9, 10, 32, 35, 67
Sha'ar ha-Gemul 32
Commentary to Genesis 5:4 116
Commentary to Job, chap. 33, 32
Ḥeshbon Keẓ ha-Geulah (New York, 1904), p. 20 101
Naḥum ha-Maaravi, R. 115
Narbonne 22, 23, 35
Narbonne, Aacademy of 21
Nathan ha-Bavli, R. 57
Natronai Gaon, Rav 64
Navi, Abraham the physician 12
Navi, Benjamin 12
Navi, Eliezer 12
Navi, R. Judah ben Nathan 12
Navi, R. Samuel 14
Nehemiah ben R. Abraham, R. 12
Neẓaḥ Yisrael, (Maharal) 6
Nicodemus ben Gurion 117
nightmares 54
Nishmat Ḥayyim (R. Menasseh ben Israel) 58
Nisi Naharwani 57
Nissim, Rabbenu 10, 61
Noda bi-Yehudah (Landau) 66

O

Obadiah the Prophet of Guratam, R. 25
Ohel David 14, 21, 32 35
Ohel Yosef (R. Joseph be-R. Eliezer ha-Sepharadi) 66
Omer ha-Shikheḥah (R. Abraham Gavison) 15, 40
Onkelos, see Targum
Or Zarua, Alfa Beta (Zhitomir, 1862) 44
Or Zarua, end of *Hilkhot Rosh Hashanah, sec. 276* 46
Or Zarua, Piskei Avoda Zarah, sec. 200 50
Oreḥot Ḥayyim 36, 61
Oshaiah, R. 39
Otiyot ha-Mashiaḥ 113
Otiyot le-Rabbenu Saadiah 58
Oẓar ha-Geonim 2, 8, 55, 59, 65, 67, 102

P

Paaneaḥ Raza 14
Pardes 6
Pardes Rimonim (R. Shem Tov ibn Shaprut) 6, 35
Parḥon, R. Solomon 41
Passover 48
Peirush ha-Milim ha-Zarot (R. Samuel ibn Tibbon) 78
Peirush le-Torah (R. Menachem Recanati) 3, 33, 35
Peirush al Yeḥezkel u-Trei Asar (R. Eliezer of Beaugency) 46
Peirush le-Sefer Yeẓirah (Bargeloni) 4, 62, 66, 115–116, 117
Peirush Sefer Yeẓirah (Botarel) 22, 55, 56,
Perakim be-Haẓlaḥah 92–94
Petaḥiah, R. 47
Philo 27
Pindar 40
Pinhas b. Yair, R. 22, 123
pious men of Germany, *see* Hasidei Ashkenaz
Plato 40
prophetic dream 12, 45
prophetic overflow 108
Prophets 112
Pumbeditha 56, 57, 60

R

Rabad, *see* Abraham b. David
Rabah bar Rav Huna 6
Rabbah 3
Rabbah Bar Ḥanna 100
Rabbenu (Yaakov) Tam, *see* Tam, Rabbenu
Raphael 16
Rashba 40, 51, 65
Rashbam 60
Rashi 2, 3, 4, 5, 9, 10, 11, 15, 16, 23, 26, 38, 39, 46, 49, 60, 67, 100
Ratisbon, Isaac (of) 17, 49
Rav 4
Rava 3, 60
reason 7, 9, 37, 63, 64, 67, 70, 89, 90, 95, 97, 98, 99, 108, 121, 122
Recanati, R. Menachem 3, 33, 34, 35
Regensburg 17, 25
Resh Lakish 100
Reshit Hokhmah (Falaquera,) 74
Responsa from Heaven (R. Jacob ha-Levi of Marvège) 52, *see*

also Sheelot u-Teshuvot min ha-Shammayim
Responsa of R. Abraham ben Maimonides 124
Responsa of R. Isaac Alfasi 3
Revelation at Sinai 117
Ritba 59
Ritva 9
Rosh Hashanah 49
S
Saadia Gaon, Rav 1, 17, 40, 41, 58, 61, 102, 103
Saadiah ibn Danan, R. 40
Sabians 77
sages 1, 2, 3, 6, 7, 8, 9, 10, 14, 17, 23, 27, 29, 30, 31, 32, 37, 42, 43, 50, 56, 59, 61, 65, 67, 74, 75, 77, 78, 84, 88, 89, 99, 101, 104, 111, 112, 113, 119, 120, 125
Sambari, Joseph 38, 47, 58, 125
Samson ben R. Abraham, R. 10
Samson of Falaise, R. 16
Samson of Sens, R. 16
Samuel 84
Samuel ben R. Kalynomos the Elder of Speyer, R. 13
Samuel Ha-Katan 90
Samuel ha-Nagid, R. 42
Samuel the Pious, R. 21
Samuel the Prophet, R. 13, 14, 48
Samuel the true prophet 14
Samuel, R. 60, 125
Samuel, R. (Rashbam) 46, see also Rashbam.
Santurbo, Sicily 30
Sar ha-Olam 16
Sar Shalom Gaon, R. 64
Sarah 44
Satan 74
Saul 4, 84
Saul of Lunel, R. 35
Seder Eliyahu Rabah 6
Seder Eliyahu Zuta 10, 112
Seder Olam 7
Seder Olam Katan 1
Sefer Amarkal 17
Sefer Emunot ve-Deot 58
Sefer Gematriot 18
Sefer ha-Arukh 4, 59, 60
Seder ha-Dorot 25, 44, 46, 60, 117
Sefer ha-Emunot (R. Shem Tov) 34
Sefer ha-Eshkol 21, 22, 34, 59, 66
Sefer ha-Galui (Saadia) 1, 58
Sefer ha-Kabbalah (R. Abraham bar Shelomo) 1, 54, 56
Sefer ha-Mafteaḥ 61
Sefer ha-Magid Neviim Rishonim im Peirush Rashi 25
Sefer ha-Malbush 32
Sefer Ḥaredim (R. Eleazar Azkari,) 123
Sefer ha-Ḥayyim (ms.) 58
Sefer ha-Rikmah (Jonah Ibn Janah) 41
Sefer ha-Shorashim (Jonah Ibn Janah) 41
Sefer ha-Terumah 66
Sefer ha-Turim 28
Sefer ha-Yashar 15, 16, 18, 22
Sefer Ikkarim (Albo) 1, 78
Sefer Issur ve-Heter he-Arokh (R. Jonah Gerondi) 15
Sefer Ma'or va-Shemesh (R. Judah Koreit) 33

Sefer Mekaḥ u-Mimkar (R. Hai Gaon) 65, 66
Sefer Mitzvot Gadol (R. Moses of Coucy) 1, 44, 45
Sefer Musar (Ibn Aknin) 80
Sefer Ḥasidim 1, 5, 6, 9, 24, 26, 28, 39, 49, 51, 55, 66
Sefer Raziel 54, 55
Sefer Shaarei Ẓedek 63
Sefer Sha'ashu'im (R. Joseph ibn Zabara) 22, 46
Sefer Sulam ha-Aliyah (R. Judah al-Botini) 33
Sefer Yerei'im 37
Sefer Yeẓirah 10, 39, 42, 58, 61, 126
Sefer Yuḥasin 1, 12, 34, 36
Shaar ha-Gemul (Nahmanides) 32
Sha'ar ha-Shammayim 116
Sha'arei Teshuvah, Iyei ha-Yam, no. 74 59
Sha'arei Teshuvah, sec. 122 62, 67
Sha'arei Ẓion (R. Isaac b. R. Jacob de Lattes) 100
Shalshelet ha-Kabbalah 13, 14, 17, 31, 46, 118
Shammai 59
Sheelot u-Teshuvot Maharal 22
Sheelot u-Teshuvot Maharshal 25
Sheelot u-Teshuvot min ha-Shammayim 14, 16. 39. 52, 53
Shefatiah, R. 37
sheilat ḥalom 4, *see also* dream inquiry
Shekhinah 2, 14, 67, 93, 2, 100, 111 *see also* Indwelling presence
Shem 96, 100
Shem ha-Gedolim (Azulai) 34, 37, 38, 56
Shem Tov, R. 34, 110, 114
Shem Tov Gaon, R. 33
Shem Tov ibn Shaprut, R. 6, 60
Shemoneh Perakim 69, 74, 105, 109
Shemot ba-Areẓ (R. Moshe ibn Habib) 37
Sherira Gaon, Rav 32, 55, 56, 58, 61, 63, 64, 66, 67
Sheshet ben Benveniste, R. 22, 23
Sheshet ben Sheshet, R. 35
Shevet Yehudah 117
Shibbolei ha-Leket 17, 22, 23, 52, 66
Shirei Shelomo ibn Gabirol 43
Shittah Mekubbeẓet 4, 9, 36
Shiur Qomah 21
Shoshan Sodot 3
Shushan 5
Sibbuv R. Petaḥiah 47, 49
Sicily 30, 61
Siddur Rav Saadia 58
Simeon b. Yoḥai, R. 11, 65, 124
Simon ben R. Isaac the Great, R. 17
Simon ha-Gadol, R. 17–18
Sinai, Mount 9, 96
Sleeping and Waking (Aristotle) 23
Sod Mesharim (R. Obadiah the Prophet) 24
Sodei Razayya (R. Eleazar Rokeach) 3, 6
Solomon ben Adret, R. 36, 99, 125
Song of Songs 80
Song of the Sea 14
sorcerer 11, 77
soul 2, 7, 8, 12, 19, 23, 26, 27, 28, 29, 32, 33, 42, 53, 54, 67, 70, 79,

80, 81, 82, 87, 93, 94, 95, 97, 98, 100, 103, 104, 111, 116, 120, 122
Spain 45, 64, 75
speculative inquiry 103
Speyer 13, 21, 48
Spirit 6, 93
spiritual attainment 97
spiritual heroes 102
Sufi 120, 121, 122, 123, 124
Sukkot 55
Suleiman ben Yeruḥam 1
Sura 57, 63
Syria 85
Syriac translation 11

T

Taam Zekenim (R. Hai Gaon) 59, 62, 64
Taku, R. Moses 26, 28, 54
Talmidei Rabbenu Yona al Berakhot 27
Talmud 1, 9, 18, 24, 27, 30, 31, 36, 38, 50, 74, 99, 101, 117
Talmudic master 7
Tam, Rabbenu 14, 15, 16, 17, 18, 19, 21, 43, 49
Tannaim 2, 6, 40, 49
Taḥkemoni 22, 40, 90, 90–91
Targumim 5, 67
Tashbaẓ Katan 50
tefillin 14, 17, 29, 45
Teitelbaum, R. Moses 66
Temim Deiim (Rabad) 36
Temple 1, 4, 9, 12, 37, 38, 59, 99, 100, 111
Teshuvot ha-Geonim, Shaarei Teshuvah, with the commentary *Iyyei ha-Yam, sec. 187* 63
Teshuvot ha-Geonim (Assaf) 66
Teshuvot ha-Geonim (Harkavy) 64
Teshuvot ha-Radbaz 16, 52
Teshuvot ha-Rambam 29, 71
Teshuvot ha-Rashba, 26, 99
Teshuvot Maharshal 13
Teshuvot Maimuniot 10
Teshuvot R. Meir ben R. Barukh 13
Teshuvot Rashi 65
The High Way to Perfection (R. Abraham ben Maimonides) 120, 124
The Travels of R. Benjamin of Tudela 21
third part of the Guide 126
Torah 1, 2, 8, 10, 11, 17, 18, 21, 32, 38, 44, 52, 53, 55, 57, 58, 62, 63, 65, 73, 76, 77, 86, 92, 93. 97, 101, 103, 112, 113
Torah knowledge 80
Torah learning 16, 21
Torah, secrets of 10, 65, 73
Torat ha-Shem Temimah 67
Tosafist 10, 12, 14, 15, 19, 38, 49, 51, 66, 118
Tosafot 10, 15, 16, 17, 18, 19, 23, 25, 49, 100
Tosafot Rabbenu Pereẓ 19
Tov-Elem (Bonfils), R. Joseph 21, 22
Trevish, R. Eliezer 16
Troestlin, R. (the Prophet, of Erfurt) 20
Tur 28
Turei Zahav, on *Oraḥ Ḥayyim 51:1* 24
Tuviah ben Eliezer, R. (Author of *Lekaḥ Tov*) 48

U

Urim ve-Tumim 3, 4, 62, 100, 111

V

veridical dreams, 76, 77, 78
Virgil 40
Vital, R. Ḥayyim 29, 46, 63, 64

W

Writings (Ketuvim) 112

Y

Yaffa, R. Mordecai 18
Yam shel Shelomo (R. Solomon Luria) 66
Yefei Mar'eh 55
Yemen 113, 115
Yoḥanan, R. 100
Yosef Omeẓ (R. Yuspa Hahn) 16
Yudgan (follower of Abu Issa of Isfahan) 31

Z

Zabara, R. Joseph 22
Zechariah 1, 5, 19, 24, 75
Ẓedah la-Derekh (R. Menachem b. Zeraḥ) 38
Zemach bar R. Hayyim, R. 63
Zikhron Berit la-Rishonim 44
Zikhron la-Rishonim (Harkavy) 63
Zion 118
Ẓiyyoni, R. Menachem, Vayera 23
ẓiẓit 6, 45
Zohar 35 *see also* index of references.